Interpersonal Growth Through
Communication

Interpersonal Growth Through
Communication

Gerald L.
Wilson
University of South Alabama

Alan M.
Hantz
University of North Carolina at Asheville

Michael S.
Hanna
University of South Alabama

Wm. C. Brown Publishers
Dubuque, Iowa

wcb group

Wm. C. Brown
Chairman of the Board
Mark C. Falb
President and Chief Executive Officer

BookTeam

Judith A. Clayton
Senior Developmental Editor
Mark E. Christianson
Senior Designer
Mary Jean Gregory
Production Editor
Shirley M. Charley
Visual Research Editor
Mavis M. Oeth
Permissions Editor

wcb
Wm. C. Brown Publishers, College Division

Lawrence E. Cremer
President
James L. Romig
Vice-President, Product Development
David A. Corona
Vice-President, Production and Design
E. F. Jogerst
Vice-President, Cost Analyst
Bob McLaughlin
National Sales Manager
Marcia H. Stout
Marketing Manager
Craig S. Marty
Director of Marketing Research
Marilyn A. Phelps
Manager of Design
Mary M. Heller
Photo Research Manager

Cover and chapter opening illustrations by Michael F. Blaser

To Lin, Mimi, and Nancy

Contents

Preface xii

1

The Interpersonal Communication Process 2

Preview 2
Objectives 2
Why Study Interpersonal
  Communication? 4
    *Professional Dimension 5, Social
      Dimension 6*
Models of the Communication
  Process 7
    *Process Model of Communication 7,
      Communication Channels 9,
      Filtering Screen Model 9, An
      Interpersonal Exchange Model 12*
Key Interpersonal Communication
  Concepts 14
    *Feedback 14, Sensitivity 15, Self-
      Disclosure 15, Trust 15, Risk 15*
Content and Relationship 16
    *Content Dimension 16, Relationship
      Dimension 16*
Agenda for Talking About
  Relationships 19
    *Observations 19, Inferences 20,
      Feelings 22, Wants and
      Expectations 22, Intentions 24,
      Latitude of Acceptance 24,
      Images 25, Check Out 26*
Summary 26
Why Are You Taking This Course? 27
The Group 27
Looking Ahead 29
Discussion Questions 30
Endnotes 30

2

Self-Concept 32

Preview 32
Objectives 32
Definition of the Self-Concept 36
    *Ideas about Who You Are 36, The
    Johari Window 37*
Components of the Self-Concept 39
    Beliefs 40, Values 43, Attitudes 44
The Evolution of the Self-Concept 45
    *Processes in Self-Concept Evolution
    45, The Influence of Significant
    Others 47*
Interpersonal Needs in the Self-
  Concept 52
    *Need for Inclusion 52, Need to
    Control 53, Need of Affection 53*
Self-Concept Maintenance 54
    Survival Orientation 54
Guidelines for Self-Concept
  Development 58
Summary 59
Discussion Questions 60
Endnotes 60

3

Perceiving Self and Others
62

Preview 62
Objectives 62
The Functions of Perception 65
The Qualities of Perception 66
How You Perceive 68
    *Sensory Aspects of Perception 68,
    Physical Influences on Perception
    69, The Act of Perceiving 71*
Perception as Interpretation 73
    *Closure 75, Perceptual Organizing
    76, Selectivity 78*
Perceiving Others 81
    Mutual Experience 82, Change 84
Building Accuracy in Perception 85
    *Building Receptive Skills 85,
    Building Interpretive Skills 87*
Summary 89
Discussion Questions 90
Endnotes 91

4

Listening to Others 92

Preview 92
Objectives 92
Why Is Listening a Problem? 95
  Listening Requires Effort 95, Noise
    Inhibits Listening 95, The Idea
    Doesn't Require Full Attention 96,
    The Speaker's Message Is
    Assumed 96, The Idea is Contrary
    to the Value and Belief System 97,
    Faulty Hearing Can Cause Faulty
    Listening 97
The Listening Process 98
  Components of the Listening
    Process 98
Using the Model of the Listening
  Process 100
  Sensing Problems 100, Attending
    Problems 101, Understanding
    Problems 103, Remembering
    Problems 107
Listening Improvement 108
  Work at Being Involved 109, Keep
    an Open Mind 111, Listen with
    Empathy 111, Use Active
    Listening 113, Check Out Your
    Conclusions 115, Increase Your
    Ability to Remember 116
Summary 118
Discussion Questions 119
Endnotes 120

5

Talking about Feelings 122

Preview 122
Objectives 122
Communication and Emotional Control
  124
  Attachment 125, Denial Strategies
    126
Expressing Emotions 126
  Emotions Exist in Language 126,
    Emotions Are Cognitively
    Controlled 130, Emotions Have
    Behavioral Consequences 132,
    Anxiety Has Behavioral
    Consequences 136
Communicating Feelings 137
  Recognize Feelings 138, Emotions:
    The Expression of Physical
    Feelings 139, Limited Language
    Ability 140
Solving the Problem of Expressing
  Emotions 144
  Learning More Feeling Words 147,
    Completing the Verbal
    Message 149, Avoiding Denial
    Strategies 152
Summary 153
Discussion Questions 154
Endnotes 155

6

Language and Interpersonal Relationships 156

Preview 156
Objectives 156
The Nature of Language 159
Language and Experience 160, The Triangle of Meaning 160, The Abstraction Process 162
The Bases of Language 166
Language and Culture 166, Language and Society 167, Language and Relationships 169
Language and the Self 172
Language Expresses the Self 172, Figurative Language Reveals the Self 173, Naming the Self and Relationships 174, Modes of Expression: Assertive, Nonassertive, and Aggressive 179
Problems with Using Language 180
Stereotyping and Self-Fulfilling Prophesy 181, Confusing the Map and the Territory 182, Polarization and the Two-Valued Orientation 183
Summary 185
Discussion Questions 186
Endnotes 187

7

Nonverbal Expression 190

Preview 190
Objectives 190
General Body Cues 193
Clothing 193, Artifacts 196, Body Movement and Gestures 199
Particular Body Cues 204
Face and Eye Behavior 204, Touching Behavior 208
Environmental Cues 210
Space 212, Personal Distancing 218, Time 218
Paraverbal Cues 221
Turn Taking 221, Interpretation 222, Vocal Quality and Vocalizations 223
Summary 223
Discussion Questions 224
Endnotes 225

8

Defending and Supporting 228

Preview 228
Objectives 228
Defensive Communication Behavior 231
  Why You Defend Yourself 231, When and How You Defend Yourself 232, Negative Responses to Another's Definition of Self 234, Consequences of Defensive Behavior 235, Alternatives to Defensive Behaviors 236
Supportive Communication Behavior 237
  Characteristics of Supportive Climates 237, Benefits of Supportive Communication 242, Choosing to Remain Supportive 244
Summary 246
Discussion Questions 247
Endnotes 247

9

Managing Conflict and Stress 250

Preview 250
Objectives 250
Conflict Locations 253
Intrapersonal Conflict 253
  Approach-Avoidance Conflict 254, Avoidance-Avoidance Conflict 255, Approach-Approach Conflict 256, Intervention Techniques 257
Interpersonal Conflict 258
  The Conflict Episode 259, Forcing Strategies 265, Confrontation and Problem-Solving Strategy 266, Typical Use of Interpersonal Conflict Strategies 266, Managing Interpersonal Conflict 268
Stress 272
  Consequences of Stress 272, Managing Stress: A Plan 273, Stress and Body Relaxation 275
Summary 276
Discussion Questions 277
Endnotes 277

10

Caring for the Relationship 280

Preview 280
Objectives 280
Relational Development 282
    Initiating 282, Experimenting 284,
    Intensifying 285, Integrating 286,
    Renegotiating 288, Bonding 290
Relational Deterioration 290
    Differentiating 292, Circumscribing
    293, Stagnating 293, Avoiding
    294, Terminating 295
Two Important Relational Elements 295
    Relational Definition 295, Relational
    Rules 296
Initiating Relationships 297
    Why You Engage 297, Basic
    Interpersonal Needs 298,
    Engaging Another Person 300
Promoting Relational Growth 300
    Appropriate Self-Disclosure 301,
    Achieving Role and Rule
    Agreement 301, Giving
    Support 302, Demonstrating
    Affection and Liking 302,
    Managing Conflict
    Constructively 303
Confronting Relational Problems 303
    Preventing Stagnation 303

Combating Relational Decay 304
    Assessing and Understanding the
    Problem 304, Developing a Course
    of Action 306
Summary 308
Discussion Questions 310
Endnotes 310

Epilogue 313

Self-Help Guide 314

Credits 325

Index 327

Preface

Enrollments and offerings in interpersonal communication have increased in nearly every college and university across the country in spite of the fact that budgets and selections in many other areas of the curriculum have declined dramatically. This increase in enrollment suggests that students realize the value of a course in interpersonal communication. They appear to know that the course promotes growth and helps them to meet their interpersonal needs in both their personal and professional lives.

This text is designed for students and teachers in a range of interpersonal communication courses, but especially for those who are directly involved in an introductory course. *Interpersonal Growth through Communication* has a strong skills approach, grounded in interpersonal research and theory.

We three authors have been researching and teaching interpersonal communication and serving as interpersonal communication consultants in the business community for many years. Our students have varied in age and experience from eighteen to twenty-two-year-old undergraduates, to business and industry employees, to adults who have returned to college—sometimes after retirement—to resume their educations. The experiences we have had with these students led us to the conclusion that a text that puts interpersonal communication into a relational context is needed.

Interpersonal Growth through Communication is research- and theory-based. Its organization, especially the inclusion of several unique examinations of current topics in the field of interpersonal communication, will assist the readers in becoming more efficient and more effective interpersonal communicators. These examinations include traditional communication situations as well as several especially troublesome areas that are not addressed by any current texts.

- The book allows the student to see how interpersonal skills relate to the process of relationship development. This feature, while not unique to this text, has not been effectively utilized in a number of currently available texts.
- The book provides a far more comprehensive and, we believe, more useful treatment of such topics as expressing emotions, defending and supporting, and interpersonal conflict management.

- The book contains a section on stress as it relates to interpersonal contexts, an area that has received minimal treatment in other communication texts.
- The book develops a system that will help the students to diagnose relationship problems in a variety of settings and to talk more carefully and specifically about those problems.

The Self-Help Guide, also included in the text, is an original tool that will guide students through interpersonal communication problems. This section is designed to make the book useful to the student beyond classroom applications. The Self-Help Guide includes questions that are indexed to pages in the text where answers may be found. The questions are about problems commonly faced in day-to-day interpersonal communication encounters.

The book includes frequent examples and illustrative materials that have been "field tested" to hold the student's attention and to clarify the concepts by using the student's own experience as the primary vehicle for understanding. Exercises that give the student an opportunity to apply principles have been included in the text at appropriate places. In addition, each chapter includes a carefully worded preview, a list of discussion questions, and photos, diagrams, and illustrations to make the book both interesting and useful.

From time to time throughout *Interpersonal Growth through Communication,* the reader will encounter a group of individuals in a series of interpersonal experiences. The identities of the group members have been changed for obvious reasons, but we have created their experiences from actual classroom observations as well as from reports these students have made to us. We have chosen experiences that relate directly to the topics of the chapters. Students will be able to identify with these group members because they are real. But more importantly, the group's actions exemplify the concepts in practice.

Many people have helped us in the preparation of the manuscript. We were associated with Herb Hess and Charles Tucker for many years. Their influence on us was massive. We want to acknowledge our debt and appreciation to them. William C. Brown Publishers was unusually thorough in making inquiries about interpersonal communication courses and about the students who enroll in such courses. We refined the book's structure and content as a result of the response to these inquiries by people who teach the course.

The following people have provided insightful comments and suggestions that improved our manuscript. They have our gratitude.

Lois Almen
College of San Mateo

John C. Countryman
University of Richmond

Jim Crocker-Lakness
University of Cincinnati

Robert C. Dick
Indiana University, Indianapolis

William Douglas
University of Houston

Jackson Huntley
University of Minnesota, Duluth

Bernadette M. MacPherson
Emerson College

Judy C. Pearson
Ohio University

Sharon A. Ratliffe
Golden West College

Rita Schlecht, Rhonda Youngblood, and Bob Girola worked long hours—often well beyond normal closing time—to see that the chores of producing this manuscript were completed. We thank them for their effort.

Mary Jean Gregory's work with each line of our manuscript improved it dramatically. Mary Jean knows what to do with language, and she was generous with her help. We are very grateful.

Louise Waller and Judith Clayton, our editors, saw us from the birth of the project to its completion. They were enormously helpful. Of course, they were supposed to do that, but their help went beyond what authors might expect. We appreciate their excellent advice and effort.

Gerald L. Wilson
Alan M. Hantz
Michael S. Hanna

Interpersonal Growth Through
Communication

The Interpersonal Communication Process

Preview

This chapter sets the stage for *Interpersonal Growth through Communication*. It explains why people engage in interpersonal communication and how interpersonal skills generate growth. It previews the remainder of the book and strikes a keynote.

Objectives

After reading this chapter, you should be able to complete the following:

1. Explain how the study of interpersonal communication can benefit your life, both professionally and personally.
2. Define communication in useful terms.
3. Identify, define, and explain in your own words these key terms from a model of the communication process:

source	context
decoder	messages
encoder	noise
feedback	receiver
channels	

4. Explain "the meanings people 'get' are those they generate."
5. Construct a model of the interpersonal communication process.
6. Explain how feedback, sensitivity, self-disclosure, trust, and risk work together as the central aspects of learning to communicate better.
7. Identify the content and relationship levels as separate dimensions of communication.
8. Explain the components of an agenda for talking about relationships.

M ary and Russ were experiencing a familiar college experience. They had met each other at a party, and then again in the student center. They found that they shared many things in common: they loved the out-of-doors; they were avid white-water canoeists; they enjoyed the feeling of excitement when the crisp air of the high mountain meadow was moved by the early autumn breeze. Yet they also had some differences that each found intriguing: he loved photography; she loved art; he was an avid sports fan; she was more interested in the social life that surrounds college sports. Their relationship held promise when they found that they had so much in common. They were clearly attracted to each other.

Then, for some unexplained reason, their time together seemed less satisfying. They had made enough of a commitment to continue seeing each other, but it became clear that something was different. Each believed in the promise of that first glance—the promise of an intimate, on-going, deeply satisfying relationship. What had happened?

Of course, the reason for this change is not known for sure. But what seems clear is that Russ and Mary knew something was wrong and either did not or could not deal with it. Perhaps they needed ways to talk to each other about what was happening. Perhaps they needed more skill in understanding how to nourish the relationship. These are the fundamental skills of interpersonal communication. Russ and Mary needed to develop these interpersonal skills in order to nurture their relationship.

This book examines interpersonal communication with a determination that whoever works with the exercises and reads the text will come away with improved interpersonal communication skills. The fundamental purpose of the book, however, is to cause you to think more intelligently about your interpersonal communication events. We want you to think objectively and reflectively about the enormously complex process of communication. It is the means by which people develop into the individuals they are.

Why Study Interpersonal Communication?

The pattern established early in his life became, more or less, an indication of how James's life was going to go for him. He had learned that he was not OK. In order to become OK, James had to work hard. So James always tried to do good—within the limits that the significant other people in his life laid out for him. Imagine how he must have felt when he went away from home to college. Suddenly he was confronted by people who didn't share his views. Some openly and happily did things that he had learned to hide, if he did them at all. For example, one day while walking across campus, he noticed a couple of college students lying on the grass under an oak tree. They were necking. They were actually being sexual. James, from his understanding, was shocked.

On another occasion, a guy in the dormitory tried to enlist James in a business venture. The man was selling term papers to freshmen English composition students. Since James could write and knew how to use the library, he would be a valuable asset to the already lucrative business. James was dumbfounded by the suggestion that he participate in something so dishonest. Moreover, he couldn't believe his ears. This man was completely candid and open about the proposition.

James's attitudes and behaviors were shaped by his early training. He was the product of all of his interactions with others and of the connections he had made among those interactions. This idea, called "Symbolic Interactionism," has been enormously influential in the field of human communication.[1]

Had James known about the ideas of the symbolic interactionists, he would have been able to rest easier. He'd have realized that there was nothing basic in him that was evil. He would have known that he had determined on his own, by talking with others and by talking to himself, that he was OK. More importantly, James might have learned how to improve his self-concept and his self-confidence.

We want to teach you the skills to improve both your image of yourself—your self-concept—and your satisfaction with your relationships. We're going to focus on skills that can provide you a great deal more self-confidence than you might now have. And, in doing these things, we're going to focus on skills and methods that will help you to achieve your relational goals more often, more efficiently, and more effectively.

Professional Dimension

Effective communication is definitely advantageous in a person's professional life. Because they embrace many of the other advantages, the two most important are influence and impression management. As you can imagine, managing your impression and influencing are clearly related and are important to the ability to lead others. When you work with other people, either on the job or in a social context, there is always the element of leadership. You may try to influence your colleagues in a variety of ways on the job. You also try, more often than might be supposed, to influence your friends in social contexts.

For example, suppose John, who is between school terms, is looking for something interesting to do next Saturday morning. He enjoys George's company, so when he runs into George at a social gathering Wednesday evening after school, John tries to persuade George to go fishing with him.

"Hello, George. What have you been up to?"

"I've been really busy, but I'm thinking of taking a vacation. Other than that, I've been okay." (Note that George didn't answer the question. He was working on his own agenda. It might be difficult to influence him.)

John plants a seed. "I always try to take a little vacation each weekend." Now he exercises his influence. "What do you think about getting together this weekend for some R and R?"

"Hmmm . . ." George is attracted, but is weighing this general proposal against other ideas he's had. Too vague? Not enough information? He may be thinking that he's not sure what he wants to do and doesn't want to make a commitment. "I don't know. What do you have in mind?"

"I hooked into a very good strike out on Green Lake last week. I think maybe I'll go back there and see if I can catch the rascal this time." John has just tried to develop an image for George that he believes George will have no trouble "hooking into."

"Oh yea?" George is interested.

"Yea, but losing him didn't really matter. The place was just beautiful. I guess I've never seen the water so clear. . . ."

George is hooked. "Was the weather warm enough to be comfortable?"

"I took my coat off by 9:30 and was plenty glad to have a cold one by 10:15." That should do the trick. George's favorite beverage comes in an aluminum can!

"What do you say to our going together this weekend?" George just made John's proposal for him. John has got him.

"Sure. You name the time and place." John will let George finish his image, but John will get what he wants, too.

People have many opportunities every day to utilize interpersonal skills to influence others. Knowing when to stand and when to back off; when to negotiate and when to hold to a position; when to challenge and when to give in; and when to use power and when to avoid using power are all part of the interpersonal communication process that affect school and professional life.

Social Dimension

The social reasons for studying interpersonal communication may seem obvious, but remember the social setting is different from the work setting. There is a social dimension in all communication events and social settings have a particularly important impact on your health and happiness. The central concern in a social context is "relationship." Knowing how to manage relationships involves being able to talk about them when that seems to be a good idea. It also involves knowing how to communicate about relationships when it's not a good idea to bring them up to the level of talk.

So many different kinds of important relationships—every one social—happen in people's lives that it is possible to say they are the stuff of the human condition. To the extent that you become skillful in talking interpersonally, and to the extent that you learn to value honesty in your interpersonal communication—that is to say, game-free candor—you will be able to increase the quality and intimacy of your life.

These ideas will be discussed throughout the book. Therefore, it is essential that the term "interpersonal communication" is defined. The easiest way to do that is to distinguish this term from a larger context. So first, a general model of the communication process will be described, into which inter-personal communication can be placed. Then interpersonal communication will become the focus, with some models presented to clarify this meaning.

Models of the Communication Process

What is communication? *Communication* is the continuous process of verbal and nonverbal message exchange by which people identify, define, and main-tain their relationships and conduct their affairs. You can participate in that process if you wish, but whether you participate or not, the process continues. Because communication is a process, this definition is limiting and serves pri-marily as a "keynote." A better explanation of the term exists in a model.

Process Model of Communication

Figure 1.1 is a *process model of communication*. This model just stands for the process and is, therefore, limited. But the uses of the model outweigh its lim-itations. For one thing, the model provides a point of view that will continue throughout this book. For another, it visualizes the process as a process. You can refer to it as you read. The model also provides a framework for comparison of the various parts of this book. Take a look at the model.[2]

Parts of the Process Model of Communication

The model is labeled to indicate that two individuals are working together in one setting. The *source* is the location of an idea. Obviously, in interpersonal contexts, the source of the idea is an individual. The next term, *encoder,* is used in the same box to show that individuals must translate ideas into codes. The most common, but by no means the only, code is language. You can also encode into many different nonverbal message systems. For example, you can communicate with muscle changes. You can communicate by using space in peculiar ways. You can communicate with the clothes you wear. Or you can communicate by the gestures you use and the tone of voice you use.

Figure 1.1 Model of the Communication Process

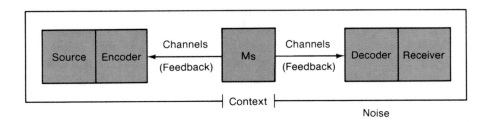

Notice that, at the other side of the model, another individual must *de-code* the messages sent. Since the messages sent out do *not* have meaning in and of themselves (meaning is in the minds of those who use the codes), then messages must be decoded in order to make them meaningful. Skill in decoding is just as important as skill in encoding.

The source/encoder transmits messages—plural. Since more than one code is used every time you communicate, you must be sending more than one message. The *M*'s in the box in the middle suggest these multiple messages.

These messages have to be transmitted through *channels*. A person talking with you is using vibrations in the molecular structure of the air as a channel. If this person is visible as well as audible, you will pick up many nonverbal messages, too. In that case, light waves are being used as channels. If a phone is used, electrical impulses over a wire are being used to send messages. Even in this situation, a phone call, more than one message is sent. Words, phrases, tone, stress, and emphasis are all communicated.

Notice the arrowheads at either end of the middle line labeled "channels." These arrowheads suggest that messages travel in both directions at the same time. This special feature of the model is *feedback*. A decoder feeds back what is heard so that the encoder can control and correct the message if it is wrong. Feedback also suggests that messages flow in both directions at the same time. This two-way flow allows the encoder to know what is being received. This in turn allows for modification in action during communication.

Reexamine figure 1.1. Notice that all components of the model are enclosed in the context of the communication event. Everything available to the communicators in that event—including all that the participants brought with them—affects the message exchange. Health, attitudes and opinions, emotional condition, and inhibitions all come into play at the moment. Outside these things, the context is filled with noise.

The term *noise* is the label for anything that disrupts or distorts communication. Noise can be both physical (disturbances in the channels) and emotional. Sometimes called "semantic," noise is anything going on inside the participants that upsets the accuracy of message reception or transmission.

A potential for noise is in the source/encoder. If the encoder has a biased perception, or uses strong language, for example, noise is introduced. Or there can be noise in the channels. Hear that air conditioner or furnace working? Is anything happening in the next room? If something is happening, you are aware of it because of the noise. If something is not happening, then you have checked that out, too, by examining the noise in the environment.

There is also the potential for noise in messages. This is especially possible when people of different cultures try to talk with each other. Or offensive language is sometimes used by people speaking the same tongue. Sometimes, too, nonverbal signs and signals are sent out that are noisy. These problems are compounded when the expectations of other cultures are introduced. Often very noisy results are produced.

To illustrate, Tim was working as a busboy in a restaurant that also employed an Iranian student on the same shift. One day he raised his thumb to the Iranian student in what he supposed was a friendly gesture meaning, "Everything is good. You did well." The Iranian, apparently still feeling strongly about American press stories on Iranian students during the hostage crisis during the Carter administration, knocked Tim off his feet. It wasn't until later, when the two were able to talk about the incident, that Tim learned that his friendly signal was identical to one used in Iran for an obscene message. The thumbs-up message was noise in that particular context.

Communication Channels

Most Americans think about communication in terms of a one-way, highly linear phenomenon; like water going through a pipe. Assuming that there are no blockages in the pipe, the water flows through smoothly. A similar metaphor is the operation of the U.S. Postal system, where you write a note on a piece of paper, enclose the paper in an envelope, put a stamp in the right place on the envelope, then drop the envelope into a mailbox. Assuming that the system is intact, the letter will get to its destination. Your responsibility seems to end when you drop the envelope into the mailbox. You have done all you can do to ensure accuracy in communication.

Although this metaphor is limiting when used to describe the communication process, part of this model is useful. It allows you to understand, for example, how important it is to keep the channels of communication open! But the idea of open communication has the potential for harm, too, because it suggests that once something is said, your responsibility for communication accuracy ends. If the message is not received correctly, the decoder is at fault. Open communication assumes that the responsibility for accuracy is shared, but at different times, by the sender and the receiver. These assumptions are false, as you will see later in this book.

Filtering Screen Model

Recall the idea that meaning is not contained in words: that the meanings people "get" are those they generate. Now examine figure 1.2, another model of the communication process, that focuses on what happens when you communicate.

All *S*'s to the left of the figure stand for stimuli. This term is used because once a message—say, a word—is sent, the message loses its significance. It becomes part of the environment. The word becomes, until it is heard, merely vibrations in the air column. It is only one of an infinite number of stimuli in the environment. If you make stimuli significant, they are. If you ignore them, they are not meaningful to you.

Figure 1.2 Filtering Screen Model

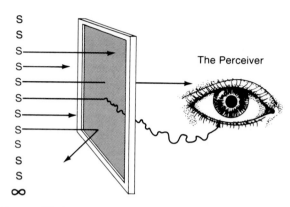

Frame of Reference—A Filter for One's Experience

Your Filtering Process

To illustrate this point, focus your attention on your left ear. Until your attention was called to it, you may not have been aware of it at all. Yet, your ear was there before. How does the ear feel? Can you test the temperature of the ear with your attention only? Can you check out to see if it itches, or if there's a hint of an earache? Can you become aware of the sense of hearing in that ear?

You can probably do all of these things because of the *filtering system* that allows you to attend to certain stimuli and to ignore others. If your ear began to hurt, you would no longer ignore it. The data would become significant.

To provide you with another example, look more closely at the actual ink on the page you are now reading. Center on the formation of the letters. You have been reading along without really paying attention to the ink on the page or the formation of the letters.

Look at the enlarged letter in figure 1.3. Why didn't you pay attention to the height of the "t" relative to other letters? The information was always there, but you didn't pay attention to it because, until now, it wasn't important. The features on the letter "t" go unnoticed until something calls attention to them. Besides, you are processing the symbols on this page in ways that prohibit an examination of individual letters. You are looking for groupings and for patterns, not for letters.

Y O U C O U L D R E A D T H I S L I N E O F T Y P E only if you studied the individual letters, then forced a grouping and a pattern on them. This is necessary since the line of type violates your perceptual expectations. But this   line is   somewhat   different   and, no doubt, is easier for you to read. This pattern of ink on paper is a violation of what you

Figure 1.3

would expect, too, but the groupings make sense. Thisl   ine,ont
heoth   erhand,i   safarmo   redifficult line to examine because the
groupings and patterns are a complete violation of perceptual expectations.
The stimuli are essentially changed, but not because of the ink on the paper.
The change is in the pattern of ink on paper. You probably weren't aware of
the pattern, nor the shape of the various letters that make up the pattern. You
were aware of your understanding of the pattern. You filtered the data, paying
attention only to those that seemed important to you.

To provide you with still another example, did you notice those two dots
in the upper margin of this sheet?

Return to the model. The eye to the right of the screen symbolizes all of
the ways you can take in data: through your eyes, ears, nose, mouth (both by
taste and touch), and skin. The perceptual process is a system, and you will
almost always involve more than one way of receiving data in any perceptual
moment. You are looking at this sheet of paper, but you are probably also
touching the book. Perhaps you are sitting in a chair under a lighted lamp. You
may be playing music. Your brain is always monitoring ways of sensing. But
at the unconscious level, you are filtering what gets through to your awareness.
It is in that context that you are processing your messages. They become merely
additional data for you to perceive. You have the responsibility to select those
to which you will attend and those that you will ignore.

The two communication models introduced here are useful. The first shows
that the components of the communication process always exist in a context.
There is always a process of encoding and decoding when people are communicating. Feedback is important to the model. And noise is a continuing
problem. In fact, the control of noise—either physical or psychological—is the
difference between what is effective and what is ineffective communication.

The second model is an aid to help you understand the essence of meaning inside your head. What is out there—outside of you—is a stimulus field into
which all sent messages must fall. What gets through your own filtering de-
vices is up to you. The meanings you generate from what you allow through
your filters are your realities. They are your understanding. They are what is
real—and all that is real—for you. Thus, your meanings are in you and not in
the messages sent to you. There are no meanings in words, there are only
meanings in the people who use words.

An Interpersonal Exchange Model

These models apply to every communication event. Communication scholars have typically divided the communication process into subsections in order to study the process more carefully. One of these subsections, the most basic, is called *intrapersonal communication*. The prefix "intra-" refers to whatever is going on inside an individual. At this level, means and methods of processing data are the substance of communication.

The level of greatest import to us is *interpersonal communication*. "Inter-" means "between." Thus, interpersonal means between persons. Interpersonal communication also occurs at the group level. In *Interpersonal Growth through Communication,* the complex interactions of three or more people are discussed in the context of committee meetings and work groups. What is said in these situations also applies to interpersonal interactions within other small groups, too. In addition to the group, there are a number of one-to-many settings in which interpersonal communication is an important part. Public speaking is the most obvious one-to-many context.

This book is about these interpersonal communication contexts. The variables in a communication event involving two individuals in message exchange are discussed. Figure 1.4 is a very useful model of the interpersonal communication process, but is a little more complicated than the others already presented.

Notice that the model in figure 1.4 is dominated by arrows, suggesting the flow of communication. Look more closely. You see that there are two persons represented. Does your interest begin to fail because of the rather complicated movement your eye must make across unfamiliar terms? Don't be discouraged. The noise and the problem will be broken up for you. The resulting insight is worth the effort.

Look for the numbers and follow these. The terms will be defined as the interaction the model represents is described. Find Person *B* in the upper right of the model. That person is someone you've never met named Frank.

1. (Stimulus: any person, object, or thing that causes you to initiate communication) You see Frank.
2. (Sensitivity: ability to discover stimuli and to discriminate among them) You take in a variety of stimuli.
3. (Perception: bringing stimuli into your body and becoming aware of them) You register some of the things you sense about Frank. You notice, for example, that he is tall, rather nice-looking, quick to smile, and self-assured.
4. (Weighing risk: comparing the probability of positive or negative outcomes) You consider what these stimuli mean to you. "He might be friendly to me. I think I'll risk saying hello—maybe I can risk talking about my interest in movies. At least, I should be able to talk about the course we're taking."

Figure 1.4 Model of the Interpersonal Process

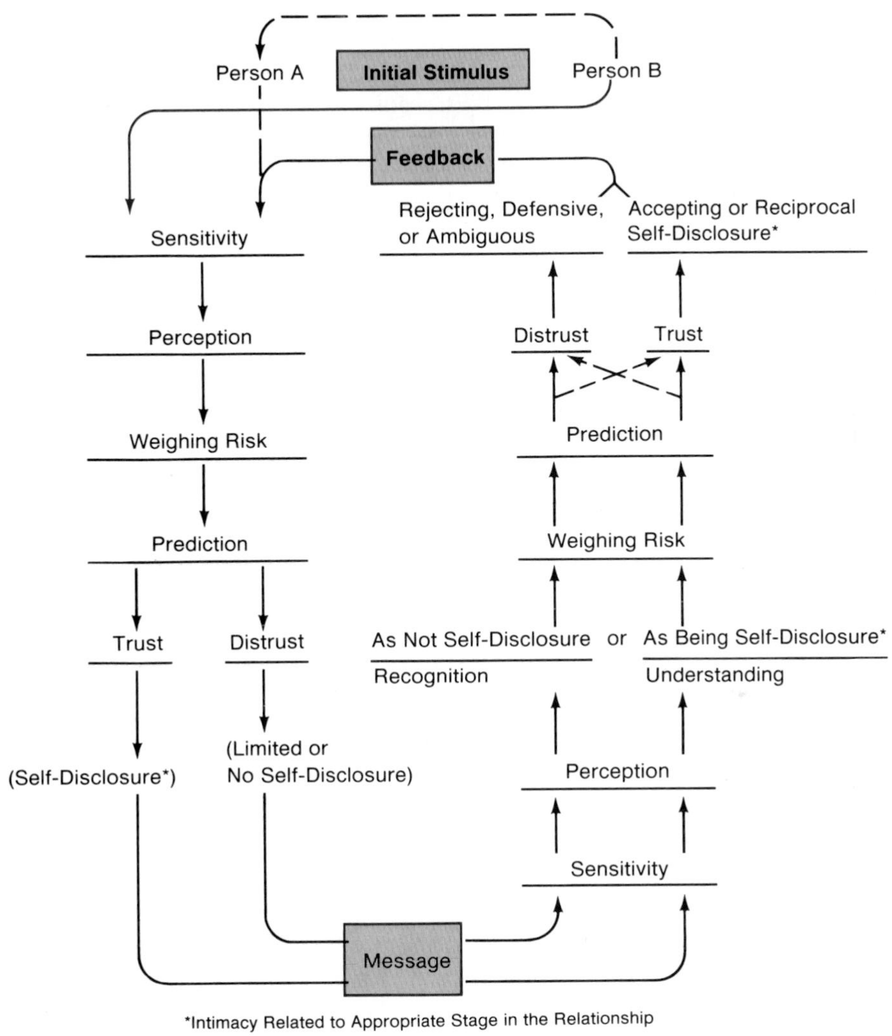

*Intimacy Related to Appropriate Stage in the Relationship

5. (Prediction: making guesses about possible outcomes) ''I think I can trust that person,'' ''I think I cannot trust that person . . .''

Steps six and seven have two parts, dependent upon the decision made.

6. a. (Trust: determination that the other person will behave in a positive way, given an opportunity to choose positive or negative behavior in the situation) ''Hmmmm. There is good reason to think Frank will

respond positively, though of course, there is a chance that he won't. Still he's smiling. He resembles me in some ways. I trust him . . ."

    b. (Distrust: believing that the other person will behave in a negative way given an opportunity to choose positive or negative behavior in the situation) "Hmmm. There's something about this guy that I just can't put my finger on. But I don't like the way he looks. I'll have to be careful . . ."

7. a. (Self-disclosure: opening oneself to another, revealing the truth about one's self) "I really would rather be seeing a film than taking this course."

    b. (No self-disclosure: not revealing oneself to another) "What do you think about . . .?" (Message) (Note: Message is whatever you send to receiver, both information and feelings.)

Now it's Frank's turn. Following the model, notice that Frank must go through essentially the same process that you did when you met him. He has to guess, however, whether or not you disclosed yourself to him. If he recognizes self-disclosure on your part, he will probably behave in an accepting and self-disclosing way. If Frank understands your self-disclosure as an invitation to greater intimacy, he will almost certainly provide you with feedback. It is your turn again. If that happens, your relationship has a good chance of growing. But if he understands that your message does not disclose yourself and so behaves in a rejecting way, or if he understands your self-disclosure, but rejects you anyway, then the relationship probably won't grow. You will probably disengage.

Key Interpersonal Communication Concepts

There are a few other ideas that are important throughout this book. These terms work as a system: each is part of the others and the sum total of these, plus the relationships among them, constitute the critical issues in learning to communicate better in any circumstance. These terms are feedback, sensitivity, self-disclosure, trust, and risk. They can be described one by one, but they cannot exist in isolation from the others.

Feedback

Feedback is the process by which an individual sends messages to another for the purpose of correction and control of ideas or images he or she has received from that other person. Feedback can occur in either the content dimension of communication or in the social, or relationship, dimension. Sometimes it is deliberate and sometimes it is accidental.

Sensitivity

Sensitivity is an individual's skill and ability to perceive and to interpret what is perceived with empathy. That is, you are sensitive to the extent that you skillfully observe and make guesses that take another into account and reflect your ability to empathize. You can't really experience what another person does, but you can experience the moment in ways that are essentially similar to the other's own ways. The key to sensitivity is the awareness that you are guessing, and that the guess needs to be checked out. Thus, sensitive people emphathize. They do that because they are willing and able to take others into account, and do so frequently. Sensitivity has to do with the perceptual mechanisms and the interpretations that are made of those perceptions.

Self-Disclosure

Self-disclosure is the process of revealing the truth about oneself, including desires, needs, and goals. You self-disclose when you report your honest attitudes about another or another's ideas, or about yourself and your ideas. You self-disclose when you respond candidly, daring to display your images.

Trust

Trust is the foundation of self-disclosure. Trust is the phenomenon that gives you permission to disclose yourself. It is reliance on another to confirm yourself. You trust another if you believe you can show yourself without getting hurt. You trust that your self-disclosure will be received and accepted. Indeed, the bases of trust include another's character, competence, and judgment as you perceive them.[3]

If a person is open, honest, and discrete; behaves consistently; and if you perceive the person's motives and intentions to be confirming, then you trust the other's character. If this person has a track record of successes, then you trust his or her competence. And if you think this individual makes the right decisions—there is evidence of good judgment—then you trust the individual's judgment. If all of these are combined in your image of this person, then you trust in and will be able to risk disclosing yourself to him or her.

Risk

Risk is the process of deciding to accept adverse outcomes that may result from trusting another. The greater the risk involved, the more you must trust. "Taking the risk" is usually an expression of a decision to gamble that you'll receive positive, not negative, consequences from your actions. In its simplest form, to risk is to weigh payoffs and costs, and to determine that the payoff for behaving in a certain way is likely to be greater than the cost involved. When the decision is about self-disclosure, the risk is that you may be damaged by trusting another enough to disclose yourself.

Thus feedback, sensitivity, self-disclosure, trust, and risk are interrelated. The ability to interact in a game-free exchange—one in which the participants are open to each other; one in which they grow—depends on these interpersonal events. This is the goal of *Interpersonal Growth through Communication.*

Content and Relationship

In every communication event, both a content and a relationship exist. Each is vital to the event.

Content Dimension

The content involves topics such as plans, problems, and solutions. In the statement, "Look, it's raining outside," the topic is rain. Discussion of the rain is in the content dimension because it refers to some object, phenomenon, or event outside of you and outside the realm of a relationship.

Relationship Dimension

There is also a relationship dimension. Compare and contrast these three different ways to tell that it is raining outside; differences, you'll discover, that have precious little to do with the topic of rain. They have to do with the relationship between you and another that is assumed when the talk turns to rain:

1. "Look, it's raining outside."
2. "If you have the time, and if it is convenient for you, would you be willing to look outside? It is raining, and—I mean—the rain seems so beautiful. . . ."
3. "Look! I said, LOOK! It's raining."

In each of these sentences, the topic of the content dimension is rain, a relatively commonplace phenomenon. But the tone and the style of the sentences suggest that a different relationship is involved in each of the three utterances.

Number one, "Look, it's raining outside," is straightforward. The assumption most people would make on hearing this sentence is that one person of equal status made a discovery and was attempting to share it with another. The second sentence, "If you have the time . . . if it is convenient for you . . . would you be willing to . . . , could be spoken only by lower-status people, or those who believe themselves to be lower status. The third sentence, "Look! I said, Look! It's raining," could only come from individuals who think they have a right to boss others around.

Clearly, the differences among the three sentences are involved in the relationship dimension of communication. Talking about the relationship is the real key to successful interpersonal communication. Most of the time people are pretty good at talking about content. But also most of the time, individuals do not talk directly about the nature of their relationships. A very complex set of alternative, nonverbal codes for communicating with each other about relationships has evolved. Relationship communication is left to tone of voice, quick changes of musculature, or placement relative to the other person. However, interpersonal communication will improve when people learn to talk more clearly and more accurately about the relationships that exist between them.

Absolute Present

One way to improve the accuracy of your discussions about your relationships is to accept the fact that you live in the present. This idea is absolute. You cannot live at any other time than right now, not in the future or in the past. But you can remember the past because you have language.

The person who is now a college student, but talks and acts as if his experiences in high school are the present, is trying to live in the past. The person who lives for and as if she is the physician she is studying to be, is trying to live in the future. Both situations cause problems in relationships and communication because most people experience others in the present.

This idea of the absolute present is sometimes intimidating, but it can be greatly liberating, too. Since you can only live in the present, and since you cannot take back the past, then all that has come before is history. You have to choose—in the present—how you'll respond, emotionally, to past events. This choice can allow you to influence how others view your past. But it can also allow you to guide their perceptions of you while you are in contact. You can choose from among many possibilities: you're not "stuck" with only one!

What you want and what you can expect involve the future. You can learn to deal with others in relationship to what you want—mostly free of the ties you have to the past—if only you choose to do that.

Personalizing

Another way to clarify your messages about your relationships is to personalize your verbal communication. This is making clear by your choice of language that you are taking responsibility for your own statements and judgments.

That's a fairly complicated notion. To illustrate it, suppose your instructor walked up to a person in your class who has just presented an outstanding analysis of a case study. He says, "You are wonderful." Clearly, he is making a judgment about the woman. He is responsible for the decision to judge those stimuli coming into him as "wonderful." Put another way, the idea "wonderful" is a function of his own value system.

But look at the sentence again. "You are wonderful." The form of the sentence appears to say that the woman is intrinsically wonderful. Anyone hearing her analysis of the case study would judge her to be wonderful if that were the case, regardless of their preferences for subject matter, style, or their listening ability and expertise in the area addressed by the case study. The wonderfulness would in some sense, then, be something born into her. The instructor, listening to her, would have nothing whatever to do with her wonderfulness. Therefore, the form of his sentence makes the sentence incorrect. It denies the real truth—that the instructor, and not the woman, is responsible for his judgment about her analysis.

So long as there is no socially sensitive component in the sentence "You are wonderful," it is a compliment. So is "You are beautiful." Another student in the class might walk up to the woman and say "You are beautiful." Although the speaker might be considered forward, you do not notice that the form of the sentence is wrong.

The focus is not on the fact that the judgment actually belongs to the speaker if the judgment does not call attention to itself. But suppose the speaker said instead to that young woman, "You are, without a doubt, the ugliest and most repulsive-looking beast I have ever seen." Ah! That's another story, isn't it?

The woman would not ignore that sentence. She would undoubtedly be offended by it. She would instantly say the sentence is offensive, perhaps wrong, clearly inappropriate. But she might have some difficulty identifying *why* she felt that way. The fact is, the form of this sentence shifts the responsibility for the other student's judgment onto her. "Ugly" is not his responsibility, but hers! Ugliness is a function of some intrinsic quality in her if the form of the other student's sentence is correct.

For some personal experience with this idea, study the following two pictures. In order to determine which of these two paintings is more beautiful, you must call upon an internal set of criteria. That is, you must JUDGE which of the two is more beautiful. This judgment is a function of your own nervous system. But if you *say* that one of the pictures *is* more beautiful, you have used language that places the beauty in the picture rather than in yourself.[4]

Likewise, to personalize your talk is to state clearly that your judgments are your responsibility. Personalizing talk is also owning up to your responsibility. Sentences such as, "You make me mad," "You're crazy," "It's important that we follow this procedure," and "Don't you think that . . ." are problematic because none is personalized. Each places responsibility for your nervous system on someone or something outside of you. But they can be improved—and made much more accurate and meaningful—by personalizing them.

Not Personalized	**Personalized**
You're beautiful.	You seem beautiful to me.
You're ugly.	I don't like the way you look.
You make me mad.	When I see that behavior I respond with anger.
You're crazy.	That behavior seems crazy to me.
It's important that we . . .	I think it is important.
Don't you think that . . .	I think that . . . and I would like you to think so, too.

Seated Woman by Pablo Picasso, 1926–27, oil on canvas 51½″ × 38½″. Museum of Modern Art, NY. *Mona Lisa* by Leonardo da Vinci. Three Lions, NY.

If you can learn to stay in the present when it is helpful to do so—and that's almost always when you're working on your relationships—and if you can learn to personalize your talk when you need to, then you will already be a more efficient and more effective communicator than most of the people you will ever meet. These are relatively simple skills to learn, but it takes some practice to integrate them into your behavior patterns.

Agenda for Talking About Relationships

Figure 1.5 presents an agenda for talking about relationships. It shows all the components of a relationship. These components can be summarized into eight categories: observations, inferences, feelings, wants and expectations, intentions, latitude of acceptance, images and check out. Note on the agenda that five of these components, feelings, wants and expectations, intentions, latitudes of acceptance, and images, are boldfaced. This indicates that these five are the primary components of the agenda, although the other three are necessary.

Observations

Observations refer to anything you take inside and process as you are communicating with another individual. You can observe in many ways.

Figure 1.5 Agenda for Talking about Relationships

Task Dimension	Social Dimension
	Observations
	Inferences
	Feelings
	Wants and Expectations
	Intentions
	Latitudes of Acceptance
	Images
	Check Out

Inferences

Inferences are the guesses made about what observations mean. The truth is, *you can never read another's mind. You can never get inside another's head and know what is going on there.* You have to *guess* what is going on unless it is told to you. But you often act as though you can read someone else's mind. You often make an observation, and without identifying it, guess what another is thinking, and then act as though your guess is correct. This idea is called *fact-inference confusion* and is a very common problem. Perhaps you've had a similar experience to this one:

Said	**Thought**
He: Hello. How are you?	Hmmmm. Not bad looking. Nice eyes.
She: Hi. (Smiles) I'm just fine, although I think I am a little lost.	Thank goodness. Someone to help. Hmmm. Nice build. Must be an athlete.
He: Can I help you? I . . .	Nice smile. I'll help her. . . .
She: I'm trying to find the Drum Room. I've been up and down the street and . . .	I'm late. Hope he knows how to get there. His voice has command. I like that.
He: My name is David. I'm going there myself. Are you in the A.M.A.?	I can help. Maybe she'll walk along with me. That smile lights up her face. The A.M.A. is having a meeting. She must be a doctor!
She: Yes. I'm Jennifer. Are you in the A.M.A. too?	Maybe he'll ask me to walk along with him. That'd be pleasant. His suit must have been expensive.
David: Would you like to walk with me? It isn't far.	Me a doctor? I haven't even graduated from college yet. But there's no sense spoiling this opportunity. I'll see if I can find something else to talk about with her.

Said

Jennifer: I sure would. . . .

David: Are you making some kind of presentation?

Jennifer: I'm reading a paper at the 3:00 session. And I think I'm late as well as lost.

David: You're not late. You're quite a bit early. It's just a quarter until two. . . .

Could I buy you a drink?

Jennifer: I'd like that very much. Shall we go to the coffee shop here?

David: Sure. Where are you from?

Jennifer: I teach at the University of Iowa. Do you know where Iowa City is?

David: Yes. Where did you go to medical school?

Jennifer: Medical school! I'm a teaching assistant in the Marketing Department working on my Masters.

Thought

Dumb question. Why did I say that? For that matter, why didn't I just tell her I'm not a member?

He's not a member, but he's very good-looking. Wonder what he's going to do at the convention.

Well, I'm not the only one who makes mistakes. Wonder where she's from to be an hour off the time. Hmmm. White Shoulders—or is it Charlie?
I wonder if she's attached?

No ring. I wonder if he's attached? I don't want to get mixed up with . . .
He's surely not single. But then, maybe he is. . . . It won't hurt to have a cup of tea. I'm tired from the trip. Shouldn't have treated myself to that can of beer on the plane.

Dumb question again. Why couldn't I have said something like . . .

So what if I am a teaching assistant in my first term. He's probably a wealthy attorney or something.

I'll make small talk. She's out of my league. . . .

Where'd he get this idea?

From this short dialogue you can see that what people *say* is only a small part of what they experience at the moment. A good deal of what is experienced is guesswork—and often, wrong. For example, David felt he couldn't trust Jennifer. He didn't respond to her questions. He may have thought that the A.M.A. (we can suppose he saw a sign so he knew there was a meeting) was the American Medical Association. This guess would justify his next guess that Jennifer is a doctor. We can't know what was going on beyond what is provided, but notice that when Jennifer asked him if he was in the A.M.A., too, he responded with a question. Was he embarrassed by his own lack of education? He talks about not graduating from college—to himself. Does he equate his lack of formal education—his lack of a degree—with being not OK? He doesn't want to spoil an opportunity with Jennifer so he evades the issue by looking for another topic. Moreover, he chastises himself for asking Jennifer if she is making a presentation. Was he comparing himself to his image of Jennifer, and coming out badly in the comparison?

And what about Jennifer's reaction to David? She is attracted to him, it would seem. But how do you account for her devaluation of her own position as a teaching assistant in her first term? How do you account for her guess that David is a well-to-do professional? How do you account for her surprise that David asked the name of her medical school? The answer is obvious by now. They were operating on their own guesses as though the guesses were the truth. David and Jennifer were suffering from fact/inference confusion.

Relationships consist of observations and inferences, always in the present tense. You observe the other person, then infer what the observations mean. Sometimes you check those out, and sometimes you don't. Not checking these out can obviously create problems in a relationship.

Feelings

Feelings deal with the physical condition of individuals. Feelings are always physical, unlike *emotions,* which are the words used to describe feelings in particular contexts. You can't feel words, you feel your body. Then you attach words to those feelings.

But feelings are extremely important because contextually you assign language to them that has significance in your relationship. For instance, the physical feeling you get when experiencing anger may include an increased pulse and respiratory rate, elevated temperature, and an increase in the endocrinal juices that flow into the bloodstream. The resulting physiological evidence includes increased energy levels, a ''butterfly sensation'' in the stomach, or similar sensations. That physical feeling is sometimes called ''anger.'' But isn't this also the physical feeling you call ''sexual excitement'' in other contexts? Isn't it essentially the same thing you know as ''fear'' at still other times?

In interpersonal contexts, what you call your physical experience is critical to the relationship with another. If you experience these sensations with another and you term them fear, what does that say about the nature of your fear? If you're calling them anger, can you see that another's wrong guess has damage potential? So you see, one factor in a relationship is a guess about feelings.

Wants and Expectations

Just as feelings are part of a relationship, so are **wants and expectations.** In the relationship dimension, there is never a time when you don't want or expect something from the other person. An instructor speaks with you, for example, requesting the loan of a textbook. In the content dimension, what she would like is to have you lend your text to her. But there is a want in the relationship dimension, too. She wants you to confirm your relationship; her image of the relationship at least. This instructor wants you to show that you trust her. Not only is the intent of the request to borrow the text but also to confirm the relationship.

Now consider what the instructor *doesn't want.* Remember, the task is to borrow the book. This is in the relationship dimension. She doesn't want you to answer, "Well . . . uh . . . I guess it'll be all right. Uh, look, last time I lent you a book it came back all messed up. You can borrow the book, but don't use a highlighter, and make sure you don't pour coffee all over it." This statement would disconfirm her image of your relationship. Although she would have been able to borrow your book, she would not have received what she wanted in the relationship dimension.

Similarly, you always expect something from your partner in a relationship. Typically, the expectation is behavior, but sometimes it is lack of behavior. If you think about it, when you feel betrayed, the chances are good that you thought you had a contract with the one you feel betrayed you. You expected something, but didn't get what you expected. To illustrate, put yourself back to the age of about sixteen. Suppose your father lets you take his car, after asking what time you will return it. You say, "I'll be back by 7:00."

Your father accepts that at face value and makes plans accordingly. "Honey," he says to your mother, "how'd you like to see that movie? We could go tonight and be there in time for the 8:00 show." She answers, "Great." They make a date, and both get set for an evening out together. They have done so because your father believed—expected—that you would return the car by 7:00.

At 7:15, you're still not home. Nor are you home by 7:45. All the while the tension is rising. You made a commitment and Father is feeling betrayed. But your parents can still "make" the 8:00 o'clock show if you'll just bring the car up the driveway. You return at 8:20 to a disappointed Mom and a fuming Dad. He is feeling betrayed because he expected something from you that he did not get. Obviously, then, wants and expectations are important in any relationship.

From your point of view, however, you probably had a good reason for not getting home earlier. *The other person in a conflict always has a good reason from his or her own point of view.* You might, for instance, have been caught in a traffic jam. You might have had to change a flat tire, and there was no phone nearby so you could call for help or tell your father you were delayed. Or the car may have run out of gas, and you had to walk to the nearest intersection in order to buy some.

Your father's sense of betrayal is utterly inside himself. It is involved with his perceptions of the situation, and his wants and expectations as the events of the evening played out. If he guesses that you were being irresponsible, then becomes angry with you on the basis of that guess, your relationship is at risk. If he acts on his wrong guess, that you deliberately betrayed him, then you two are liable to become involved in one of the classic conflicts of our time—the parent-child, generation gap argument.

Intentions

If there are always wants and expectations, there are always **intentions** too. For instance, a professor lecturing to a class wants the students to learn the material. In the relationship dimension, the professor wants to be thought of by the students as a skillful and personable lecturer, competent and knowledgeable, and able to make the subject matter lively so that the learning experience is pleasant. The instructor wants to be regarded as a person to be trusted, to be respected as a person, and to be identified positively as a role model. Thus, the students would be confirming the professor's own self-image, or at least the image he is trying to project.

This is a tall order. It might even be an order that is impossible to fill. Nevertheless, the professor is willing to do certain things in order to get what he wants. He *intends* to prepare in order to be knowledgeable about the subject matter. His intent is to polish an act so that the lectures flow smoothly. A student-centered approach to teaching is intended; one that takes the learner into account. Interactions with students, both in the classroom and outside of it, are intended to be warm—to the extent that this warmth is sustainable. And, really, the professor *intends* to pay attention to his personal habits of dress and grooming so that he manages his impressions consistently.

There's not a lot that can be done beyond this set of intentions except to follow through with behavior, and to do so as consistently as possible. Thus intentions, too, are part of an existing relationship.

Latitude of Acceptance

You guess about the other's openness to your ideas. This openness is the **latitude of acceptance.** Everyone has a degree of openness toward the other or toward the other's ideas and attitudes at any given moment. The latitude continually changes in response to the conditions in the environment and in yourself, as you perceive them. If you are open, if you have a broad latitude of acceptance, then you are likely to be open to proposals from another. You will probably enjoy interacting with that other person. If you are closed, have a narrow latitude of acceptance, then you probably will not want to interact with that person. You may even avoid contact altogether. Or if unavoidable you may shut out this person, not hearing any proposal because you are closed to it.

In a relationship, you usually make estimates of the latitude of acceptance the other is experiencing. Consciously or not, you monitor, by observation and guess, what the other's acceptance is likely to be. You accommodate that guess by choosing communication strategies that will be most effective under the circumstances you believe exist.

To illustrate, suppose you believe your professor has made an error in your grade. You expected a "C" but received a "D" at the end of the term. That difference is symbolically significant. You are not accustomed to receiving a "C", much less a "D." You have a self-image that you are an "A" and "B" student. But you have adjusted to the "C" because the course is very difficult and because the professor has the reputation of being a difficult grader.

That reputation is what is giving you pause. You want to talk with her, but you don't want to cut across her grain. You have accepted that she is a tough grader. Before you approach her, you will undoubtedly attempt to find the right time and place to do it. Should you go to her office *during* office hours, or after them? There are advantages either way, since matters of her expectations, matters of privacy, and matters of available time are involved. Should you go to her immediately before or immediately after class; talk to her in the classroom or in the corridor? There are advantages either way, since you may be able to get her to invite you to her office, thus setting up a more comfortable interview. But there is that chance that she will be distracted, planning and worrying about her lecture, if you approach her before class begins, or that she will be frustrated or bothered, assuming the lecture did not go as well as she had hoped, if you approach her afterward.

This weighing of factors depends on your observations and guesses about the professor's latitude of acceptance, first of you, and then of the subject matter you want to discuss. Latitude of acceptance is clearly a component of your relationship with the professor, as it is a component of every relationship.

Images

Images are developed and sustained about all sorts of things at the same time. Images of self are developed in certain contexts, as are images of others. It is possible to place those images into the same contexts into which you place yourself. When you are interacting with another, you are most likely interacting with your image of that person at that moment.

Kenneth Boulding developed a notion of image that applies directly.[5] He believed that the total effect of experience was a person's image. Boulding was talking about *subjective* knowledge. Thus, according to Boulding, what is true is what is believed to be true.

Image is not a static thing, but is constantly changing. It interacts with what is perceived, while the meaning of what is perceived is whatever change is produced in the image. Boulding was convinced that perceptions, or what he terms messages, result in one of four alternative states: a message could leave the image unaffected; it could add to an image; it could change an image, sometimes only a little but sometimes quite dramatically; or it could either clarify or confuse an image.

Consider the professor who gave you a "D" again. Who is she? Is she the individual she believes herself to be? Is she the individual she would like you to believe she is? Is she the individual you perceive her to be? Is she the sum total of all the perceptions of her class, or of all her classes? Who is she?

In Boulding's interpretation, the critical issue is not who she is. The critical issue is the image you have of her. That image is the net effect of all your experiences brought to bear on the moment. The image, and not the woman, is whom you are worrying about when you wonder which will be the most appropriate time to talk to her. The image is critical when you guess about her intentions and about her wants and expectations, as you observe and guess about her feelings at the moment. Clearly, image is an important part of all relationships.

In review, we have explored a process where people observe, then make guesses based on those observations. Relationships consist of these observations and guesses. Guesses are made in the present, about data that is available now. Although language is the tie to the past and the future, it is difficult if not impossible to live or to have relationships in any time other than the present. Observations and guesses go on inside individuals about things that are inside the interacting others. Relationships are not only present tense but are also internal. They consist of feelings, wants and expectations, intentions, latitudes of acceptance, and images.

Check Out

It is impossible to read another's mind. So in order to know the truth about guesses, they must be checked out. This is the final part of the agenda for talking about relationships. The process of checking out is quite simple and easy to do if it is remembered. If a guess is wrong, and action results from the guess, there is a good chance that the relationship will be damaged. If a guess is made that is wrong, and the guess is checked out, and the feedback to this checking is accurate, an intelligent choice on how to interact can be made. The relationship is strengthened by checking out guesses.

This critical component of checking out guesses about others is at the heart of effective interpersonal communication. And yet, when the chips are down and feelings are strong, as when wants or expectations are unfulfilled or images of others are not trusted, there is a tendency to avoid checking out what is going on inside other people. There is operating in these circumstances the belief that it is possible to read minds. So images are projected into the situation and relationships are endangered.

Checking out guesses would result in much better communication. As you might imagine, we're going to be returning to this idea repeatedly throughout this book. We'll do that primarily under the topic of feedback, although we'll also do it either directly or by implication in a variety of other contexts as well.

Summary

Communication is the process by which individuals identify and negotiate the nature of their relationships. This process is a critical factor in both professional and social life. Effective communication in the professional dimension can enhance an individual's influence and impressions. In the social dimension, the quality and intimacy of life is determined by the honesty of interpersonal communication.

Many models of this communication process can be constructed: the process model; the filtering screen model; and the interpersonal communication process model. Despite the labels given the components of the process in each model, the same point is emphasized: Meanings exist within individuals. Whatever meanings are generated as the result of processing information become the individual's reality.

Several terms, plus the relationships between them, constitute the critical issues in learning to communicate more effectively. These terms are *feedback, sensitivity, self-disclosure, trust,* and *risk.* Although each term can be isolated for examination, none can function independently of the others, and all are involved in managing the relationship dimension of communication events.

Both a content and a relationship dimension exist in every communication event. The content dimension involves topics. The relationship dimension exists in the present and inside the individuals involved in the event. The language used to communicate in the event should reflect these two aspects of the relationship dimension. Individuals working on their relationships should attempt to remain in the present tense and make clear that they are responsible for the function of their own nervous system.

An agenda is useful for talking about relationships. The agenda includes all the components of a relationship—*observations, inferences, feelings, wants and expectations, intentions, latitude of acceptance, images,* and *check out.* By using this agenda, an individual can discover the source of trouble when relationships are at risk.

Why Are You Taking This Course?

"Why are you taking this course?" If you are willing, take a moment to stop and jot down four or five of your reasons. You might write them in the margin of this page if you don't have paper handy.

When students are asked to do this, they usually list such items as a good grade; four hours of credit; to learn to communicate better; or to feel better about talking to people. Are these similar to your reasons?

The connection between what you are learning in class and your day-to-day interpersonal communication has been considered in *Interpersonal Growth through Communication.* To illustrate the important ideas in this book, the experiences that a group of people, who may be very much like you, are introduced. Concrete examples will show you how to apply these important ideas to your own communication exercises.

The Group

Five people are members of this group. Their names are Mary Ann, Tim, Phil, Elizabeth, and Cheryl. This group is hypothetical, but each character is modeled after a real person. Each situation in which the group is involved actually happened, although the situations have been dramatized and edited some-what.

You will see the relationships among the group members grow and change as you progress through the book. This important aspect of communication cannot be easily illustrated through isolated examples, so examples from this ongoing group are provided. Over time, you will come to know this group well enough to have expectations of each individual and to make predictions about how each might communicate. You should begin to understand communica-tion and relationships more meaningfully, and make use of these insights in your own interpersonal relationships.

The main thing that the members of the group have in common is their involvement in an interpersonal communication class. Try to picture each per-son. Is the person like you? Are you different? Do you know people like them?

Mary Ann   Mary Ann is white and thirty-two years old. She is generally a quiet person, but when she talks, she shows that she is skilled at interpersonal com-munication. When you talk with her, you get the impression that she knows what she wants in life. Mary Ann can lead people in a natural sort of way. She is very good at connecting people to one another. Because she understands people, she can help them to patch up interpersonal problems. However, she would never step in unless invited.

Tim   Tim is white and eighteen years old. He is the kind of person who says what is on his mind, sometimes without thinking. This brutal and naive honesty is sometimes a problem in his relationships. Tim doesn't understand people very well. In fact, he doesn't understand himself very well, either. He is sincere, though, and sometimes his caring nature shows through his hotheaded exte-rior.

Phil   Phil is twenty years old and white. He does not understand people very well. In fact, Phil is sometimes afraid of people. He is very quiet, even timid. Phil would rather give up what he wants than engage in a confrontation. Nor does he know how to say no.

Elizabeth   Elizabeth is black and twenty-seven years old. She is competent, but not confident. Elizabeth is bright, and usually very good at communicating with others. However, there are times when she feels uncertain about herself. She often masks this uncertainty by pretending that she doesn't care. These displays of apathy hide her true sensitivity to others.

Cheryl   Cheryl, nineteen, is the most outgoing member of the group. She is both confident and aggressive. This aggressiveness, however, sometimes re-sults in interpersonal problems. Cheryl seems more concerned with larger is-sues, and does not care for details. Although she understands people, Cheryl sometimes does not display the patience necessary to convey that under-standing. Cheryl doesn't hold back.

Looking Ahead

In chapter 2 we take a look at self-concept and how self-concept evolves. You will see that self-concept is directly tied to the ability to enjoy intimacy and honesty in relationships. And, since the self is a result of interactions with others, it is possible to change self-concept and to build self-esteem. Some pointers on how this may be done are included in chapter 2.

Chapter 3 focuses upon perceiving yourself and other people. In that chapter the process of perceiving and some of the pitfalls in that process are discussed. Most importantly, some very practical suggestions are included that will help you to cope with predictable perceptual problems and that will dramatically improve your perceptual skills.

Chapter 4 addresses the whole process of listening to others. The goal of this chapter is to suggest the means of improving your listening skills. You should be able to listen more empathetically, more actively, and with greater care in checking your own understanding of the other person.

Chapter 5 reintroduces the agenda for talking about relationships that has been described briefly already. This chapter focuses especially on feelings. Expressing emotions is enormously important to interpersonal growth, but there are some cultural problems that inhibit free expression. Ways to identify emotions and to be clear in expressing them are suggested. When considering trust and self-disclosure, expressing feelings can be very risky. Ways to minimize this risk, primarily language techniques, are presented.

The focus of chapter 6 is language—how meaning evolves and some of the problems that arise out of the structure of language. A very practical set of suggestions for coping with the most debilitating language problems are offered. For instance, if you call your feeling "anger" because you don't have enough words, enough language, to identify it more accurately, and if you can only respond in two ways (defensively or supportively) about the anger and the subject of the anger, then the language limitations are limiting your relationships! An increase in your ability to use language in less limiting ways frees you from the limitations you have been imposing on your relationships. The magic of language is that you can choose to use it in as many ways as you wish.

In chapter 7, communicating without words is explored. Body posture, gestures, vocal control, and facial expressions, all have message value. More often than not, those messages are about the relationships, rather than about the tasks. Common nonverbal communication problems and behaviors are suggested, as are alternatives suggested by research in nonverbal communication.

Chapter 8 takes a closer look at defensive and supportive behavior. Here the idea that defensiveness and supportiveness are typically a function of language use is presented. There are good reasons to learn how to be more supportive. Surprisingly, this is easier than people commonly expect. A big part, but not all, of more supportive behavior is language. Another, and perhaps bigger part, is behavior without words.

Chapter 9 deals with the improvement of sending and receiving messages in order to achieve greater accuracy of communication. But that doesn't mean that greater accuracy will automatically bring greater joy. Sometimes accuracy in the message exchange merely makes clear that you are in conflict. Conflict and stress are related, and these are functions of the communication in which people engage. How to cope with stress and how to manage conflict are the topics covered in chapter 9. This completes the circle of looking at relationships.

The relationship is reconsidered in Chapter 10. Specific suggestions are made about how you can more effectively initiate, maintain, and change your relationships. The key is more effective communication. The goal is greater success and happiness.

Those skills are identified and explained in *Interpersonal Growth through Communication*. They apply in every personal, professional, or social context in which individuals interact. Best of all, they are not all that difficult to acquire.

Discussion Questions

1. The complexity of the communication process is a major reason for the difficulty in communication study. How does the "filtering screen" model limit the understanding of the complexity of the communication process?
2. Is a really great kiss a communication event? What are its limitations? What important features of this kiss caused you to answer the way you did?
3. Imagine the last argument you had with someone for whom you care. Can you identify the feelings, wants and expectations, intentions, and latitude of acceptance each of you had during the argument? How might you have managed that moment more effectively?
4. Perhaps during registration for classes you discover that a course you really wanted to take is full. Suppose that you ask for special consideration to get into the class, and that you are told "no." How might you use the agenda for the social dimension of talk to examine this communication event?

Endnotes

1. J. G. Manis and B. N. Meltzer, eds., "Conclusion," *Symbolic Interaction* (Boston: Allyn and Bacon, 1972), 575–77.
2. This is an abstracted variation of a model developed by Claude Shannon and Warren Weaver in their landmark book, *The Mathematical Theory of Communication* (Urbana, IL: The University of Illinois Press, 1949).

3. J. J. Gabarro, "The Development of Trust, Influence and Expectations," in A. G. Athos and J. J. Gabarro, *Interpersonal Behavior: Communication and Understanding in Relationships* (Englewood Cliffs, NJ: Prentice-Hall, Inc., 1978). See pp. 294–98 for an excellent explication of this key interpersonal communication concept.

4. We're aware that we've loaded this exercise somewhat by appealing to the cultural assumptions with which everyone must live. We've skewed your perceptions with an awareness of the assumptive reality you learned while growing up with American cultural traditions. This is another example of perceptual set, which is discussed in greater detail in chapter 2.

5. K. E. Boulding, *The Image* (Ann Arbor: University of Michigan Press, 1956).

Self-Concept

Preview

The images you have of yourself depend on your interactions with other people. These images control your interactions as well, so it is important that you understand how your self-image has evolved and what you can do in order to change it. Moreover, there is value in learning how to help other people develop a more positive self-image. Thus, your images profoundly affect your communication with others, too.

Objectives

After reading this chapter you should be able to complete the following:
1. Define the term self-concept.
2. Describe the ways in which beliefs, values, and attitudes shape your frame of reference.
3. Identify particular beliefs, values, and attitudes that are important to your self-concept.
4. Explain the processes that contribute to the development of your self-concept.
5. Identify particular significant others from each of the four sets presented (family, peers, schools, and media personalities) with whom you identify.
6. Explain the ways that Schutz's interpersonal needs are expressed in the self-concept.
7. Discuss why the different degrees to which interpersonal needs are fulfilled affect interpersonal communication.
8. Explain the way survival orientations affect self-concept and communication behaviors.
9. Compare your past, present, and future self.
10. Create goals for the development of your self-concept, and define the specific steps for the attainment of those goals.

As Mary Ann walked into the student center, she saw Tim and Elizabeth sitting at their usual table in the far corner. Elizabeth sat back in her chair listening as Tim gestured savagely, punctuating his remarks by pointing toward the wall and nodding his head with seeming certainty. Mary Ann could tell he was upset. As she walked over to the table to join them, Tim got up, brushed past her muttering "Hello" and went over to the counter.

She asked Elizabeth, "What's up with Tim? He seems pretty disturbed."

Elizabeth didn't seem too concerned. In fact, she looked a little amused. "He's angry about his sociology class," she said.

"Really," replied Mary Ann. "I thought he was doing well. I know he got a 'B' on the midterm last week."

Elizabeth smiled. "It's not the grade. It's the teacher. They aren't getting along. I had the same class last term. I just ignored the guy and I got by all right. Wait till Tim gets back and we'll tell you all about him."

When Tim returned he slammed down his cup, spilling some coffee. He fell into his chair and started right into his story.

"Sorry I was so grumpy when you were coming in. Elizabeth and I were just talking about Brunner, my sociology prof. Elizabeth, I'm dropping that class! He's just too much, and after what I said to him in class today, I don't think I should stick around for any more of it. He's the teacher and so he knows the subject and everything. But it bothers me the way he reminds us of what an expert he is."

Elizabeth nodded. "When I had him, he reminded us of that every day."

"Yeah," Tim continued, "every day at the end of the lecture he asks if there are any questions. But don't dare ask anything. You can't even express a point of view. He gets all angry and indignant, like you're attacking him or something."

Elizabeth smiled knowingly. "When I had that class and somebody dared to ask a question, he made them feel stupid."

"Either that or he'd say the question was irrelevant," Tim added. "And he thinks he's great. At the beginning of the course he made this big speech about how he's an open person and how he wanted to hear our viewpoints."

Elizabeth added, "Then he thinks that he proves he's open by asking every day if there are any questions. Nobody is going to ask anything."

Tim looked at her sharply and said, "Well I did, and when he tried to put me down, I let him have it. I was sick of his arrogant attitude. It's a good thing the class ended right in the middle of it."

Mary Ann finally spoke up. "Well Tim, you usually say what's on your mind. I wonder what would happen if no one played into his question game."

"I can tell you what happens," said Tim. "In my class everybody stopped participating after the fourth week. Then things got worse. This guy sees himself as the Great Teacher, the Expert in his field. He'd ask questions and get silence in return. Then he'd try to encourage the class by reminding us about how open he is. When that didn't work, he'd single out people he'd put down in the past."

Elizabeth laughed. "Yeah, that's right. But I saw through him on day one and decided then and there that I better keep my mouth shut for the whole term. So he didn't bother me. He never even called on me once. But I know you're not like that Tim. When you first told me you were signing up for that class, I figured you'd get into it with him."

Tim sighed. "Well, I really did it too. I couldn't just sit there and take it. I wanted to learn the stuff in this course, but not enough to put up with this guy. I guess I'll take the class when I can get Professor Schmidt. She seems pretty straightforward. I've never met her, but Cheryl had her last term and said she got a lot out of the class."

Elizabeth began gathering up her things as Tim continued, "I don't know, Mary Ann. I grew up in a bad neighborhood, you know, and it was rough. My father's a construction foreman. He raised me to be responsible for my viewpoint and to speak up without fear. I do that here as a student and at work in the stereo shop."

Elizabeth broke in, "I've got to run to class. If I don't get there in time there won't be any seats in the back of the auditorium."

Tim waved and Mary Ann rose to leave. "Tim, I'd like to hear more about this but I promised Cheryl I'd go over the notes she missed on Thursday. Do you want to come along?"

Tim said "No thanks," and Mary Ann left as he went for another cup of coffee.

From the sound of this conversation, you would think that Professor Brunner has a problem. He asserts an image of openness and expertise, but is not really open. Instead he "puts down the student" when asked a question. He may actually be having doubts about his expertise, so establishes himself as an authority. He wants to be open, yet is afraid of losing control. This creates a no-win situation. In order to maintain his view of himself, he thinks he cannot be challenged. At the same time he thinks the only way to appear open is to encourage challenges.

If he really believes he is open, then his view of himself is somewhat unrealistic. The image he holds is not consistent with the image others see.

It is also possible to speculate a little about Tim and Elizabeth. Tim seems to think of himself as someone who takes people at their word. He accepts the professor's expressed view of himself as the expert, and he also accepts the professor's requests for questions as genuine. He wants to learn about the subject, so he asks questions. Tim does not consider his questions challenging to the professor. Tim knows that he is quick to speak up when he feels he's been wronged and is also aware that his temper often gets the better of him.

Elizabeth appears to be an entirely different person. She knows she does not share Tim's manner nor his temperament. So when she took the class, she displayed a less vigorous style. She is sometimes willing to sacrifice her curiosity to preserve her anonymity. And she is willing to trade off involvement to avoid confrontation. Perhaps she felt uncertain about her footing in the course and didn't want to risk calling attention to herself.

Think about the last time you introduced yourself to another person. What information did you give about yourself? You probably told them who you are in terms of the things that you have done and places you've been. For example, Tim presented himself to Mary Ann and Elizabeth as the son of a construction foreman, a worker in a stereo shop, and the product of a bad neighborhood. These are characteristics that Tim believed appropriate to present to Mary Ann and Elizabeth. The information was intended to assist them in placing his remarks in context. The message contained information about Tim, and by inference, what's important to him; why he ought to be listened to. This chapter will examine the importance of your presentation of self; who you are, who you can be, and what's important to you.

Definition of the Self-Concept

People present themselves to one another through communication. Naturally, the self that you present varies from one encounter to another. However, there are some things about you that are repeated in many relationships. Self-concept is comprised of the characteristics that you frequently present about yourself. In presenting these images of yourself, you are choosing the aspects of self you think are important to various relationships.

Imagine that all your personal information is contained in a little box that you carry around. When you meet others, you select identifying items from the box to present to them. There is some information that you want most people to see, so you select those bits most frequently. There are other things about yourself that you want only select individuals to see, and so you reserve these bits for special situations. There are still other parts of you that you keep entirely to yourself. These are things known only to you. And finally, there is information tucked in the corners of the box that you don't even know exists. These are things you won't discover until you've spent some time and energy rummaging around in the box. Sometimes one of these unknown bits sticks to another that you are taking out of the box, and unknown to you, is presented to someone you're talking with. This is what Athos and Gabarro call "a message sent unawares."[1]

When you communicate, you select bits and pieces from the box to represent who you are for that specific communication. Some of these bits are things that you do; others are affective or emotional. Still others are cognitive, involving knowledge of the world.

Ideas about Who You Are

Concern about self-concept is not new. In fact, in early Greek writing, Aristotle made the point that there were physical and nonphysical parts of the person. At the turn of the century, psychologist William James refined earlier ideas about

Figure 2.1 The Johari Window

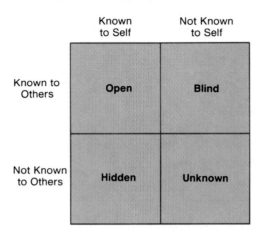

the self.[2] He suggested that there is a *Material Me*—my body, my home, physical objects around me; a *Social Me*—my awareness of how others see me; and a *Spiritual Me*—my awareness of myself as a thinking and feeling person. Later, symbolic interactionist George Herbert Mead observed how people achieve identity through viewing those around them.[3]

The Johari Window

Two contemporary psychologists, Joseph Luft and Harrington Ingham, developed a practical illustration (fig. 2.1) that will help you to understand the relationship between the various ideas you present as yourself and your communication.[4]

The Johari Window illustrates what you and other people might know about who you are. The upper left-hand quadrant presents the information about you that is clear both to you and to others. This information includes behaviors, attitudes, feelings, desires and so forth, and is termed the *open self*. The square to the right presents those things others know about you that are not evident to you, or the *blind self*. You might lead the meetings of a group you are working with and not be aware of such an action. In the lower half of the window, are the hidden self and the unknown self. The *hidden self* is that part of your private image that you choose not to reveal to others. Almost everyone has information about themselves that they keep private. This may include ambitions, wants and desires, as well as hopes and fears. Finally, Luft and Ingham reasoned there is an *unknown self*. You can probably remember discovering something, perhaps a talent or phobia, about yourself that you did not know and believed that nobody else knew, either.

An examination of your own Johari Window can help you to know about yourself and your communication. The understanding that comes from shared openness helps you to perceive those around you more accurately. Although some authors overstate this case about openness, it is clear that the more information that is known about a person, the fewer the assumptions that are made about that individual.

On the other hand, if the open self is too big, an opposite effect may result. A person who is too open is said to be imprudent; not completely in control. Often the motives of an open person are suspect. Perhaps you've met a person with whom you feel uncomfortable because there has been too much disclosure. You felt uncomfortable when communicating with this person because you have a sense about what information is appropriate for disclosure according to the depth of the relationship. When the disclosure is too intimate, you feel uncomfortable. If you have a choice in this situation, you would probably withdraw and avoid. If you could not avoid, you would probably engage in some subtle joking or teasing about the situation. Generally, you do not come right out and tell the other person why you're uncomfortable, but you do hint about it.

Recall now that the Johari Window suggests that there is an area of self to which your perception is blind, but which is known to others. A variety of habitual gestures are examples of this unaware behavior. One specific example of this unconscious behavior contributing to communication difficulties is the behavior of a friend of ours. This man would typically stare off into space, looking past the person with whom he was conversing. He was unaware of this aspect of his communication style, yet people avoided communicating with him because of it.

You can use the Johari Window to help sort out the information you impart to others. Select a relationship you have in common with someone that you would define as "close." Examine your open area in that relationship first, writing down several of the major things that you believe are known both to yourself and to the other person. Next, think about your hidden area in that relationship. What information about yourself have you kept to yourself? Write down several of the major items from this area, then ask yourself a couple of questions. Is there anything in your hidden area that you might be willing to disclose to that person? Under what circumstances might you be willing to do this?

Learning about your blind and unknown areas in the relationship requires some effort on your part and cooperation on the part of the other person. First, go back over your open and hidden lists. What aspects of yourself were revealed to you as a result of this relationship? These are aspects that existed in your blind or unknown areas and became known to you through your communication with this person. Finally, ask the other person to talk with you about the way she sees you, herself, and the relationship. Such a conversation may reveal even more to you about your blind and unknown areas.

Sketching out a window in this way enables you to see how open you think you are in a relationship. It also helps you to make more conscious choices about what to disclose. For example, you may see that there is some information that you have in the hidden area that might improve your relationship if you brought it into the open. Thus, the Johari Window is a tool for examining communication in interpersonal relationships. It can help to clarify the information that you share with others, and also help you to better understand yourself.

The key objective in your selection of self-concept data is appropriateness. You wish to present an image that is correct for a relationship and its context. You have the ability to present a variety of selves, the larger, more general characteristics of which remain rather consistent. The self-concept is generally viewed as constant in the short run and changeable over time. That is, while there is usually little change observable from day to day, you are clearly different in your presentation of self than you were, say, five or ten years ago.

Components of the Self-Concept

The self-concept is a complex, multifaceted structure. This complexity is illustrated by the idea of *multiple selves*. You seem to be a different person in each situation you find yourself. A short illustration may help you understand this idea. First, picture yourself at an athletic event. Get a good picture in your head of what you would be like there. Now, contrast that image with one of yourself in the process of taking a final exam. You would probably describe yourself differently each time. Which image is really *you?* Of course, both are. You have multiple selves, each dependent on a context. It is the context that makes certain aspects of the complex you more important at the particular moment. Consequently, you think of yourself in those terms at that time. All of these different images together form your self-concept.

Self-concept is composed of your beliefs, values, and attitudes. Your beliefs give your self-concept its substance. Your values give it aspirations and standards. Your attitudes provide motivation. So beliefs, values, and attitudes provide a structure on which you develop and build yourself. Curiously, you make many assumptions about others on the basis of your own beliefs, values, and attitudes. It seems reasonable, therefore, that you should look more closely at these components that determine your self-concept.

Attitudes, beliefs, and values all represent assumptions that you hold about the world and your place in it. They are different, however, in what they do. Your beliefs represent the people, places, and things that exist for you. Your values appraise these, and your attitudes guide your behavior toward them.

Attitudes, beliefs, and values are the ''components'' of a self-concept. Together, they provide a ''frame of reference.'' You experience people, places, and things through this frame much as you see through a pair of sunglasses or look through a window. In other words, a frame of reference is a set of interlocking facts, ideas, rules, and presuppositions that orient a person and give meaning to situations and experiences. Every combination of beliefs, values, and attitudes provides you with a different frame of reference. The particular frame through which you look at an event colors the way that you "see" it. If you shift frames of reference, like changing to a different shade of sunglasses, you will experience the event differently. The difference that the frame of reference makes is most important to your perception of people and messages.

As you proceed through the remainder of the text, be aware that the source of your frame of reference is the belief, value, and attitude structure that makes up the self-concept.

Beliefs

At the core of your self-concept lie your *beliefs* about the existence and characteristics of people, places, and things. A belief is a statement about "what is." Any idea that you create is a belief if it includes any form of "to be." So Elizabeth's statement, "You're not like that, Tim," is an expression of a belief that she holds about Tim.

Some beliefs are more significant than others. Some concern yourself, while others concern the people around you. Still others have to do with tangible objects and come from direct or indirect contact with the objects. For example, in the episode at the beginning of this chapter, Tim said, "He's the teacher and so he knows the subject and everything." The belief statement here is that Tim's professor must know his subject because he is the teacher. Presumably, knowledge of a subject is a prerequisite to the teacher's getting a job. The connecting of "teacher" and "expertise" by Tim illustrates a belief statement.

Other beliefs are developed outside the realm of personal experience. A belief may be derived through synthesis. Tim's statement about Professor Schmidt represents such a belief. Tim has had no contact with Schmidt, yet he believes her to be straightforward. This belief is based on his confidence in Cheryl's report on Professor Schmidt; a belief in her reported experience.

Many of your beliefs are only infrequently stated, yet underlie much of your communication. These "taken for granted beliefs" are called *primitive beliefs*. Milton Rokeach suggests that beliefs are organized in a branching fashion from a central core of more primitive beliefs. This concept of relative centrality is explained by Rokeach in terms of four principles:

> (1) Beliefs about one's self, one's existence and identity, are much
> more central than other beliefs. (2) Shared beliefs about one's
> existence and self-identity are much more central than unshared
> beliefs (ones held only by oneself). (3) Beliefs that are derived from
> other beliefs (rather than from contact with the object of belief) are less
> central than underived beliefs. (4) Beliefs concerning matters of taste

Figure 2.2 The Structure of Beliefs

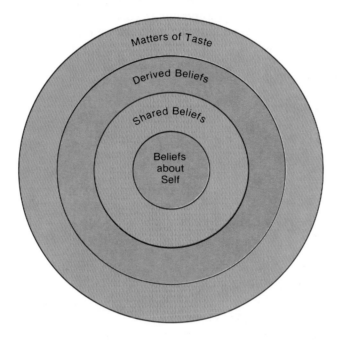

are less central than other beliefs. They are usually seen by the holder as arbitrary in nature and thus are relatively inconsequential in their impact on other beliefs.[5]

These interrelationships are shown in figure 2.2.

At the outside of the figure are beliefs that are least central, such as matters of taste. The group's frequent choice of a table in the far corner of the student center expresses a belief that there is something preferable about that location. This preference is probably flexible and has little impact on other beliefs. Tim's choice of coffee is another example of these *surface beliefs*.

The next ring inward represents beliefs that are derived from other beliefs. Tim's assumption about Professor Schmidt's straightforwardness represents one such *derived belief*.

Shared beliefs are shown in the next ring. These beliefs are derived through experience and are acknowledged by others. Some beliefs are primitive, while others provide a basis for interpersonal communication. For instance, Tim and Mary Ann seem to share the belief that Tim usually speaks up for himself.

Unshared central beliefs, in the center of the figure, are fundamental beliefs about yourself that you rarely share with others. Thus they are rarely directly challenged by others. This central core also includes your secret (and perhaps unconscious) hopes and fears, desires and delusions.

Beliefs are what you know about the world and your relationship to it. They exist as statements about "what is." Beliefs about yourself are the building blocks of the self-concept. From them, you shape the foundations for the images you present. Because your beliefs about yourself are held centrally and intensely, you can see that the core of the self-concept is well-protected. It is relatively stable.

To find out more about the beliefs you have, try the following experience. It should help you to identify your self-concept building blocks.

Experience: Beliefs

From the following list, select twenty characteristics that describe your perception of yourself. Try to select characteristics that you believe others perceive in you, too. How do these characteristics affect your interpersonal communication? Do you believe that others share this view of you? Test yourself. Ask a classmate or friend to look at your selections. How do these characteristics relate to your beliefs about yourself?

adaptable	diffident	loyal	skeptical
ambitious	direct	manipulative	self-confident
analytical	disagreeable	materialistic	self-conscious
argumentative	disorderly	officious	self-starter
arrogant	domineering	opportunistic	sensitive
articulate	driving	optimistic	shrewd
autocratic	earthy	outgoing	shy
belligerent	efficient	outspoken	sincere
calm	egotistical	overbearing	sneaky
candid	emotional	patient	stable
careless	enthusiastic	pensive	stern
cautious	flighty	persevering	stubborn
cold	frank	persuasive	sympathetic
competitive	friendly	pessimistic	systematic
complicated	garrulous	practical	tactful
conforming	genuine	pretentious	thorough
conservative	gregarious	probing	thrifty
considerate	guarded	prompt	truthful
cooperative	honest	proud	tyrannical
courageous	idealistic	rational	understanding
courteous	imaginative	relentless	vain
critical	impulsive	reliable	warm
decisive	independent	reserved	withdrawn
deferential	indifferent	resourceful	witty
dependable	kind	rude	
devious	lazy	ruthless	

Values

Values represent what you deem important in your life. These include goals or standards of behavior, and are evaluative in nature. Wealth, parenthood, and the desire for inner peace and a comfortable life are all examples of values. Obviously, values involve beliefs. But they move the self-concept one step beyond beliefs. Values sort beliefs into wants, goals, and guidelines that define their desirability. While beliefs represent "what is," values suggest "what ought to be." When you make a statement about what you ought to be, you are expressing a value.

Oskamp emphasized the significance of the value structure, stating:

> Values are the most important element in the individual's system of attitudes and beliefs. They are ends rather than means; they are the goals a person strives for and which help to determine many of his other attitudes and beliefs.[6]

Values contribute to the image you present to others. They also help you to determine an image of others as you assign meaning to their behavior. Sometimes these value systems come into conflict. Imagine what might have happened if Tim and Elizabeth had continued their conversation. Tim's emphasis on speaking openly contrasts with Elizabeth's desire for maintaining a low profile. Tim must be careful that he does not begin talking to Elizabeth as though she values speaking up as he does. Since the value she places on the issue is different, she might react defensively.

What do you value? Try the following experience to determine your value structure.

Experience: Values

Return to the beliefs experience and place the terms in a value context. Take the characteristics you selected from the beliefs list and rank them from most important to least important. Next place a check (✓) by those that you perceive as positive characteristics. Compare your list with that of another person. In what ways are the other person's responses different from yours? Discuss both the differences and similarities with the other person to arrive at a better understanding of your own value system. Notice that some of your values are about you and the things you want for yourself. Other values are statements that imply standards about the way things "ought to be." You may also notice that some of your values are related to several beliefs. In fact, many values represent a synthesis of several beliefs. This relationship is shown in figure 2.3. The values that you hold shape the images that you think are appropriate to present.

Thinking and talking about your values helps you to know more about who you are and who you want to be. A clearer idea about what's important to you enables you to express yourself more coherently and effectively.

Figure 2.3 The Structure of Beliefs and Values

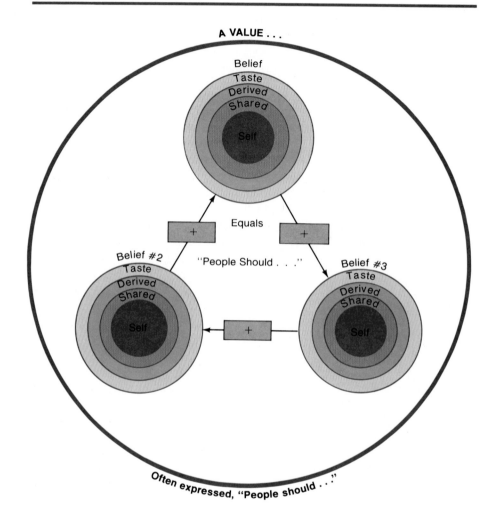

Attitudes

Gordon Allport defined *attitude* in a way that is useful in a discussion of self-concept.[7] He stated that an attitude is a "mental and neural state of readiness organized through experience, exerting a directive or dynamic influence upon behavior, the individual's response to all objects and situations to which it is related." Your attitudes summarize and express belief and value structures. In simpler terms, an attitude is always about something that you perceive.

It is helpful to examine this definition in detail. Allport described an attitude as a state of readiness. Attitudes comprise your predispositions to act.

Figure 2.4 The Attitude, Belief, and Value System

Kind	Belief Statements	Value Statements	Attitude Statements
Essence	Something is . . . Statements	"Should" and "Good" Statements	Statements of Personal Intention
Example	"This course is boring. The professor is monotonous and the materials are dry and irrelevant."	"A good course should be interesting and should keep me awake. A good course means the professor should make it interesting."	"I am going to withdraw from this no-good course."

Such actions might include a word or statement, a gesture or movement, or simply an expression or thought. It is thus mental and neural, involving activity in the brain as well as action by the body. Although your attitudes are organized through experience, it is important to note that they are also tied together in this organization of beliefs and values. In fact, attitudes are an outgrowth of beliefs and values. Just as values sometimes serve to summarize a set of related beliefs, attitudes do the same for collections of values. Attitudes direct your beliefs and values toward action. This attitude structure, as it relates to beliefs and values, is shown in figure 2.4.

Tim's beliefs about himself and his relationship with Professor Brunner, valued negatively, result in an attitude that is illustrated by his readiness to drop the course. A more general structure is revealed when you look at Tim's perceptions of himself. Tim believes that he is a person who speaks up for himself. He thinks that his assertiveness is good and desirable. He values this characteristic in himself. Tim is even able to predict occasions when he is likely to speak up. Therefore, his attitudes like yours are sometimes future-oriented. They involve expectations about what you will think, how you will feel, and what you will do.

The Evolution of the Self-Concept

Processes in Self-Concept Evolution

The formation of a self-concept is a complex and ongoing procedure. There are four processes involved in self-concept formation, though all may not apply directly to an individual.

As each of these four processes is discussed, ask yourself which apply to you. But keep in mind that these are not stages; therefore, two or more can

act simultaneously in the process of developing self-concept. The four processes are (1) labeling the dominant behavior pattern; (2) reflected appraisal;
(3) social comparison; and (4) scanning the environment.[8]

Some individuals observe their day-to-day activities and then *label* a certain pattern of behavior. For example, you may see yourself constantly taking
the initiative in both social relationships and business activities. If others reinforce this behavior by calling attention to it, you may come to think of yourself
as an initiator—a take-charge person. You will have developed an idea of yourself that is based on a dominant behavior. Although this example accurately
describes what happens in some situations, it may also simplify what is more
often a very complex process.

A more thoroughly developed explanation of how the self-concept evolves
is found in the second process, known as *reflected appraisal,* which evolved
out of the work of George Herbert Mead and Charles H. Cooley.[9] Mead wrote
that the self-concept begins to emerge with the child's observation of a behavior of *significant others* (such as parents or peers), and the imitation of this
behavior by the child.

At play, the child begins to display the behaviors that these significant
others present. Mead calls this "taking the role of the other."[10] As the child
grows, a concept of self is developed in terms of these behaviors. Thus, the
child's self-concept is a reflection of the appraisals of significant others.

The third process, *social comparison,* takes the idea of self-concept beyond mere reflection of the attitudes of others. Here self-concept evolves out
of the comparison of the selves of others. Leon Festinger[11] argues that people
possess a basic need to have their beliefs and values confirmed by those around
them. Some beliefs can be confirmed by checking facts. Others are confirmed
by comparison. After a period of time, standards for comparison will be acquired, internalized, and reinforced. In fact, learning is so intense it may rule
out the possibility of any later change due to social comparison.

Another way people shape their identities is by developing *identity aspirations.* They desire to be recognized as a particular kind of person. These
goals may cause them to behave in ways that will lead others to identify them
as they would like them to. For example, one instructor may want to be recognized as the best professor in her college. To be the best of anything implies
that she needs someone else to agree that she has those qualities that the
other accepts as "best." The instructor may be able to perform so that she
feels good about herself as a professor and that others with whom she works
acknowledge her efforts by calling her the "best" professor.

But she may not be so capable in other areas. Suppose she also wishes
to be identified as an athlete, but lacks ability in this area. She might be able
to achieve agreement about this view of herself by scanning the environment

for incidents that will confirm this image. On the basis of her ability to selectively perceive, she could call attention to her memory of past experiences that emphasize her athletic ability. The result may be an image of herself as an athlete.

Your relationships with others affect the process by which your self-concepts are shaped. You reflect on your communication with others. You compare yourself to others. You use others as models for your own behavior. Your perception of what others think of you and of how they react to your disclosures provide data that support aspects of your self-concepts. Charles Cooley calls this the "looking-glass self" because, in effect, you use others as a mirror for seeing yourself.[12]

The Influence of Significant Others

George Herbert Mead named four sets of "significant others" who enter into the process of shaping the self-concept. "Significant others" may include family members, friends, religious leaders, teachers, and media personalities. The role that each of these forces plays in development varies from person to person. You will probably find that one of these forces was more influential in your own development than were others. By identifying them, you can better know yourself and better understand the way you respond to others.

Family

Family members, particularly parents, provide the earliest stimuli in the development of your self-concept. Parents serve as a primary source of information, behavior, and attitude, while satisfying physical needs. Parents aid the early development of definitions for determining your place in life. From parents, you also learn ways of expressing your feelings about what's going on around you or inside you. Parents can exert both a positive and negative influence on your beliefs, values, and attitudes about such things as achievement, education, religion, politics, love, and even bigotry.

Other family members are also a source of identification and "mirroring" in self-concept development. Some will exhibit behaviors that you may choose to emulate, while others will display attitudes or mannerisms that you will try to avoid. Even the birth order of brothers and sisters has been found to influence aspects of self-concept development. Research has determined, for instance, that firstborn children gradually place great emphasis on achievement in life, while middle-born children tend to value peer relationships and interactions more highly and usually see themselves as more independent than others. The last-born child is consistently more dependent on others than are older siblings.[13]

Peers

Peers are another set of significant others. They provide a general standard of "social acceptability" and a safe medium for trying out social roles and styles of communication. Throughout adolescence, in particular, peer relationships nourish the development of the self-concept in terms of status, acceptance versus rejection, leadership, sexuality, and romantic behavior.[14] Many interactions with peers take place within the context of a third important source of influence, the schools.

Schools

For much of the early part of your life, time was spent observing and interacting with teachers. Children observe, for example, how teachers deal with other people at school, and then, perhaps, adopt some of these styles of expression for their own use. Some teachers display personality types that children will not want to emulate.

In addition to the influence of teachers, the school system itself is important to the development of the self-concept. McCandless and Coop summarize the significance of the school system's influence on the self-concept by stating:

> The school is a miniature social system in which the adolescent is
> expected to acquire basic cognitive, intellectual, and social skills, and
> which enables the student to earn primary or earned status.[15]

In school, children acquire the tools of self that will facilitate the achievement of goals and the appropriate expression of values in an organized society. The impact of the school system on the self-concept is continually apparent throughout life. Even the selection of a college is made, at least partly, on the basis of the behavior style encouraged at the college.

Media Personalities

A fourth source of significant others is the mass media, particularly television. In 1973, the Surgeon General reported that some forty million children aged two through eleven watched an average of three-and-one-half hours of television every day. By the age of twelve, the average American child has been exposed to some 13,500 hours of television, an amount that is nearly double the time spent in school. By 1980, the number of hours children spent before a television was even greater, about twenty-seven hours per week.[16]

George Comstock detailed the influence television had on children in his 1978 book, *Television and Human Behavior.* He summarizes this influence in the following manner:

> It captures children's attention for long periods, and presents them
> with information and portrayals not duplicated or readily tested in their
> real life environment. It is turned to by children for information not
> readily available to them in real life. It provides models of behavior

children may emulate. It can alter the level of intensity of behavior, and such alterations may shape the future pattern of behavior through positive or negative reinforcement children receive. Viewing of violence increases the likelihood of aggressive behavior on the part of the young, but the larger implication is that television may influence other classes of behavior.[17]

Television provides role models. Children frequently nominate television characters as people they want to be like when they grow up. Children will even imitate the behavior of admired characters. Thus, television provides the potential for a pervasive influence on the self-concept—and this influence can be very subtle. You expect family, friends and schools to shape you, but what you usually expect from the media is entertainment or information. It does this and more. The effects are there and are clear in terms of self-concept development.

Although your self-concept does not change dramatically day-by-day, the complex process by which self-concept is formed and developed is unending. You change gradually over a period of time. As you express messages about who you are, you are guided by information acquired through your interaction with "significant others," including family, peers, the educational system, and media personalities. These forces shape the self-concept through processes of labeling the dominant behavior patterns, reflected appraisal, social comparison, and scanning the environment.

It is valuable to consider some aspects of yourself as you see them and as they are seen by others around you. The characteristics that express who you are must become known to you if you want to improve your interpersonal communication. To the extent that every message is, at least in part, about you, it is helpful to think about and talk about your images. How you see yourself is important, as is how you think others see you, and how they really see you. For a little help in this process, we suggest you try the following experience.

Experience: Self-Analysis

The following is a series of semantic differential scale items for you to use in a self-discovery experience. Take a moment to produce two copies of this scale. On one copy, place a check on each line to represent the degree of the attribute you think you possess. Since the words at each end of any particular line are opposites, one end of the line represents one extreme of the attribute while the other end of the line represents the opposite extreme.

After you have completed marking all items, take a different color ink and mark the items again. But this time, mark the items to indicate how you believe others see you. Finally, give the unmarked copy of these scales and have someone who knows you fairly well indicate how they see you.

	7	6	5	4	3	2	1	
1. Relaxed	___	: ___	: ___	: ___	: ___	: ___	: ___	Tense
2. Confidential	___	: ___	: ___	: ___	: ___	: ___	: ___	Divulging
3. Confident	___	: ___	: ___	: ___	: ___	: ___	: ___	Ill-at-ease
4. Enthusiastic	___	: ___	: ___	: ___	: ___	: ___	: ___	Apathetic
5. Trustworthy	___	: ___	: ___	: ___	: ___	: ___	: ___	Untrustworthy
6. Safe	___	: ___	: ___	: ___	: ___	: ___	: ___	Dangerous
7. Considerate	___	: ___	: ___	: ___	: ___	: ___	: ___	Inconsiderate
8. Friendly	___	: ___	: ___	: ___	: ___	: ___	: ___	Hostile
9. Involved	___	: ___	: ___	: ___	: ___	: ___	: ___	Detached
10. Straightforward	___	: ___	: ___	: ___	: ___	: ___	: ___	Tricky
11. Respectful	___	: ___	: ___	: ___	: ___	: ___	: ___	Disrespectful
12. Reliable	___	: ___	: ___	: ___	: ___	: ___	: ___	Unreliable
13. Secure	___	: ___	: ___	: ___	: ___	: ___	: ___	Insecure
14. Sincere	___	: ___	: ___	: ___	: ___	: ___	: ___	Insincere
15. Stimulating	___	: ___	: ___	: ___	: ___	: ___	: ___	Boring
16. Sensitive	___	: ___	: ___	: ___	: ___	: ___	: ___	Insensitive
17. Not Deceitful	___	: ___	: ___	: ___	: ___	: ___	: ___	Deceitful
18. Pleasant	___	: ___	: ___	: ___	: ___	: ___	: ___	Unpleasant
19. Kind	___	: ___	: ___	: ___	: ___	: ___	: ___	Cruel
20. Honest	___	: ___	: ___	: ___	: ___	: ___	: ___	Dishonest
21. Skilled	___	: ___	: ___	: ___	: ___	: ___	: ___	Unskilled
22. Informed	___	: ___	: ___	: ___	: ___	: ___	: ___	Uninformed
23. Experienced	___	: ___	: ___	: ___	: ___	: ___	: ___	Inexperienced
24. Bold	___	: ___	: ___	: ___	: ___	: ___	: ___	Timid

When you have collected data from all three ratings, transcribe the numbers associated with the spaces you checked on a grid that resembles the following. When you have entered all the numbers, consider what they mean in terms of self-concept.

Remember as you are reading that self-concept is not necessarily static. If there are areas in which you would like to see change, you can. If you decide to make some changes in the way you operate, some suggestions we make later in this chapter may prove to be helpful. A word of caution, however, is in order here. *Remember: The rating from the other person is a perception of one (only one) other person.* It is subject to selectivity and subjectivity.

Self-Analysis Grid

Attribute Scale	Self-Rating	My Perception of Other's Rating	One Other Person's Rating
Relaxed-Tense			
Confidential-Divulging			
Confident-Ill-at-ease			
Enthusiastic-Apathetic			
Trustworthy-Untrustworthy			
Safe-Dangerous			
Considerate-Inconsiderate			
Friendly-Hostile			
Involved-Detached			
Straightforward-Tricky			
Respectful-Disrespectful			
Reliable-Unreliable			
Secure-Insecure			
Sincere-Insincere			
Stimulating-Boring			
Sensitive-Insensitive			
Not Deceitful-Deceitful			
Pleasant-Unpleasant			
Kind-Cruel			
Honest-Dishonest			
Skilled-Unskilled			
Informed-Uninformed			
Experienced-Inexperienced			
Bold-Timid			

Interpersonal Needs in the Self-Concept

The complex system of beliefs, attitudes, and values that make up your self-concept determines the starting point and the control system for your interactions with others. As noted in the first chapter, for every interaction there is something wanted by you and something the other person wants, too. Each want is an appropriate expression of who you believe you are and how you wish to be seen. When communicating in an ongoing relationship, you are more likely to know how to express yourself in ways that the other person will understand. That is, you present yourself to the other person in a style that is developed on the basis of past interactions with that person. The greater your experience with the other person, the more accurate your predictions are likely to be. You will also have more confidence that the other person will behave in ways you can anticipate.

Remember Tim's communication at the beginning of this chapter? He may have wanted Mary Ann to understand him. He may have wanted Elizabeth to support him. Clearly, the expression of feelings and the solicitation of feelings involve special problems and therefore call for special skills.

At times you might be seeking assistance in achieving your goals. This sort of want is related to the development and projection of the self-concept. Wants that involve a basic development of the self-concept are referred to as expressions of interpersonal needs.

There are several ways of looking at needs. We have chosen to focus on the three areas of interpersonal need identified by William Schutz: the need for inclusion, the need to control, and the need of affection.[18]

Need for Inclusion

People have a basic need to be accepted, to feel wanted, and to be a part of groups, both at work and in their personal lives. Yet clearly, people do not experience all these needs in the same way. Some people demand a great amount of inclusion, while others seek to avoid inclusion almost entirely. Schutz recognizes these varying degrees of needs and labels them accordingly. *Undersocial* people have little need for inclusion, isolating themselves from group involvement. *Oversocial* people behave in the other extreme, continually seeking to join and feel a part of many groups. The *adaptable-social* person, on the other hand, balances needs for inclusion and privacy. This type of person realizes that there are certain situations where inclusion is desirable, but can also recognize those times when inclusion is not so desirable. Such a person is comfortable in both situations.

Undersocial and oversocial people often experience difficulties in their work. The undersocial person may be seen as aloof, arrogant, or indifferent. The oversocial person may be viewed as superficial, dominating, and demanding of time and attention.

Understanding inclusion as one part of everyone's need structure gives you an insight into what motivates people. It also suggests some ways you might behave if you wished to motivate others.

Need to Control

The need to control is the degree of desire you have to exercise power and authority. The need to control is based on two strict principles. First, you have the need to control your environment and the people around you. And secondly, everyone else around you has the same need to control as you.

There are also differing degrees of this need to control. Schutz describes an *abdicrat* as the person who has little need to control. This person abdicates all power and responsibilities. This person's opposite, the *autocrat,* is one who dominates others and feels the need to rise to the top of a power hierarchy. A person who takes the middle ground is called a *democrat,* and is capable of taking charge when needed or allowing others to be in control. This person is flexible and does not avoid taking over when appropriate.

The need to overcontrol can cause serious problems in relationships. Autocrats overextend themselves by trying to control "everything." Abdicrats, on the other hand, can also cause serious problems. The professional who cannot or will not assume control leaves more work for his co-workers. This person may take a job but may not take charge. Where efficiency is critical to business, this lack of leadership ability can often determine success or failure.

Your understanding of this problem may give you the insight to avoid it. Your awareness of this dimension in others will help you focus still closer on how they work.

Need of Affection

The need of affection is the desire to be liked by others and to develop loving relationships. The fulfillment of this need generates identification with the person who is liked. As a rule, you tend to like most those who like you in return.

The result of liking is personal closeness and positive feelings. When a person has little need of affection, neutrality is displayed in relationships. All others are treated the same. Some persons may even behave with hostility to avoid closeness. Schutz refers to this lack of need as *underpersonal.* On the other hand, a person who is high in the need of affection is considered *overpersonal* and will take special pains to avoid being disliked by anyone. An overpersonal individual can become too concerned with the social dimension and spend far too much time socializing. A *personal* individual holds the middle ground, and can balance situations in order to be liked when affection is desirable, but can also maintain distance between self and others when affection is not needed. This balance allows people to manage their relationships more productively.

An understanding of others' need of affection will assist you in determining how to better relate to those around you. You can vary your approach dependent on whether the individual is underpersonal, overpersonal, or personal.

Thus a better understanding of the differences in people's interpersonal needs can be quite useful to you. First, you may be able to understand yourself better if you conduct a personal analysis of each of your need areas. Consider where you are and where you would like to be within the context of your life. Does your basic need structure square up with the roles you have chosen? Can you conduct your relationships and have your needs fulfilled? You should not necessarily play amateur psychologist or select roles based solely on your needs, but this information might assist you in making choices. This consideration can help you know how to operate or adjust if necessary.

It is safe to say that an effective communicator is one who understands how all parties operate in his or her relationships. Such a person understands how to motivate and reward others. Understanding each person and working toward the general compatibility and satisfaction of needs within relationships is critical to effective interpersonal communication.

Self-Concept Maintenance

You are often reminded that the characteristic that most distinguishes humans from other creatures is the ability to communicate with each other. Indeed, this special ability made it possible for our predecessors to tame this planet despite the ferociousness of their surroundings. At first, humans developed their communication skills to survive the threat posed by other creatures. Now, improved communication skills are needed to grow and develop further.

Survival Orientation

The survival instinct still exists but serves a slightly different function. At times, the mind works to protect itself from change and can sometimes inhibit the growth of an individual. When this instinct takes over, you find yourself behaving without knowing it and in a direction quite different from that of your goals. When the self-concept feels threatened, it will direct you to defend it. The mind's takeover of your conscious behavior is referred to as *going unconscious.* When this happens, you are moved to do or say whatever is necessary to emerge from a situation with your self-concept intact. This affects both your expression and your perception.

As noted earlier in this chapter, the self-concept is a relatively stable structure on a day-to-day basis, yet is changeable over time. Remember Professor Brunner in our story at the beginning of this chapter? You might interpret his criticism of his students as his way of emerging from a situation with his self-concept intact. After all, if he believed that the students would not participate because they had a problem, he could still view himself as open and

minimum a list of the people, places, things, and events in your experiences that are significant. You should also provide details of why you feel these are important. You are urged to write down as much information as you can, because as you attempt to commit your reflected experiences to paper, you will think about them more deeply and recall more details about them. Organize this activity in a way that works best for you.

Here are four suggested methods.

1. Focus on those people you identify as significant others in your past. You will probably have thought about these people already as you read earlier in this chapter about the forces that shape your self-concept. In what ways were they influential? What characteristic or aspect of self-concept do you have now that you did not have before interacting with these people?
2. Focus on the events that you consider significant in your life. Start with the most recent and work your way backwards as far as you can. How did these events influence your view of yourself then?
3. Divide your life into categories of style: your personal life, your work life, and your public life. What were you like in each of these areas of your life? How do you know these characteristics are the important ones?
4. You might also organize this activity around the roles you have assumed in your life. What was your communication style in each role? What sort of feedback did you receive from others as you performed these roles? Did you succeed in each role?

Stage Two: Looking at Yourself Now

Who are you now? How do you see yourself? How do you present yourself? How do you think others see you? If you completed the self-awareness experience as well as those in which you explored your beliefs, values, and attitudes earlier in this chapter, you already have a lot of information about who you think you are. Continue this self-examination by first reviewing those materials. Next, make a record of the people, places, and things that are important to you right now—not tomorrow and not next week, but right now. What do you expect from the people you've listed as important? What do you think they expect from you? How do you feel when you're around them? Why do you think you feel this way? Are you who you want to be right now? You may be experiencing some uncertainty about your answers to one or more of these questions. If so, just acknowledge these feelings and keep going. In most instances, knowing that you don't know is healthier than pretending that you do know these answers.

Stage Three: Looking Ahead at Yourself

How do you see yourself in the future? How do you predict others will view you? What options are open to you? Who can you be? Create several scenarios for your future identity based upon choices you believe you might make about directions in your life. You will probably see that you have quite a few options, and that some are entirely different than others. Feel free to engage in a little fantasizing. Just look at yourself and allow your imagination to assert itself.

As you complete this part of the program, you may experience *blocking.* That is, you may start to create a picture of yourself and then something inside you will say, "You can't be (or do, or have) that." This is probably your survival orientation cropping up again. We encourage you to push past these internal objections. Create images of as great a variety of future selves as you can.

Stage Four: Looking Again at Yourself

If you completed the preceding experiences, you have thought and written about who you have been, who you are, and who you can be. The important question that you are asked to face at this stage is who you want to be. You have the unique ability to look at yourself clearly, and know whether or not a concept fits you and your goals. There's no reason to start down a road that does not lead you to where you want to go.

Guidelines for Self-Concept Development

Here are some suggestions to help you as you work toward achieving your goals and developing your self-concept.

1. *Start small.* Recall that some of your beliefs, values, and attitudes were shaped gradually over a long period of time. Also remember that you have surrounded your more important characteristics with a protective layer of supportive information. The friend who never ran started into running enthusiastically, but was trying to be too much at one time. Some people can change themselves swiftly and with ease, but most of us cannot. For most of us, self-change is most successful and long-lasting when accomplished in manageable portions. Use your skills to look ahead at yourself to predict how much of a change you can manage without interfering with your other goals and priorities. If you overestimate, don't hesitate to slow your pace a little.
2. *Be specific about the changes that you desire.* Wanting to be "a better person" is certainly a desirable goal but how will you know when you get there? A clearer statement about this might be "I'm going to work

with the local youth council the first Saturday morning of each month." The more specific you are, the better able you'll be to visualize yourself being there and the easier it will be to measure your progress.

3. *Translate your desires into agreements.* Make agreements with yourself about what you expect. Sometimes it helps to include a reward for successfully carrying out desired changes. Encourage others to expect that of you as well. But take care not to hold others responsible for producing your change. It is easy to avoid the responsibility for achieving your own goals.

4. *Seek feedback about your presentation of self.* You already know that the concept of the looking-glass self you think others have of you is important. Check out the image others hold of you. Find out if they are perceiving the changes that you are working toward. How do they feel about them? You may find that they will encourage and support you, and so help you to achieve your goals.

5. *Remain conscious.* Remaining aware of the images you project is critical to the change process. Watch yourself communicating in relationships using the reflected appraisal process described earlier in this chapter. For some people, keeping a journal similar to the "Looking at Yourself Now" experience is helpful.

Changing the self-concept involves getting through your natural inclination to resist change. Although such change is sometimes difficult, with the proper techniques and attention, you can achieve your desired outcomes.

Summary

Interpersonal communication involves the presentation of ideas about the people, places, and things in your world, as well as information about yourself. The image that you have of yourself and your notion of what is appropriate for expression comprise the self-concept. This self-concept includes aspects of which you may be entirely unaware. It also includes information about you of which others may or may not be aware. The basic components of the self-concept are beliefs, values, and attitudes that exist in branching fashion from a central core. Some of these components are intensely held and protected against change, while others are more flexible. These components, in various combinations, provide windows through which you experience people, places, and things in the world. Such windows are called "frames of reference."

Four processes operate in the evolution of the self-concept. These are (1) labeling the dominant behavior pattern, (2) reflected appraisal, (3) social comparison, and (4) scanning the environment.

Significant others are important forces that influence the evolution of the self-concept. The four principle forces are (1) family, (2) peers, (3) schools, and (4) media personalities.

The self-concept determines our wants, expectations, and predictions. Many of these are expressed as interpersonal needs for affection, inclusion, and control.

The self-concept is generally flexible, but relatively stable when examined over short periods of time. Long-term change, however, takes place as an evolutionary process. When expressed unconsciously, the self-concept can act as a protective, survival-oriented mechanism. When expressed consciously, it serves as the principal tool for achieving wants and needs.

Maintaining and changing undesirable aspects of the self-concept requires attention and discipline. In this chapter, not only were you provided with a useful definition of the self-concept but also with techniques for its maintenance and change.

Discussion Questions

1. Call to mind a child you know who is ten years old or younger. Can you evaluate that child's emerging self-concept? What are the contributing factors in this emerging self-concept?
2. Imagine that this same ten-year-old child has just brought home a report card with a very low mark in one of the major subjects. In what ways might the child's self-concept influence his or her behavior? How will the parents' response affect the child's emerging self-concept?
3. Imagine yourself in each of the following roles. How might your role and your relationships be affected by their contribution to your self-image?
   A religious person
   A political person
   A student
   A partner in a special relationship
   A member of a family
   A volunteer in public service
4. Considering the same roles mentioned in number three, which of the interpersonal needs discussed in this chapter are most likely to be expressed in the role behavior associated with each?

Endnotes

1. A. G. Athos and J. J. Gabarro, *Interpersonal Behavior* (Englewood Cliffs, NJ: Prentice-Hall, Inc., 1978).
2. W. James, *Principles of Psychology* (New York: Holt 1910).
3. G. H. Mead, *Mind, Self and Society* (Chicago: University of Chicago Press, 1934).
4. J. Luft, *An Introduction to Group Dynamics*, 2d ed. (Palo Alto, CA: Mayfield Publishing Company, 1970).

5. M. Rokeach, *Beliefs, Attitudes and Values: A Theory of Organization and Change* (San Francisco, CA: Jossey-Bass, 1968), 5.

6. S. Oskamp, *Attitudes and Opinions* (Englewood Cliffs, NJ: Prentice-Hall, Inc., 1977), 13.

7. G. W. Allport, "Attitudes," *Handbook of Social Psychology,* ed. C. Murchison (Worchester, MA: Clark University Press, 1935), 810.

8. K. Gergen, *The Concept of Self* (New York: Holt, Rinehart and Winston, 1971).

9. Mead, *Mind, Self and Society.*

10. C. H. Cooley, *Human Nature and Social Order* (New York: Scribner's, 1912).

11. L. Festinger, *A Theory of Cognitive Dissonance* (Stanford, CA: Stanford University Press, 1957).

12. Cooley, *Human Nature and Social Order,* 152.

13. B. R. McCandless and R. H. Coop, *Adolescents: Behavior and Development* 2d. ed. (New York: Holt, Rinehart and Winston, 1970), 233.

14. *Ibid.,* 246.

15. *Ibid.,* 333.

16. *Television and Growing Up: The Impact of Televised Violence.* Surgeon General's Scientific Advisory Committee on Television and Social Behavior, 1972.

17. G. Comstock, S. Chaffee, N. Katzman, M. McCombs, and D. Roberts, *Television and Human Behavior* (New York: Columbia University Press, 1978).

18. W. C. Schutz, *The Interpersonal Underworld* (Reading, MA: Addison-Wesley Publishing Company, Inc., 1969).

Perceiving Self and Others

Preview

The world that exists outside you is not the same as the world you understand and live with inside you. Your communication and your relationships do not depend on the world outside you so much as they do your perceptions of that world. It is useful, therefore, to study how people perceive and how they misperceive. With that information, you can learn to communicate more accurately and, therefore, enhance your relationships with others.

Objectives

After reading this chapter you should be able to complete the following:
1. Explain how perception affects interpersonal communication.
2. Describe how the three qualities of perception operate during the interpersonal communication process.
3. Explain how each of the senses contributes to the interpersonal communication process.
4. Identify examples where health, age, and fatigue influence perception.
5. Provide examples of the influence of contrast, repetition, motion, familiarity, and novelty on perception.
6. Discuss the ways that people interpret stimuli to shape the frame of reference.
7. Define the terms closure and perceptual organization.
8. Provide examples that illustrate the differences between assimilation and accommodation in perception.
9. Explain how selectivity shapes perception during interpersonal communication.
10. Discuss the three ways that perceiving people differs from perceiving objects.
11. Present a plan for improving your receptive and interpretive skills.

3

The instructor in the group's interpersonal communication class suggested that the members of the class get to know one another better. He indicated that perhaps by socializing a little and studying together, they might be able to get more from the course. Following his suggestion, the group decided to take in a basketball game.

The first part of the game was exciting and by halftime, practically everyone but Elizabeth stood to cheer their team off the court. Mary Ann noticed that Elizabeth remained sitting and asked, "Are you okay, Elizabeth?"

"Yeah, I'm alright," she replied. "It's just that all this jumping up and down has worn me out. I'm still fighting off that cold, and I think it's starting to get to me again. Do you think the second half will seem as long as this one did?"

Tim looked around at her and cut in. "I thought this one went by pretty fast. But anyway, I don't think the second will seem long at all. There's going to be a lot of action."

Phil laughed and said, "I hope so. If they don't start looking up, they won't stand much of a chance in the conference championships."

Tim looked at him sharply. "They're doing just fine, Phil. Brown is making more than half his shots and the defense is really moving. I think the championship will be no problem."

"Half his shots?" asked Phil. "That's pretty good. Maybe they will do all right in the end. Although they were pushing people on the other team around a lot more than I think the championship referees will allow."

Tim snorted. "Are you kidding? They're not doing anything illegal out there. That's just aggressive basketball. A championship team has to play aggressively."

Phil looked down and said, "Yeah, they are championship material. Well, maybe they weren't actually pushing."

At this point, Cheryl jumped into the conversation, saying, "Hey Tim, I saw Johnson out there banging away at number twenty-three with his elbow. Remember, I showed you that during the first quarter? The referees didn't see him at first, but he did it so often that they finally caught him. Then they started watching for it, and now he's got three fouls."

"Well, the first time they caught him, he really was guilty," Tim replied. "But after that they were just picking on him. And that last one was an outright bad call. He didn't come near that guy."

Phil gave a surprised look, saying, "I don't know, Tim. Number twenty-three fell down when that call was made. Johnson must have really hit him."

Tim laughed. "That's acting, Phil. Players are trained to do that. It gets the referee's attention and it fools them as it fooled you. When I played in high school, we did it all the time."

Cheryl shook her head and said, "I think you're wrong, Tim. I saw him hit the man. Now that I think about it I remember wincing at the sound of his elbow cracking into twenty-three's ribs."

"I didn't see that," Tim said. "And I didn't hear anything either. It really doesn't matter, anyway. He got called for it. Did you see it, Elizabeth?"

Elizabeth looked up, frowning, and said, "I didn't see anything. I didn't hear anything. I don't even know what number twenty-three looks like. This cold has me so dazed, I'm lucky I remember what you look like, Tim."

Cheryl spoke up again. "I'll bet the coach is giving them all a good talking to this halftime."

The group nodded in agreement, and Phil replied, "He probably is. Say, who is number sixty-four for our side? I was watching him, but I've never seen him play before."

"I was watching him, too," Mary Ann said. "His name is Bill Silvia. I know him from my philosophy class last term. I was surprised to see him playing because he never mentioned going out for the team when we talked."

Cheryl said that she'd noticed him too, and then said, "Hey, here they come. Everybody ready for the second half?"

This conversation seems fairly typical. People are discussing what each thinks just happened during the game. You don't have to be a basketball fan to recognize that all the members of the group witnessed the same event. When they talk about it, however, it seems as though they saw different things. These are differences in perception.

Perception is a fundamental aspect of interpersonal communication. The word perception comes from the Latin, *perceptio,* which means receiving. As it applies to interpersonal communication, however, perception means much more than merely receiving information. In the process of perception, information is acquired and meaning assigned to it. Perception involves both taking in stimuli and interpreting them. In chapter one, you read a little about how your senses perceive. Here the topic is discussed in depth, so that you will learn how perception can either help or hinder your growth through interpersonal communication.

The functions and general qualities of perception are presented first. You will learn how you perceive, including the physical and sensory influences on perception. You will learn the receptive and interpretive processes of perception, and the various forms of selectivity. You will study the way you perceive people, and distinguish it from the way you perceive objects. Ideas such as shared experience, expectations, and change are considered. Finally, you will read about the ways that you can build accuracy in perceiving people in your relationships.

The Functions of Perception

Perception is important because of what it *does* for you as you communicate. First, it provides structure for your frame of reference. Second, it serves to stabilize the frame of reference. Third, perception gives meaning to your experiences.

Recall that in chapter 2 we said that your frame of reference is a set of interlocking facts, ideas, beliefs, values, and attitudes that serve to orient you and to give meaning to messages, situations, and experiences. These beliefs, values, and attitudes also organize your world of experience. The process of perception builds and maintains this structure, incorporating each new bit of information.

Perception also provides stability in your experience. Rather than seeing experience as constantly shifting in response to the contact of different signals with various senses, perception endows experience with flowing quality. For instance, try this experiment. Hold your hand out at arm's length and examine it for a moment. Now move it quickly toward you and then back out.

Although the movement of your hand created differences in size and color, you probably experienced it as the same size and color when you were moving it as you did when you were not. This stabilizing function can sometimes prove troublesome in your relationships, as you will see later in this chapter.

The various events that occur around you are not necessarily connected. Some may be related to one another, while others may not be related at all. However, in order for you to make these events part of your experience, it is necessary for them to be related to the other events you witness and to your frame of reference. Perception allows you to connect separate experiences.

For example, imagine the standard routine of getting ready for each new day. You awaken to classical music on your clock radio. You rise quietly; move to the bathroom; turn on the light; use and flush the toilet; balance the temperature of the shower; step under the shower head where the needlelike jets of water massage your body and increase your circulatory rate. You turn off the water; draw back the shower curtain; find your towel; notice that it is your favorite yellow one; rub your skin vigorously, stimulating your body and enjoying the clean fresh feeling that results. All of these perceptions, and many more, are connected in your head. They become the single reality of a morning routine.

The Qualities of Perception

Although research on perception continues, scientists have clearly identified several aspects of the process. These aspects shed some light on the way you perceive yourself and others.

One aspect of *perception* is that it *is active.* You cannot accept and take in all the stimuli available to you. Rather, you sort, screen, and sometimes reach out for information. You go through this selecting because the world contains much more stimulation than you want or need. So as you move along, you perceive selectively in order to maintain your sense of structure and stability. Things don't just fit together. You actively fit them together through perception.

Perception also works inductively. Through your perception you generate whole images of things and people built from observation of parts of them. Your

Figure 3.1

perception process takes in clues about the way things are and then puts the clues together to form a conclusion representing the whole thing.

Examine the four faces depicted in figure 3.1. What do you think of these people? What mood would you say each is in? What are they feeling? Of what would you say they might be thinking? What clues did you use to assemble your perception? Compare your perceptions to those of your classmates. How are their inferences similar to yours? How are they different? Did they use different clues than you in creating your perceptions?

A third aspect of perception involves your awareness. *Perception occurs unconsciously.* You don't usually think about perceiving while you are doing it any more than you think about your heartbeat or your breathing pattern. Unlike these, however, you can't even focus attention on perceiving because attention is one of your tools of perception. You can focus on *what* you are perceiving, and this focus is very important in building accuracy in perception.

How You Perceive

The basic tools of perception are your senses. The information taken in by senses can be influenced both by your physical state and by the object of perception. Aspects of the process itself, such as interpretation and selectivity, also influence perception.

Sensory Aspects of Perception

The bits and pieces of information from which you draw conclusions about your experiences are gathered through the senses. This information provides the basis of your interpersonal communication.

Taste and Smell

Taste and smell affect your interpersonal communication in similar ways. Both are subtle senses, and information from them usually accompanies that received through other senses.

Taste provides a good example of the inductive nature of perception. Your sense of taste is mediated by taste buds arranged primarily on the tongue. There are really only four basic tastes to which these buds are receptive. Any taste that is not sweet, sour, salty, or bitter is one that you've interpreted. The interaction among the food, your taste buds, and your experience yields a conclusion that amounts to a taste. You may find some foods enjoyable, but may know a friend who finds the same disgusting.

Smell functions in much the same way as taste. Your sense of smell is also one of the more adaptable senses. If you enter an environment that has an unusual smell, you will adjust very quickly to the new odor. After a little while, you will not even notice it at all.

Taste and smell are part of interpersonal communication. A taste or smell that you like evokes pleasurable associations that may make conversation easier.

Hearing

Your hearing differs as a perception tool from smell and taste because the hearing receptors, your ears, are physically separate from one another. This adds a directional dimension to your perception that is lacking in taste and smell.

Hearing, the primary receptor for language, helps you to interpret shades of meaning associated with tone of voice. You might discover the importance of your hearing by watching some television with the sound turned off. You will find that in doing this, you can probably keep track of the general flow of the program. You are missing the language, however, and also the tone of voice, background music, and sound effects. Consider the difference in meaning these elements make.

In recent years, both televised and live public presentations have used captions or sign language interpreters to convey messages to viewers with hearing deficiencies. These techniques shift the primary language stimuli from the auditory to the visual channels and enable people with hearing problems to participate in a wider range of activities.

Sight

Your most important sense is probably your sight. You watch people as you talk with them and take in data about them from gestures, posture, and appearance. The importance of vision is even reflected in the language that you use: "Do you see what I'm saying?"

Touch

The skin is at once the largest and most subtle of our sensors. Your sense of touch conveys information through pressure and temperature. Pressure pertains to the hardness or softness, roughness or smoothness of things with which you come in contact. Temperature pertains to the warmth or coolness of something relative to your own body temperature.

You normally have to focus on what you are touching to be aware of this sensation. You don't usually notice the feeling of the chair pressing against your back and legs unless you consciously choose to do so. You do, however, notice that your perceptions adjust as you make contact with another person through a handshake or an embrace. In these cases you are concentrating more on your tactile experience.

It is through these five senses that you take in information about what is going on from the environment. This is the first step in perceiving. Remember, perception is complicated by the fact that you are taking in data through all five senses simultaneously. While you may be looking at something and thinking about what you are seeing, your other senses do not shut down. As you communicate, you are tasting, smelling, hearing, seeing, and feeling the touch of your relationships as well.

Physical Influences on Perception

The senses may vary among people in quality and quantity. Such variation may result in different perceptions of the same event. There are other physical factors that may affect your perception of events such as your health, fatigue level, and age.

Health

When you are not feeling well, your body concentrates more on itself, at the expense of one or more of your senses. Think about the last time you had a bad cold. Did you have a stuffy nose? Blurred vision? Hearing impairment? Your body had to limit or shut down one or more of your senses in order to divert attention to fighting the cold virus. When you read about the group's experience at the basketball game, you probably noticed that Elizabeth wasn't feeling very well. To Elizabeth, the first half of the game seemed longer than to the other members of the group, nor could she recall specific details from that first half. Elizabeth attributed her lack of knowledge about the game to her cold. We think she may have been right and that her time distortion could have come from her poor health as well.

Fatigue

At one time, it was believed that fatigue affected perception similarly to poor health. But recent research has contradicted this belief. In his book, *Sleep: The Gentle Tyrant,* Wilse Webb summarizes the research conducted for the U.S. Army on the impact of sleeplessness on performance of duties.[1] In this research, individuals were assigned a number of tasks of varying complexity during a forty-eight hour period of wakefulness. The researchers observed declines in attentiveness, mood, and in ability to stick with a routine. However they also observed that the subjects of the study improved in their ability to respond to tests of free association as they became sleepier. Lack of sleep had no impact on the ability of the subjects to perform complex intellectual tasks, or on activities that the subjects reported as interesting or demanding. You may have noticed this same phenomenon if you have ever worked all night writing a term paper. Your sleepiness probably did not interfere with the task of creating the report, but when you attempted to type the final draft, you may have found yourself all thumbs. Fatigue first strikes your ability to carry out mundane or routine tasks that with normal rest, would be quite simple.[2]

This information applies to fatigue triggered by short-term sleep deprivation. Fatigue that results from long-term loss of rest or from strenuous physical exertion can result in such perceptual problems as distortion, confusion, and what Webb calls "transient inattention," or losing your train of thought. In general, then, your perception is at its best when you are getting the amount of rest that is appropriate for you. You should be aware of your fatigue level when you are communicating with others. Accurate and effective communication is a difficult task when you are tired.

Age

Age is an interesting variable in perception because it influences perception both physiologically and psychologically. Aging slows down movement. This is certainly not to suggest that people are less productive or even less active as they age. Rather, you accomplish tasks in ways that require less exertion.

Thus, your perceptions about tasks, and the way they ought to be done, shift along with your ability and desire to exert yourself.

The internal effect of age on perception is more significant. You know that self-concept consists of the attitudes, beliefs, and values that you have accumulated. The older you get, the more data you have collected through your experience, and consequently the more you have to sift through as you build relationships with others. You have more experiences through which to filter new stimuli. Thus, the world may seem different to someone who has been around longer.

The Act of Perceiving

Perception has been defined as taking in and assigning meaning to stimuli. You have examined the ways that you operate as a perceiver. But it is also important to consider the characteristics of stimuli that affect your perception. These characteristics are contrast, repetition, motion, and familiarity or novelty.

Contrast

You tend to notice things that stand out from the rest of the environment. Textbook publishers use this principle in presenting information to you. Important terms sometimes appear in bold type. Or the discussion of a special idea may be isolated from the rest of the text in a box. You also use contrast to aid your perception when you underline or highlight as you read, so that when you review the material, important ideas stand out.

Contrast influences your interpersonal perceptions as well. For example, have several people from the class stand in the front of the room and talk to the class, all at the same time. After about two minutes of this, explore with other members of the class which speakers each paid attention to and why. One person will have received the attention of a class member because he was closest in distance to the listener; another because she was the tallest. Still another may be listened to because he spoke the loudest. Contrast can take many forms, including size, shape, color, and intensity. Any outstanding difference between a stimulus and the environment is likely to attract attention.

In conversation, the stress placed on particular words or phrases may affect your perception of the message. To explore this aspect of contrast, try this experiment. After choosing a partner from the class, take turns repeating one of the following phrases, emphasizing a different word in the statement each time it is spoken. Notice how the meaning assigned to each statement changes with the emphasis.

"I need that report tomorrow."
"I think you're quite attractive."
"Are you going to the game Saturday?"
"I want to talk with you."

Repetition

Repeated stimuli are noticed more than those that are not repeated. In some television programs, the same commercial may be shown every fifteen minutes. You may prefer that the station show a single four-minute advertisement for the product at the beginning or at the end of the program and televise the show uninterrupted. But the advertiser knows that your perception of the product will be better influenced by repeated messages. The player that Cheryl told Tim about was illustrating this principle. His repeated action of hitting other players with his elbows eventually caught the attention of the referees. Once the officials were aware of this behavior, they began to look for it more often.

Repetition has a point of diminishing returns. Once a particular message has been completely absorbed, further repetitions may become redundant and negatively influence perception. Rather than attracting your attention, a too-often repeated message will repel it.

This attraction or repulsion resulting from repeated messages sometimes operates in the interpersonal context. A few years ago, for example, people in the business world became very aware of the importance of effective communication in their organizations. Managers were taught to improve the communication involving problems at work. Some of these managers repeated the need for "good communication" too often. They defined all organizational problems as "communication problems." Soon they found that others in the organization no longer paid attention to them. Although communication in the organization is extremely important, excessive repetition can result in perceptual problems. People will disassociate from the repeated message.

Motion

Things that are in *motion* are more readily noticed than things that are static. Because this is true, some public speaking teachers even go so far as to encourage students to use carefully planned gestures to accentuate important points. These instructors know that hand and body motion can attract attention to the important idea, conveying it more forcefully. Get together with someone in your class and try to have a conversation without gesturing. You'll find that doing this may take a conscious effort because body movements are so helpful in interpersonal communication.

Imagine yourself driving slowly through a crowded parking lot in search of a space. You'll use both contrast and motion to help you find a place to park. An open space will stand out from the filled ones (contrast) and the vibration of a vehicle with the engine running suggests a car about to leave a space. People moving toward parked cars suggests that they are leaving, and ultimately, vacating a parking spot.

The movement and gestures of a person with whom you are communicating affect your perception of the person and the message. Your perception is also affected by the movement of a person toward or away from you as you talk.

Familiarity and Novelty

The familiarity or novelty of a stimulus relates to both the environment and your experience. You look for familiar people and things when you're in a new environment. But you'll often look for something novel in an old environment. At a social event, you may find yourself searching the crowd for a familiar face because finding someone you know helps you to feel comfortable. On the other hand, when you are with old friends, you may find yourself looking for new things to discuss. Perhaps you'll focus on something that is new or different about them. Remember Phil and Mary Ann's conversation during the game? Phil noticed number sixty-four because the player was new to him. Mary Ann, on the other hand, noticed the same player because he was familiar to her in another context.

D. E. Berlyne thought that novelty was the essence of human curiosity.[3] As you become familiar with your environment you act on the basis of what seems most likely to happen there. When two or more responses seem equally probable, you'll experience uncertainty and will seek information to balance your perceptions in favor of one or the other. Then you'll act. If a person doesn't act as you've predicted, you'll experience conflict because the prediction and the person's actions don't match. This mismatch can produce internal tension in your brain: a conflict you can't resolve often produces concern. Sometimes you resolve this conflict by adjusting your perception of that person.

On the other hand, when you communicate with new people, you will search for things that are mutually familiar, and use those as a basis for self-disclosure and extension of the relationship.

Apart from your senses then, these four, contrast, motion, repetition, and familiarity or novelty, affect your perception. Things that possess one or more of these characteristics will attract your perception more than those that do not. Have you ever walked down a busy city street in the evening? If you have, you may have noticed all four of these aspects in competition with one another for your attention. You have seen movement in flashing signs, contrast in bright neons, repeated messages, and appeals to both the familiar and the new. These are all aspects of messages that attract you.

Perception as Interpretation

As you already know, different people may view the same events in different ways. They may even perceive them as different things. Since what you do depends on what you perceive, your perception is more consequential than either what the other person intended, or what really happened.

For example, you may believe that two people talking are actually arguing. Another observer may view the same interaction as the two "poking fun" at each other. This is important because the action taken depends on how you see what is going on.

Figure 3.2

Your response to the people in your relationships is the result of your perception, too, just as are their responses to you. Sometimes people communicate a distorted view of what happened because of the perceptual factors previously discussed. At other times perception is distorted intentionally, out of defensiveness or as a part of some strategy. Perhaps differences in perception rest in the interpretations placed on that perception. In any case, if you and someone else *act* on the basis of different perceptions, there could be trouble. In the conversation at the beginning of this chapter, you saw an example of differences in interpretation. Tim, Cheryl, and Phil interpreted what they saw happening on the court in entirely different ways. Tim saw the player's pushing as aggressive, but legal, play. Cheryl, on the other hand, interpreted his action as definitely illegal and violent. Phil saw it as violent, and possibly illegal. Yet they were all exposed to the same event.

Stimuli that have been received through the senses are subject to interpretation. When you interpret, you fit information into your frame of reference. Look at the four drawings in figure 3.2. Which do you like the most? Why do you think you like it? Compare your perception with others in the class. Those having a different opinion than yours about the drawings will give reasons that reflect differences in interpretation of what they viewed.

People will assign different meanings to what they see in figure 3.2. Others will have seen parts of a picture that you did not notice at all. They may have found reason for liking the picture on the basis of these aspects that were unnoticed by you. But even after these hidden features are pointed out, you may still prefer your original choice.

Figure 3.3

Georges Seurat, *Sunday Afternoon on the Island of La Grande Jatte,* Collection of the Art Institute of Chicago.

Another reason people select one picture over another is the overall impression formed about the picture. That impression results from all of the prior experiences, norms, rules, and expectations that have gone into the development of the personalities of each.

One thing that you will notice as you compare your perception of the drawings with the perceptions of others is that your own perception shifts to accommodate their perceptions. You'll incorporate the perceptions stated by others into your own evaluation. There are two basic ways that this occurs: closure and perceptual organization.

Closure

When you add "finishing touches" to your perception of otherwise incomplete events, or when you draw inferences about the nature of an event as a whole, you are providing closure as a way to reduce your own uncertainty about the things you are perceiving. When you finish another person's sentence before it is entirely stated or when you generalize about what someone is "like," you are interpreting by closure.

Look carefully at the reproduction of Georges Seurat's painting *Sunday Afternoon on the Island of La Grand Jette* in figure 3.3. What would you say is going on in this picture? Describe your perception of the painting.

Figure 3.4

Georges Seurat, *Sunday Afternoon on the Island of La Grande Jatte,* Collection of the Art Institute of Chicago.

Now look carefully at figure 3.4. This figure is a blowup of one small portion of the Seurat painting. As you can see, the painting is really just a mass of dots of various shades and densities. You used closure to bring these dots together into the recognizable picture seen in figure 3.3.

Perceptual Organizing

Perceptual organizing occurs when you interpret incoming stimuli by arranging them in a way that makes sense to you. In chapter 1 you saw some variations in the printed text. Words were grouped differently, and in one instance, spaces were omitted. You made sense of that material through the interpretive process called perceptual organization.

Perceptual organization is a learning and categorization stage of the perception process. Sometimes perceptual organization is referred to as selective interpretation and selective retention. But in this chapter, we use selectivity to describe the way that your choice of stimuli varies as your senses encounter them. We use perceptual organization to refer to changes that take place inside you.

Two aspects of perceptual organization, assimilation and accommodation, are important.[4] It is important to understand and to distinguish between these processes because they account for the difference in your perceptions. *Assimilation* changes what you perceive to make it fit your attitudes. *Accommodation,* on the other hand, changes your attitudes to make them fit your perceptions. In both cases, change takes place. Knowledge of these processes can help you to identify more clearly the nature of changes that take place in your relationships and in your communication. Thus, you can better understand and improve them.

Assimilation changes what you perceive to fit your attitudes. It makes incoming stimuli a part of a previously existing frame of reference. Accommodation, the other aspect of perceptual organization, changes your attitudes to fit your perceptions. The attitudes must change to make room for the new data.

Accommodation and assimilation always happen together. That is, a space is made for the information and the information is made to fit the space. There are examples of assimilation and accommodation in the discussion between Phil and Tim about pushing on the basketball court, aggressive basketball, and the nature of a championship team. See if you can pick them out.

Sometimes the information is bent a little in assimilation. It may be leveled, sharpened, or distorted in order to better fit the space provided in the structure. When a perception is *leveled,* details have been shaved off the perception, leaving only those parts of the experience that clearly fit within the frame of reference. For instance, you may have a friend whose company you enjoy, but with whom you've had your ups and downs. As you organize your perceptions about this person, you may retain the averages of several experiences, rather than recall the low and high points that might contradict your general attitude about your friend.

When a perception is *sharpened,* you edit your experience by focusing on details that reinforce your frame of reference and discarding the rest. You might recall the enjoyment of spending time with your friend with a few of the adventures you had together, and forget the more mundane encounters.

The outright changing of the content of experiences is *distortion.* Experience is changed to fit your frame of reference. If you went out with a friend whom you normally enjoy, and had a particularly bad time, you might alter your memory of the details of the experience. Then the event can still be assimilated into your frame of reference.

As accommodation takes place, the frame of reference always changes. It's the degree of this change that's important. If the perception was altered substantially in assimilation, then the frame of reference will not have to change much to accommodate the new perception. However, the experience may be powerful and the perception too significant to level, sharpen, or distort. In this case the frame of reference will have to change drastically in order to accommodate the new perception. The way you respond to similar events will be different in the future.

Assimilation and accommodation, along with the leveling, sharpening, and distortion of perceptions, alter stimuli during the interpretation stage of the perception process. There are also changes that originate as you take in information. These alternations result from selectivity.

Selectivity

Selectivity is choosing information. Even with all five senses operating at optimum efficiency, there is just too much going on around you to take in everything. You must, therefore, select from the available stimuli. You select what you'll expose yourself to and you select what you'll pay attention to.

To illustrate this important idea of selectivity, look more closely at a line of type on this page. Notice how a lowercase "m" is shaped. Note that it is much wider than the lowercase "a" or lowercase "i." Notice the height of a lowercase "x." How much higher than the top of the "x" is the top of the "t"? How much higher than the top of the "x" is the top of the "h"? We suspect that you really didn't take any of this information into account before you started reading this paragraph, although the information has been available to you from the first word you read in this book. You have been selective in your perceptions. The overall appearance of a word allows you to "read" it without seeing it in detail. You had no need to select the details to perceive.

Selective exposure and selective attention are the two types of selectivity that are important to interpersonal communication. These processes occur in order with exposure first, followed by attention. Selective exposure provides an opportunity for perception. Selective attention is the manner in which you perceive.

Selective Exposure

When you turn on your radio and tune in a frequency, you are choosing to expose yourself to some information and to exclude other available channels. When you participate in any conversation, you make a similar choice. You make yourself available to some stimuli while disregarding others. For example, you may find yourself in a meeting with a group of people that includes someone with whom you always seem to argue. When he speaks, you may find yourself looking away from him. Perhaps you find yourself reading something you have in front of you while he speaks. You are avoiding exposure to him and to his communication.

There are more subtle bases for selective exposure to people and things. Many of these bases are personal biases. For example, you may choose to expose yourself to information coming from someone who uses your name. Bulk mail advertisers assume you make this choice when they insert your name into the appropriate blank spaces on form letters. Or you may not be aware that the news source you read tends to reinforce your own attitudes. We think you choose it for that reason. You expose yourself to ideas and to people selectively. Note, though, that selective exposure does not necessarily result in communication, or even perception. It provides the opportunity for perceiving. In order to perceive, you must not only be exposed, you must also attend.

Selective Attention

When you choose one or more of the stimuli to which you are exposed, you are attending selectively. Even though your senses operate simultaneously, you focus best when you attend to one sense at a time. At this moment, for example, you may see the page in front of you. You may also taste and smell a cup of freshly brewed coffee, hear the faint hum of an air conditioner, and feel both the hardness of the chair under your body and the tightness of the shoes on your feet. But you must select one of these sensations for attention at a time. If you decide to see the printed page, and the smell of the coffee is overpowering, you will have difficulty reading. Your concentration will flash rapidly back and forth between the sensations. You'll find it hard to concentrate on either. Recall the example of your meeting. When the person with whom you argue is speaking, you may choose to expose yourself to his communication, but you may selectively attend to only the main points of what he has to say. Or you may selectively attend to the *way* he says it, listening for a point to break in without being rude.

Take some time now to explore your own selective exposure and attention processes. Think about selective exposure in terms of people. Are there people in this class with whom you often interact? Are there any you have selected to avoid?

Experience: Selective Attention

Now try this exercise to learn more about selective attention. Concentrate on your senses, one at a time.

What do you hear right now?
What do you see?
What do you taste?
What do you smell?
What does your skin sense?

Now, try to do the following:

1. Concentrate on the taste in your mouth right now. Notice its sweetness, bitterness, or saltiness. You are tasting right now. Tune in to that experience. What do you taste?
2. Now, taste and smell at the same time. Is your experience flashing back and forth between the two sensations?
3. Next, taste, smell, and listen at the same time. You may find that it is easier to hold your attention on what you're hearing.

Figure 3.5

"Relativity," print by M. C. Escher, 1953. © BEELDRECHT, Amsterdam/VAGA, NY. Collection Haags Gemeentemuseum—The Hague.

4. Now, taste, smell, listen, and look at the same time. We expect you to find this very difficult to do.
5. Finally, try to taste, smell, listen, look, and feel the smoothness of this page with your fingertips at the same time. If you can do this, please write to us.

   Were you able to focus on more than one sense at the same time? Try some other combinations of senses. You'll still probably find it difficult to attend to more than one sense at a time.

   As a final test of your selective perception, examine figure 3.5 for a little while. Try to make sense of the drawing.

How does selective exposure operate as you attempt to make sense of this illustration? How does selective attention function? Selective attention and selective exposure work for you in directing your perceptual activity.

Perceiving Others

Perception of people is different from perception of things. Although the same basic processes are at work, there are three ways in which your experience of objects is different from your perception of people.

First, interpersonal perception is mutual. As you take in and interpret information about the other person, she is doing the same with respect to you. Knowing this, you'll be even more concerned about your self-image. Did you notice in the story at the beginning of the chapter that when Tim was challenged about his perception of what had happened in the game, he included in his reply some information about his experience in basketball. This may have been, in part, defensive, but this information also represents an acknowledgement that a person was looking at and paying attention to him. He may have needed to express a definition of himself that would help him be right about his point of view. This is not the case when you perceive objects.

Second, your expectations of people are clearer and more numerous than your expectations of objects. You have expectations about yourself, about the role you are taking in the relationship, about the role of the other in the relationship, and about the relationship itself. Relationship expectations are also mutual, although the expectations, themselves, may be different. In contrast, expectations of objects are less complex and always one-way. Pick up a pen or pencil and examine it carefully. You can really get into an examination of this object because the pencil is not experiencing you at the same time. If you studied another person the way you just did the pencil, your experience will be different because perception of others is two-directional. The other person perceives you as you are perceiving him.

Third, the difference between your perception of objects versus your perception of people is change. People change in ways that objects do not. Changes in people may be physical, social, psychological, or professional. Of course, changes in people are not always readily visible, and sometimes they're not even apparent to the person who has changed. Still, whether visible or not, ʳchange interacts with expectation in person perception. The expectations that you bring to an encounter may not be appropriate in light of changes in the other person. Similarly, the other person's expectations may be inappropriate in light of changes in you. Or both people may have changed, and all of the expectations of both require adjustment.

Mutual Experience

Mutual experience has important implications for interpersonal relationships. This involves interpersonal attraction, assignment of roles, and expectations.

Interpersonal Attraction

Interpersonal attraction describes your willingness to communicate and to develop a relationship with another. You are attracted to people you like. You are also attracted to people to whom you are physically close. And you are attracted to people whose physical attributes you admire.[5] This attraction leads to interpersonal communication.

You begin to like people in many ways that relate to the process of perception, but in two ways in particular. First, you usually like people who like you. These are people whose behavior is positive and supporting. Second, you usually like people who *are* like you. These are people you may feel you understand; people who seem to share a frame of reference similar to your own.

Though not as common as these two, you are also attracted to people with whom you are in frequent contact. The frequency of interactions may lead to the sharing of information and, as a result, in your *learning* to like someone. Through frequent contacts, you discover things about people that lead to your choices about liking them or not. Alternatively, the knowledge that frequent future encounters are inevitable may generate enough selectivity in your perception of the person to overcome other factors, and result in liking.

Or you may begin to like a person because you are usually attracted to people whose physical attributes you like. The standards for physical attraction are based on personal preference, of course, this preference will change from time to time. For example, which of the people in figure 3.6 do you find attractive? What about them do you like? Compare your choices and reasons with your classmates. Then the influence of personal preference will be obvious.

Assignment of Roles

Assignment of roles also influences the perception of people. A role is a pattern of behavior, and is both sociological and psychological.[6] *Sociological* roles are patterns of behavior that are assigned such titles as father, teacher, or friend. The assignment of sociological roles is evidenced in the history of surnames, some of which evolved from occupational and family roles: John the smithy became John Smith. The *psychological* aspect of a role is the description of the behavior used to carry out a role, or your frame of reference with respect to the behavior surrounding the role. When you begin communicating, you assign roles to both yourself and to the other. The assignment of roles carries with it guidelines of appropriate behavior. Thus your perceptions as well as those of the other person are influenced by the roles you assign to yourself and to the other. For instance, you might encounter one of your teachers in the hall after class. You identify him in your experience as a teacher, and you assign

Figure 3.6

him your psychological version of that sociological role. He recognizes you as a hardworking (psychological) student (sociological), and asks you how your term paper is coming along.

Sometimes you forget the psychological aspect of roles when you interact with other people. When this happens, you make the assumption that the other person will behave in a way that resembles your selective perception of the role, and don't allow for the other person's frame of reference. For example, suppose this same professor says, instead, "Bring your term paper in so I can take a look at it." If you see the professor's role as disciplinarian, you might perceive this sentence differently. "*Bring* (!) your term paper in so I can take a look at it!" In this case, your role definition has influenced your perception.

The generalizing of role assignments can be troublesome for you as you attempt to communicate with others because sometimes the categories you use are inaccurate. And unfortunately, these generalizations are very apparent in the language you use in your relationships.

Expectations

Expectations are an important part of the way you perceive people. You predict and expect the most likely response from someone.

Sometimes these expectations are based on a rigid impression you have about the particular group of people to which this person belongs. This process is *stereotyping,* a term originally used to describe the plate, a stereotype, that printed the same image again and again. You stereotype when you fail to see people as individuals, but instead see them as a member of a group. This distorts the perceptual process and becomes a problem because your expectations form the basis of your actions. When your prediction is proved accurate, you feel you understand that person. When your prediction of their response is incorrect, you feel as though you misunderstand the person.

Remember that, as part of your perception process, you try to predict what the other person in the relationship is expecting from you. These predictions, in turn, affect your own expectations of yourself and of the other person.

Change

Yet another important influence on your perception of people is change. When you looked at yourself carefully in the experience in the last chapter, it was probably clear to you that your self-concept has undergone considerable change over the years. When you change, your perception of others changes with you.

Think about some of the physical changes you have undergone. How did your way of perceiving shift to accommodate the physical change? Next, think about an important social change that has happened in your experience. This could be going away to college, joining a new social group, or finding a new circle of friends. How did you perceive your new relationships? Did your new associations affect your perception of other, older relationships? In what ways did your perceptions change? What changes have taken place in your career life? If you have not actually begun working in your career, you will find that when you do, your way of "looking at things" will shift again. New goals and values will develop around your professional roles, and your perception will change as you assimilate stimuli in your new roles. If you are already involved in a career, think about the last important change in your role or responsibility on the job. If you have changed jobs recently, you may have much to say about the changes in perception that occur when you make a professional change.

Building Accuracy in Perception

You *can* improve your perceptual skills. You can learn how to verify the accuracy of your perceptions. You can also learn to sharpen your ability to take in and interpret information from your environment. But working on your perceptual abilities can be demanding and time-consuming, so do not expect drastic improvement overnight. And do not expect to retain any improvements without practice and reinforcement. As you work on improving your perception, keep in mind that improved perception may result in an ability to better predict the behavior of the other person in a relationship. This, in turn, can lead to better communication and valuable interpersonal growth.

Building Receptive Skills

As stated earlier, the tools of perception are your senses. The keys to developing your perceptual tools, or senses, are attention and concentration, and time.

You must pay attention to what your body is experiencing in various situations. You must concentrate on what each of your senses is experiencing. Remember that improving your sensing ability is an ongoing, long-term process, so stay with it. There are many meditative techniques that might help you to focus with your senses. For example, the following experience focuses on what you sense about your internal state, and then expands to include your perceptions of objects, people, and relationships.

Get into a comfortable sitting position in a place where you won't be disturbed for about twenty minutes. Choose a spot slightly above your eye level and focus on it. As you focus on the spot, close your eyelids, keeping your eyes raised slightly. When your eyes are closed, begin counting slowly backward from one hundred. As you count, you will find yourself becoming more and more relaxed. When you arrive at one, check out how your body feels, starting with your feet and working your way up your body to the top of your head, including your jaws and forehead. You might tense slightly, hold, and then relax each part as you progress up your body. Inhale deeply as you tense each part, and exhale slowly and steadily as you relax it. Focus on each part of the body as long as it takes for you to feel comfortable with it. You may find that the back, shoulders and neck require greater attention than other parts. As you mentally climb your body, pay attention to what you are perceiving. Give some thought to each sense for every part of the body you relax. You may get some images that seem unrelated to what you are doing, but that's okay. It is important to accept what you think during the exercise, and to go on. Don't try to change or avoid anything that comes up for you. When you have finished this progressive relaxation, count from twenty down to one, remembering your environment as you go along. Remember the colors of the room, the arrangement of furniture, and what you expect to see when you open your eyes. When you get to one, you will open your eyes feeling relaxed and refreshed, with an increased awareness of yourself because you have focused your perception.

After repeating this exercise several times, you may find that you can shorten, or even eliminate, the counting at the beginning and end of the exercise. If this is true, you can spend this time getting more in touch with your bodily processes through focused perception.

Once you have developed a routine of performing the progressive relaxation exercise, you will find attending and concentrating on things outside yourself possible. For example, you might do this simple experience. Place a fresh orange in front of you. (It is important to start with a simple object that involves multiple senses.) After relaxing, and with your eyes still closed, concentrate on the orange. Imagine its smell, its taste, its texture, and its appearance. Think about what sounds the orange will make when squeezed, or when its skin is torn as it is peeled or cut. Work to make your image of the orange as vivid as possible.

Next, with your eyes still closed, pick up the fruit and validate your sensory predictions. Concentrate on one sense at a time. Feel the surface of the orange for its texture, smell it, then open your eyes and examine it. Tear it open and focus on the sounds that come with that action. Taste the fruit and get a sense of the internal texture as well.

Try this same experience with different objects. Over time the process of relaxing, predicting, and then validating will strengthen your ability to perceive objects. And although your perception of people is more complex than your perception of objects, this exercise, with some modifications, can help you in perceiving others, too. After you have worked with objects for a while, and feel comfortable with the process of predicting and validating your perceptions, use your ability to create images to focus on your experience of others.

As suggested before, relax yourself and call to mind a person with whom you are familiar. Exercise each of your senses as you concentrate on your image of that person. The next time you see him, you can check out your image of him, and you may be surprised at the accuracy of your image. Having concentrated on this person, you may also find yourself paying more attention to your perception as you talk with and observe him.

When you get to the point where you feel comfortable creating images of people you know, try recreating and studying communication events that have taken place with those people. By remembering and concentrating on what your various perceptions were at the time, and how those senses contributed to your action in the encounter, you can better understand how and why an exchange took the course that it did. Through this method, you can better understand how perception functions in your relationships.

This regimen for building your receptive skills can take some time, but it is well worth the investment you make in practicing. The benefits are increased personal health and increased interpersonal skill.

Building Interpretive Skills

Earlier in this chapter, you learned two things that are very important to the improvement of your interpretive process. First, you learned that interpretation takes place inductively. The interpretations of incoming stimuli that you make represent inferences drawn from what is observed through the senses. This is important to remember because you can improve perceptual interpretation by learning to distinguish more clearly between the observations and inferences of yourself and others.

Also recall that, too often, you perceive unconsciously. You cannot focus on perceiving, but you can concentrate more on *what* is perceived. You can improve your interpretive power by learning to recognize inferences when you state them or when you hear others state them.

In *Talking About Relationships,* Herbert J. Hess and Charles O. Tucker distinguish between observations and inferences.[7] They suggest that statements of observation differ from statements of inference in three ways.

One difference between the two types of statements is the extent of the description in each. *Observational statements* are faithful descriptions of what is sensed: "I saw you pour the last of the coffee into your cup and then walk away with it." *Inferential statements,* on the other hand, go beyond description: "You poured the last cup of coffee, and I'll bet you're not going to make a new pot."

A second difference is that your sensory observations make no judgment: "I smell something burning!" Inferences, however, frequently involve judgments: "It stinks in here!" Sometimes, a statement of inference is beyond observation *and* judgmental: "That inconsiderate oaf must be smoking those disgusting little cigars again." If you assume that this last statement is a fact rather than an inference, you may be surprised when your friend reacts defensively to your statement.

The third difference between these two types lies in the limitations placed on description and inference. Observations are limited to a description of what the senses take in. Inferences, on the other hand, are only limited by the imagination of the perceiver. While a description can only grow in detail as you can concentrate more and more on what you are observing, an almost infinite number of inferences can be generated.

You know that predicting and expecting are important aspects of the way you communicate. They represent statements of inference that you must make regularly. But as Hess and Tucker point out, it is useful to recognize guesses as guesses. The unrecognized inference is often the cause of clouded inter-pretation and relationship problems. Look back through the conversation at the beginning of this chapter for examples of unrecognized inferences. Tim's assertion that referees are fooled by the acting game of falling down on the basketball court represents one. Are there others?

There are some skills you can practice that will help you to develop your ability to interpret stimuli in interpersonal encounters. First, state your obser-vations and follow them with your inferences. Practice this both internally and externally. When you are alone and are thinking about a relationship, remind yourself to clarify the observations that result in your predictions about yourself and others. When you are in conversation, actually state the observation and then follow it with your inference.

As you are practicing this skill, maintain an awareness of the limitless nature of inferences. Ask yourself what other inferences might sensibly be drawn from your observation. Might a different interpretation be more appropriate if your description had more detail?

The second skill you can practice is that of checking out your inferences. There are several ways of doing this. You can check what is inferred on the basis of one sense against the evidence provided by other senses. That is, determine if what you see is validated by what you hear or feel, etc. Did you notice that when Cheryl was arguing with Tim about the pushing during the basketball game, she checked her inference by trying to recall what she was seeing as well as hearing. This technique works better at the moment of per-ception than it does after the fact. After all, she may have remembered the sound of the players hitting as a form of selective distortion to support her point of view!

Another way to check out your inferences is to repeat your observation; that is, look again. Find out if there is agreement between your first and second observations. Double checking your perceptions is sometimes time-consuming, but this can save you from acting on an inaccurate perception. Sometimes it is necessary to ask a person to repeat what was said, or to look more carefully at what is going on. But we believe the benefits to your com-munication are worth the effort.

One of the best ways to validate your perceptions is to check them out against what other people perceive. Ask the other person if she is perceiving things as you are. This is especially important when the inferences are about the other person. As Hess and Tucker point out, she is the final authority on her experience, regardless of your observations.

The practice of these skills requires a conscious effort, especially at first. But you will soon see an improvement in your ability to express what is going on with you and what you perceive as going on with others.

Summary

Perception is both the taking in and interpreting of stimuli. It plays a critical role in the process of interpersonal communication. In this chapter you learned that perception gives structure and stability to your frame of reference and meaning to your experience. The perception process is active. That is, it works constantly to sort out and define incoming stimuli. Your perception process constructs whole images for you from the bits and pieces of information received through your senses. This is the inductive nature of perception. Perception is largely an unconscious process at work while your awareness is focused on other matters.

You learned about the operation of your senses: the mechanisms of taste, smell, hearing, sight, and touch. You also learned that health, fatigue, and age can interfere with the operation of your senses. This chapter provided you with an awareness of how some stimuli are perceived more readily than others. Things that contrast with their contexts are more readily perceived than things that blend in. Stimuli that are repeated are also more easily perceived, as are those in motion. The very familiar and the very novel attract the attention of your senses as well.

You examined the way you make incoming messages fit your frame of reference, called interpretation. Perceptual organization is accomplished through closure, when you draw inferences about an event so as to have a more complete picture of it. When you alter your perception to make it fit your frame of reference, you are assimilating. When you alter the structure or content of your frame of reference to make room for a new perception, you are accommodating. You are now aware that information can get leveled, sharpened, or distorted during perceptual organization. Leveling leaves out details, while sharpening focuses specific details. Distortion occurs when you completely change the content of an experience for a better fit with your frame of reference. You also studied selective exposure and selective attention, two ways that you limit your perceptions to manageable proportions. Selective exposure is the choice to receive certain stimuli and to ignore others. Selective attention allows you to focus on some of the information to which you have been exposed, while disregarding the rest.

Perceiving objects is different from perceiving people, and in this chapter, you learned about the ways these two applications of perception vary. Perception of people is a mutual experience, with both parties perceiving and being perceived simultaneously. Also mutual is the assignment of roles to yourself and to the other person. The roles you choose will provide a focus for your perception and channel stimuli to particular categories. Stereotyping, or responding to a person on the basis of the role behaviors associated with a group to which he belongs, can sometimes result in perceptual difficulties. Another difference between your perception of people and that of objects is that you hold expectations of yourself and of others. Expectations are important be-cause they provide direction for growth in the relationship. But your expecta-tions must be checked out or conflict may result. Change is an important consideration in your perception of people. In this chapter you had the oppor-tunity to examine changes that have taken place in your experience of yourself and in your relationships. You were asked to consider the impact of the changes on your perceptions.

Finally, this chapter provided you with several tools to help you with the difficult task of improving your ability to perceive. You were provided with med-itative experiences to assist in the development of your senses. You were also provided with skills to help you manage the inferences that exist as a part of the interpretive aspect of perception.

Your growth through interpersonal communication can be greatly facili-tated by a knowledge of perception and by improvement in your ability to per-ceive. Apply the information in this chapter to your communication in relationships and you will find positive results.

Discussion Questions

1. Recall the details of your first image of your interpersonal communication professor. Have your perceptions of this individual changed in the period of time since this course began? How?
2. Call on the professor teaching a course you've considered taking in order to find out more about the course. Then, *after* you have done so, answer the following questions.
   a. What tasting, smelling, hearing, seeing, and touching cues did you receive when you met with the professor?
   b. Was the professor in good health? How do you know?
   c. Was the professor experiencing fatigue? How do you know?
   d. How old was the professor?
   e. Did you discover any evidence, either directly related to the person or to the environment, that would enable you to say whether this person is kindly or not? Well-read or not? Involved in any extracurricular activity or not? Involved with a family?
   f. Were you, yourself, tired during this conversation? If so, how did this affect your performance?
   g. How do you think the professor experienced you? What images did you leave?
   h. What perceptions of you do you believe would still be fresh and vivid in the professor's mind?
   i. Did you and the professor agree completely or even partially about the role expectations for the meeting? What were the role expectations? How do you know?
   j. Would you ask that professor for a date? If so, under what role expectations? How do you account for your response?

Endnotes

1. W. Webb, *Sleep: The Gentle Tyrant* (Englewood Cliffs, NJ: Prentice-Hall, Inc., 1975).
2. Much of this research is summarized in Daniel Goleman's "Staying Up: The Rebellion Against Sleep's Gentle Tyranny," *Psychology Today* 16 (March 1982): 24–36.
3. D. E. Berlyne, *Conflict, Arousal, and Curiosity* (New York: McGraw-Hill, Inc., 1960).
4. J. Piaget, *The Construction of Reality in the Child* (New York: Basic Books, Inc., 1954).
5. M. Ruffner and M. Burgoon, *Interpersonal Communication* (New York: Holt, Rinehart and Winston, 1981), 179–94.
6. C. L. Book, ed., *Human Communication: Principles, Contexts and Skills* (New York: St. Martin's Press, 1980), 3–37, 106–38.
7. H. J. Hess and C. O. Tucker, *Talking About Relationships,* 2d ed. (Prospect Heights, IL: Waveland Press, Inc., 1980), 19–31.

Listening to Others

Preview

Most of what you know about other people is based on what they say. The rest comes to you as a result of the guesses you make, based not only on what others say but also on how they act. Listening to people—taking in their messages, plus making guesses about the intent of those messages—is very difficult work. Error is introduced at an alarming rate when you don't listen carefully. Listening becomes particularly difficult in situations that are identified as conflicts. Learning to be more active and effective listeners is an essential part of the study of communication.

Objectives

After reading this chapter you should be able to complete the following:
1. Cite and explain the major reasons why listening is a problem.
2. Construct a model of the listening process and explain each of its components.
3. List the problems associated with sensing, attending, understanding, and remembering.
4. Distinguish between understanding and agreement.
5. Provide suggestions for improving listening.
6. Demonstrate the skill of active listening.
7. Create particular questions that would help you to think more carefully about what the other person is saying.
8. Distinguish between empathic and evaluative listening.
9. Cite and explain the response skills used to encourage the speaker to more fully explain the intended message.

4

D uring the fourth week of the interpersonal communication class, the group was given a project. The assignment was difficult, but interesting. They were each to interview two people who were not members of the class to discover what these people thought was important for a healthy interpersonal relationship. Then they were to discuss the information with the entire group. The group would then try to create a statement that represented their best judgment about the issue.

The group had just finished studying a unit on perception and so decided to divide into two-person teams for the interviewing. They figured this would help overcome some perceptual problems. Elizabeth and Tim were made partners.

Elizabeth and Tim decided to interview a counselor at the Psychology Clinic. They believed that she would be an excellent source of information. They were right. Ms. Phillips had been counseling for ten years. Not only had she developed a well-refined philosophy of what it takes to keep a relationship healthy; she was willing to talk about it.

After the interview Elizabeth and Tim sat down to compare notes. They agreed in general about what Ms. Phillips had said, but there was also considerable difference on some points. Tim, of course, believed that he was right. (You may have noticed that Tim often believes that he is right and others are wrong.) Elizabeth was just as certain that she was right.

"Tim, you always seem to think you're right. How can you say that you're right!" Elizabeth was a little upset and didn't select her words carefully.

Tim's reply wasn't carefully worded either. "Come on, Elizabeth. If you would listen, we wouldn't have to fight."

"Wrong!" Elizabeth responded. "You aren't the greatest either! You're the one who should listen better. I can't wait until our class studies listening. You'll learn a thing or two, I'm sure!"

This was all Tim could take. He stormed off, muttering that he'd find out just who was listening. Later, he talked again to Ms. Phillips and found that he was wrong. He apologized to Elizabeth. She had cooled off a bit and was willing to forgive and forget. But surely some damage was done to their relationship. Much of their problem could have been avoided had their listening been better.

You probably have had a disagreement recently over what someone really said. What was "really said" often seems to be a source of interpersonal problems. You get into a conversation with someone about an important issue, then you get angry. When you become angry, you often forget to listen. Then you might fight over just what was said.

Listening is a problem. It is a problem for you in your personal life as well as in your professional life. In your personal life, failure to listen may mean frequent struggle over why one person didn't do what they said they would do. The disappointment and frustration generated by these unfulfilled promises are important factors in unhappy relationships. In your work, failure to listen means missing instructions and so poor assignment completion. This poor listening is an important source of lost time and energy since you—or maybe even the boss—has to do the work over. This reflects on your reputation and, perhaps, on your ability to be promoted. Most organizations won't promote someone who "doesn't pay attention to what the boss says."

Why Is Listening a Problem?

Each time you find yourself not listening, you might analyze what is happening and ask why. Some of the more common reasons for poor listening are examined here. Perhaps one of these has caused you to listen carelessly.

Listening Requires Effort

Probably the biggest reason for poor listening is that concentrating on the other person requires effort. It is much easier for you to think about what you will say next. Consider the effort you are putting out now if you are reading this section carefully. In some ways, the effort required to attend to the printed page is like the effort required to attend to a speaker. For example, eyestrain, which is sometimes quite painful, may be equated to ear strain, as when you try to hear someone in a crowded room over the noise that other people are making.

Try listening carefully to another individual so that you can repeat what is said. Most people find this is a difficult task. Notice the effort it takes to both *hear* and *remember* what is said. A major problem in listening is that much of the time, listening is not considered worth the effort. So something else is done instead.

One of these listening alternatives is to fill the conversation with your own talk. Talking often gives the feeling of control. Holding the floor is the opportunity to present ideas and to influence the other person, or to be actively involved. Perhaps the involvement that comes from talking is more enjoyable than the "inactivity" of listening. If you find you are more likely to talk than listen, you need to understand and believe that effective listening is an activity that can be involving, too.

Noise Inhibits Listening

Two kinds of noise prevent careful listening. One kind of noise is *physical noise.* You have probably had experiences when it was impossible to listen to important messages because some other sound was distracting you. Consider, again, the difficulty you have hearing at a crowded party. Often this kind of noise is compensated for by a raised voice. The noise level in the environment increases when this happens, necessitating even louder talk.

This kind of noise is easy to recognize and, therefore, fairly easy to overcome. For example, you might remove yourself from the source of the noise— take your companion into a nearby quiet room. Or you might agree to discuss the matter at some later time and place.

The second kind of noise, *internal noise,* is not as easy to overcome. Suppose that your teacher has just announced that an exam will be given tomorrow. You did not notice this test in the course schedule and you now realize that there is not enough time to prepare. Under these circumstances, if someone talks to you, you are likely to be preoccupied with concern about the test. It is going to be difficult for you to pay attention to what the other is saying. Your internal noise may cause you to miss some important idea.

Internal noise is a source of enormous distraction for listeners. You might not be feeling well. If you have a headache, it's not easy to listen. You might be thinking about what you will do later today. You might have other problems occupying your thoughts. If you're worrying about something, it's not easy to listen. Many similar events compete for your attention. Any one of them can distract you from the listening task.

The Idea Doesn't Require Full Attention

Most people know that it is possible to tune in and out of communication and still keep track of what is being said. This is because you can think several times faster than a person can talk. But this difference between thinking speed and talking speed is both a blessing and a problem. It is a blessing because it allows you to keep up with the communication and to make connections between what is being said and other ideas and information you have stored in your head. It is a problem as well because it gives you time to allow your thoughts to wander. Sometimes you become so intrigued with other ideas that you lose interest in the conversation. You let your mind wander. You can see that this common behavior creates a listening problem of considerable importance.

Sometimes this time difference is used to think of what you will say when you get a chance to respond. This can be a good use of the time, but sometimes you concentrate on what you are going to say to the exclusion of what the speaker is saying. The danger here is that it is impossible to concentrate fully on two different messages at the same time.

Frequently, you can use the time differential more profitably to *interpret* what another person is saying. You can achieve greater understanding if you take time to draw connections and ask questions—in your head—about the speaker's meaning.

The Speaker's Message Is Assumed

A fourth major barrier to effective listening is assuming that you know what the speaker is going to say. *You* stop listening because you think you know what the speaker's point is going to be. When you think you have another's ideas, you may tune her out and allow yourself to think of something else. By itself, this tendency to "tune out" is not a problem. The problem comes when your assumptions are wrong. When you are wrong but you believe you're right, you will act as if you know what is going on in the particular situation. The kinds of problems this is likely to create are evident. Recall Tim's fight with Elizabeth in the introduction to this chapter. Remember that they had a dispute over what the counselor, Ms. Phillips, had said about healthy interpersonal relationships. Tim became angry and stomped off. He seems to be a fairly confident person, so perhaps he made too many assumptions about what Ms. Phillips was going to say. Perhaps he tuned out. Without the benefit of Elizabeth's notes, he may have continued to think he had heard correctly. When she challenged him on some of his information, he reluctantly checked and found that he was wrong. We've found that, very often, our students tune us out during our classes for the same reasons. Perhaps you have tuned out one of your professors during class. However, if you assume that you have figured out what the professor is going to say, then stop listening, you might find that the consequences of tuning out have a direct bearing on your course record.

The Idea Is Contrary to the Value and Belief System

Because everyone is closed-minded to some extent, you often resist ideas that seem contrary. For example, if you have a conservative outlook, you may not be receptive to some liberal ideas. If you are a Democrat, you may reject the messages of Republican candidates. One professor who was extraordinarily wise in her academic field stopped a conversation short with a remark that illustrates this idea of resistance to contrary ideas. "He is a fine candidate in every way," she said. "But I just don't see how I can vote for a Republican!"

Another listening problem is resistance. *Resistance* is opposition to a message prior to hearing it and based on a skeptical or cynical attitude toward it. Sometimes you listen only for information that you can criticize. If you are listening merely for ideas to criticize, you may filter out other ideas. Anytime you focus your attention so that it excludes concentration on the whole message, you have a potential problem. If the pattern becomes habitual, as it often does, then the listening behavior can be tremendously dysfunctional. In fact, this problem is so common that it has become a part of popular language. One old-timer sometimes says it this way: "He was talkin' when he shoulda been listenin'."

Faulty Hearing Can Cause Faulty Listening

Sometimes people are unaware of a hearing loss. Obviously, faulty hearing is a difficulty that can create inaccurate listening. It is a good idea, then, to have hearing checked periodically to discover any loss. To ask frequently, "Could you say that again?" may indicate a developing hearing problem. Since hearing problems can be compensated for in a variety of ways (a competent audiologist can offer suggestions), this listening problem may be the easiest to correct.

The Listening Process

When someone says, "You're not hearing me," they usually mean, "You're not listening to me and understanding what I am saying." Sensing, such as hearing and seeing, and listening do not mean the same thing, a distinction that is important in understanding our model of the listening process. The model is a representation of what happens when you are listening to another person. This information will make you aware of common listening problems and suggest ways to remedy them.

Components of the Listening Process

The listening components are sensing, attending, understanding, and remembering. Tim may have heard and seen what the counselor said and did, but did he really attend to what she said? Did he understand her? Did he remember? If listening is knowing what the other person said, then he needed to do more than sense what was happening.

To illustrate this point more clearly, focus on the sounds around you. Perhaps you can hear the air conditioner functioning. Perhaps you can hear people talking nearby. Perhaps you can hear sounds coming to you from outside (if you are inside). Any cars? Any birds? Locate, if you can, one of these sounds. Why didn't you sense this stimulus before? If it was there, you might have sensed it, but you didn't complete the listening process until we urged you to do so. So listening is more than sensing. It's the process shown in figure 4.1.

You may not be aware of the components of the listening process because they seem to blend together in the nearly instantaneous act of listening. But a thorough understanding of each component will assist you in the listening act.

Sensing

Sensing is receiving stimuli through the five senses. Generally, though, you concentrate on visual and auditory stimuli. You are capable of receiving the sound of a clock ticking and seeing its movement if there *is* a clock ticking, and if you have normal sensing capabilities. How is it, then, that you were not sensing it before it was pointed out to you? You could have if you were listening to it, not merely sensing it. There was an intentional filter that kept you from listening.

Attending

If you were not aware of the clock, it may have been because you didn't select its particular stimuli from the many of which you were conscious. The idea of attending to a stimulus is not a new one; it was discussed in the chapter on perception. Recall that there are thousands of stimuli that are available for your

Figure 4.1 Components of the Listening Process

Message
↓
* Noise
↓
** Noise
↓
Sensing
↓
** Noise
↓
Attending
↓
** Noise
↓
Understanding
↓
** Noise
↓
Remembering

The Listening Process

* External
** Internal

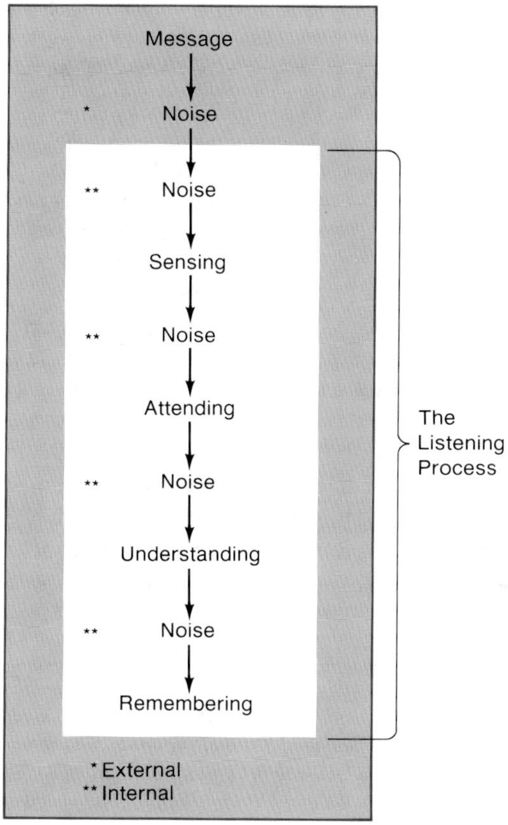

attention. You select only those that seem relevant to the particular situation, and ignore those that seem irrelevant. This may be why you were able to sense but didn't listen. You may have determined that the stimulus from the clock was not relevant, so you ignored it.

Selective attention helps you to concentrate on the message. It also allows you to block out what you choose to ignore. This selectivity contributes to poor listening when you ignore important aspects of the message. Just consider the mistakes Tim made! He filtered out important parts of Ms. Phillip's message when he and Elizabeth interviewed her.

Understanding
Understanding, the third component of the listening process, is the interpretation and evaluation of what you are able to sense. Although you take in data

through your senses and allow it to register in your brain, until you attempt to interpret and evaluate the information, you're not understanding.

Understanding involves more than merely paying attention to what is heard. Understanding implies that you assign a meaning that is close to what the speaker intended. Remember that meaning is related to more than the sensing. You get important data from your experience that helps you interpret the words you hear.

Remembering

Tim may have experienced a memory problem when he and Elizabeth interviewed the college counselor. Remembering is a difficult task for many people. Would you dare to not take notes if you wanted to remember what was said in a lecture? You might be reluctant to do this, and for good reason. The "forgetting curve," a graphic depiction of the retention rate, falls off rapidly. You lose a lot of what's said almost as soon as it's been said.

Just as you perceive selectively, just as you attend selectively, you experience selectivity in remembering. You remember some ideas more easily than others because you have found them useful. Sometimes, you remember because you are particularly intrigued by the thought. Sometimes you see a potential "payoff" and remember on that basis. You encounter problems when you choose not to remember something that later turns out to be important.

Using the Model of the Listening Process

We promised you that the effort you make to understand the listening process will be worthwhile. You can test this for yourself. Each of the elements of the listening model shown in figure 4.1 has potential breakdowns. The steps in the model form an outline where you can list potential listening problems. Focus on the problems for awhile. After you do, discussion of listening skills will be more meaningful. Each of the skills we talk about in the last section of the chapter is designed to help you overcome the problems we're about to investigate.

Sensing Problems

Noise is an obvious source of hearing difficulties. The difficulty with noise, of course, is that the interference keeps you from taking in relevant stimuli from the context. Perhaps the most common source of noise is shared space. You undoubtedly have tried to carry on a conversation while others are talking nearby. Their talking is noise to you. In office situations, machines produce noises that interfere with reception. The noise problems that come from sharing space are usually easy to overcome.

Perhaps a more troublesome source of difficulties is an actual hearing or sight loss. When your ears or eyes are not fully functioning, you cannot receive stimuli adequately. And since hearing or sight loss can only be partially restored, the problems created are not as easily overcome.

Attending Problems

Selectivity in attending to stimuli is a component of the listening process that produces many of the breakdowns attributed to faulty listening. Ralph Nichols, a man who spent much of his career studying listening, identified a large number of attending problems. We have tried to edit this long list so that you can focus your attention on the most important sources of difficulty. We think that five attention factors deserve your study: uncontrolled selectivity, dysfunctional habits of attention, counterproductive listening attitudes, low intensity of the messages, and message length. Three of these bear most directly on listening behavior. The other two affect the messages to which attention is given.

Selectivity

Attending and perceiving both have selectivity as a basis. Consider your experience of listening to a classroom lecture. Do you focus on all that is being said? You can test to see if you do. Compare your own notes against those of another person who has heard the same lecture. Do you find any differences? Our students sometimes find an entire idea missing from their notes. They may not even recall that the points were made. They chose to attend to some points and to ignore others.

Attending Habits

Many of the poor listening habits Nichols presented can be categorized as attending habits.[1] One is fake attention. Everyone is an expert at thinking about something else while appearing to pay attention to the speaker. This behavior can easily become a habit. Those who "daydream" find it easy to tune in briefly to a speaker and then to focus on another topic. This "in and out" attention makes it more difficult for you to listen.

Nichols also claims that poor listeners avoid difficult listening situations. For example, one professor asked how many students in a freshman course would be attending a lecture being given by a famous economist on the state of affairs in the national economy. No one in the class was planning to attend. When asked why, the students' answers suggested that the listening task was just too difficult for them: "Who cares about the economy?" "Why should I care about the economy? I can't do anything about it." "I don't understand any of that stuff." "I don't keep up with the economy, so I'm not interested." "The economy doesn't have much meaning for me, I'm a student." We think sentences like these can be translated into "I choose not to attend the lecture because the situation will be difficult."

Most people improve skills by practice. The same is true of listening skills. If you don't allow yourself to be challenged by difficult listening situations, then you will have more difficulty when you actually do face them. Some people who are aware of this principle deliberately force themselves to cope with difficult listening. They pick up techniques that allow them to become more efficient at the task.

Another poor attending habit is listening only for facts. Nichols found that poor listeners often do more sifting than is wise. They listen mainly for the facts but of course, much of the message is carried outside the main points. The material that surrounds the facts often determines the interpretation of those facts because it provides a context for the idea. So the surrounding material is an important resource for understanding main ideas. Professors know this so they often ask you to produce examples and illustrations on exams in order to test your understanding of the main facts.

Attitudes and Needs

People who are closed-minded may be poor listeners when the subject runs counter to their attitudes. Similarly, it is difficult to listen involuntarily. For example, if you are forced to go to a particular class you may not be able to attend to the message as well as when you voluntarily attend. The need to listen to a person "out of courtesy," will likely yield poor attention.

The mind does interesting things when it is influenced by particular attitudes or needs. It is possible for you to sense what you want to hear—even if that's quite different from what someone says—if your attitude or need is strong enough. People attend to information that satisfies their needs.[2]

This distortion is called *perceptual accentuation.* When you are hungry and see a billboard along the road, you are more likely to notice the food in the picture because you are hungry. The strength of this need, or how hungry you are, determines how open you are to part of the message on the billboard. If food is not the theme of the sign, you missed the main message of the billboard.

Perceptual accentuation can happen when you are listening, too. If your needs focus your attention on irrelevant aspects of the conversation you may miss the main ideas.

Low-Intensity Messages

All messages have some level of intensity. Intensity is not solely related to volume of sound. It may also relate to your own emotional condition and to the emotional power of the message. Suppose a speaker lacks emotional intensity. For example, a professor has droned into the second half of the class period without ever changing his tone of voice and without ever looking up from the manuscript he is reading at the class. Make the situation worse. Imagine that he stops speaking on a predictable pattern to say, "Uh, ya know? Blah, blah,

blah, uh . . . ya know?'' You may then have some attending problems. Listening to a speaker who talks softly or is the classic ''bore'' is a challenge, but the task is not impossible.

Message Length
What does message length do to your ability to pay attention? Campbell studied this question.[3] You won't be surprised to discover what he found out. Long messages present difficult attending situations. Thus the natural tendency is to condense, simplify, and eliminate the detail in the messages you receive. You will even drop out the middle sections of long messages. You need to develop skills that will allow you to overcome this tendency to distort long messages.

Understanding Problems

You can sense and attend but still not understand what someone is saying. Sometimes such misunderstandings have amusing results. But more often, misunderstandings work very serious damage in relationships. One professor was amused recently when a young woman walked into the office and asked, ''Do you want to get lucky?'' To the young woman, the question referred to the purchase of a sorority fund raising activity ticket. Understanding what she meant from the language was not possible. Thus, sensing and attending are of little value if there is no understanding. Misunderstanding in this illustration had no damaging effects, but it doesn't take much imagination to see that it might have had!

We'd like you to examine five frequently encountered understanding problems: understanding versus agreement, experience differences, lack of empathy, coordination problems, and closed-mindedness.

Understanding versus Agreement
It is common for people to say, ''You don't understand,'' when, ''You don't agree,'' is meant. There is obviously a difference between understanding and agreement, but in conversation, you often overlook this difference. You can understand someone perfectly and still disagree because you do understand that person. This same kind of confusion, in fact, is often evident in the way some people use the word communicate. ''We are just not communicating'' often means: ''If I could just communicate my idea so you could understand, then you would agree.'' The implication of such a transformation is that understanding and agreement are the same thing. Of course, they are not.

This distinction is important. When you experience and act on the basis of an understanding/agreement confusion, you can create problems. You can end a disagreement by accusing the other person, who has actually listened carefully but doesn't agree with you, of ''not listening.'' This in turn may lead to defensive behavior from that person. Have you ever heard an argument such as this?

He—I don't understand why you won't vote for him. He is conservative; he is bright; he is attractive; he is experienced; he is morally beyond reproach; and he wants the job.

She—I explained that to you. He is also a Republican. I am a loyal Democrat. I just don't want to jump across the party line.

He—But the man stands for everything you do. I don't understand . . .

She—Darn it, Hank, you just aren't listening to me. It makes me so mad when you ignore me.

He—You're crazy.

The problem works both ways. What you may mean by "not listening" is not understanding. Accusative behavior on your part is an evaluation and, thus, is a defense-producing behavior. One of the outcomes of defensive behavior is failure to listen. So what has happened is that you have now given the other a personal justification for not listening. Perhaps all of this could have been avoided by knowing the distinction between understanding and agreement.

Trying to listen to unfamiliar subject matter is difficult for most people. Obviously this is due in part to an unfamiliarity with the terms and technical language the speaker might use. But there is more to it than that. Jerry was a helicopter pilot for three years before he became a professor. Have you ever flown in a helicopter? If you have, he and you would undoubtedly be able to understand each other when the talk turns to helicopter flying. But have you flown helicopters in Southeast Asia? Unless you have done so, some difficulties in understanding may still exist.

But suppose that you have not flown in helicopters. Jerry can only talk to you about the experience in terms of imagery. He might say it is like floating in the sky on a chair that has a built-in vibrator. (Helicopters shake up and down slightly due to the rotor blades slapping the air.) This is at best, however, not a very satisfying description of what it is like to fly in a small observation helicopter. Overlap of experience is important. Understanding would be difficult in this situation without an overlap in this area.

Lack of Empathy

Sometimes people get tuned so well to each other that one of the individuals can feel what the other is feeling. It is as though the experience were really shared, although in fact, only one of the two had the direct experience. This phenomenon, called empathy, is the process of identifying emotionally with the feelings and experiences of another. When you're not able to empathize, you sometimes can't communicate very well.

Recall the experience that Elizabeth and Tim had in talking about their differences in perception of the interview with Ms. Phillips. It is likely that both Elizabeth and Tim had experiences where they and another person disagreed on what was happening in a certain event. So you might assume that this event was not entirely new to them. Yet, they were not able to identify with the problem the other was facing. They couldn't empathize with each other. They chose to see only their own viewpoint and ignore the other's. Empathy would have been an aid to understanding; lack of empathy led to misunderstanding and a fight.

The inability or unwillingness to empathize is at the heart of many problems that happen between people, especially people with markedly different histories. Fathers and sons often are unable to empathize with each other. The father thinks he knows how the son feels, so doesn't try to understand. The son figures his father is a rigid and unyielding autocrat, so he doesn't try to see things from his father's perspective. If, given these orientations, the two have a fight, who is to blame? We think both are at fault, and they could eliminate the hurtful conflicts in their relationship with a determination to empathize and to understand each other.

Coordination Problems

Yet another problem, coordination, contributes to misunderstandings. You don't coordinate your activities with others very well as a rule. Coordinating plans implies checking to ensure that you are working toward the same goal. In a work situation, your supervisor might give you instructions and then ask you to repeat them. She might later check to see if you were actually doing what you said you had been asked to do. Each of these steps would be an attempt to discover if you really understood. When coordination problems are experienced, assuming the parties are capable and well-intentioned, a likely explanation for the problems is the failure to discover that one or both of the people do not understand.

Misunderstandings that arise from poor coordination are very common, even among people who are supposed to know better. For example, in designing this book, the three of us determined which author would be primarily responsible for which chapters. At least, we thought we had determined that until one day we had a revealing conversation.

Jerry—Mike, how are you coming on the first draft of chapter two?

Mike—What do you mean? I thought you were going to do that chapter.

Alan—Actually, fellas, I was supposed to do it. We talked about it and then I promptly forgot. When was it due?

Jerry—According to our plan, it's not due for another month. I was just checking.

Mike and Alan—Whew!

Coordination problems are communication problems that probably can be traced to insufficient feedback. Misunderstandings can go undetected if an attempt is not made to discover how well the message has been received.

Suppose Jerry had not asked about chapter two. We could have had difficulties and even lost a great deal of time. Adequate feedback in this situation prevented a misunderstanding and perhaps some damage to our relationships.

Closed-Mindedness

There are a number of very common terms used to speak of closed-mindedness. Closed-minded people are called overly-critical, rigid, or polarized. Each of these terms is reflective in some way of a mental set. Such a person is steadfast in an idea to the point of being unwilling to consider carefully another's viewpoint. It's easy to see how closed-mindedness can lead to trouble.

Tim was stuck in a mind-set in the Phillips interview incident. He was unwilling to consider the likelihood that Elizabeth was correct in her perception of what Ms. Phillips had said. How set he was is unknown, but he was set enough to risk an argument with Elizabeth. He was also set enough to spend the time to prove that Elizabeth was wrong by returning to quiz Ms. Phillips on the differences. But *he* was wrong. Perhaps if Tim had been less rigid, he and Elizabeth might have come to some kind of understanding. They each might have been able to point out specifics of the interview that would have allowed remembering, then understanding and agreement. But given the mind-set of each, this was impossible.

Being closed-minded can cause no end of trouble between people. When people argue with each other they frequently become closed-minded. And sometimes this closed-mindedness can take them by surprise. Here is an example of how an argument can lead to closed-mindedness.

A frequent argument in one home erupts over who is supposed to wash the dishes. The ten-year-old never wants to wash dishes. She thinks she should do anything whatsoever to get out of the task, which she views as utterly unpleasant. The father—one of your authors—believes steadfastly that once an agreement is entered into, that agreement becomes inviolate. A contract is, without exception, a contract. The mother wishes to avoid conflict, and while she would rather not do the dishes, she would still rather do them herself than endure the tension between a steadfast husband and an unwilling daughter. In this very real, and often repeated scene, the closed-mindedness of each participant prevents a resolution of the problem. Each repeats his or her rigid position; no listening takes place. But unless the three work out their differences, they may discover that their unwillingness to bend will continue to yield misunderstandings. As you can imagine, they often find themselves fighting over the matter of doing dishes. And when they fight they are usually not listening.

Did you take a position like this with your parents as you were growing up? How much more listening is going on here?

Remembering Problems

Suppose the message the other person wants you to get has been clearly expressed. Supposed you sense it accurately. Suppose, too, that you attend to the idea. You even understand what is being said. But you can't remember the details of what was said long enough to act on them. Despite your other accomplishments, you're in trouble.

Remembering is often a problem. Normally, you don't take the detailed notes that you write when you listen to a lecture or to a formal speech. In formal situations, you don't trust your memory to store the information so that you will later make use of it. But in interpersonal communication situations, you usually don't take notes. Instead you expect—or at least hope—that you will remember. But, there is no reason to believe that memory automatically improves because of the context. It may well be easier to listen because you may be more interested in what is being said. The message may not be as complex and, therefore, it may be easier to understand. Still, there is likely to be some message loss. You can imagine that there are sometimes very good reasons to try to improve your techniques for remembering.

Some experiments show that people forget as much as eighty percent of what they hear when the material is difficult. Tony Buzan, for example, plotted the curve shown in figure 4.2.[4] He asked students to recall word lists they had memorized. They were not one hundred percent efficient at memorizing

Figure 4.2 Buzan's Forgetting Curve

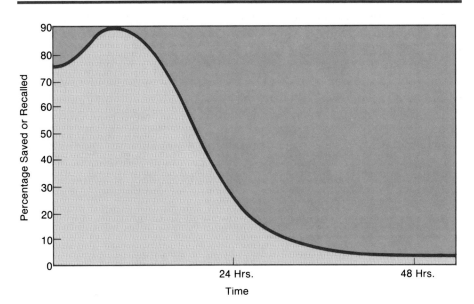

Figure 4.3 Comparison of Buzan's and Ebbinghaus's Data

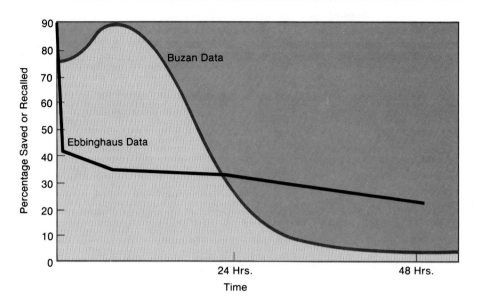

these lists in the first place. In fact, Buzan's students remembered only seventy-five percent at the completion of the learning task. Interestingly, their learning continued after the end of the learning period. Their minds continued to make connections that helped them to remember more.

Buzan's findings are provocative.[5] You could learn, if you wanted to, to take advantage of the mind's ability to make connections to what you already know.

The forgetting curve is not a new discovery, it's been known for a hundred years. Ebbinghaus was the first person to conduct research in remembering nonsense syllables.[6] Although there are some problems with his research that would concern the modern-day scientist, the agreement between a curve drawn using the Ebbinghaus data and the curve Buzan drew is interesting. We've compared these for you in figure 4.3. Notice the relatively fast drop of the retention curve in both cases. Hopefully, this drop will motivate you to improve your own memory, using some techniques we suggest.

Listening Improvement

Improvement is the result of first realizing the need to change and then being committed to that change. This is why we wanted you to understand the listening process and what can go wrong with your listening. You may believe by now that listening is not as easy as you had thought it was. And if you believe that error is likely to creep into what you are doing, you may be both more careful and more receptive to learning new techniques.

Learning about listening and its improvement can be approached at several levels. We have tried to pick out for you what we believe to be the central issues.

We think that you can greatly improve your listening by following these six suggestions.

1. Work at being involved.
2. Keep an open mind.
3. Listen with empathy.
4. Use active listening.
5. Check out your conclusions.
6. Increase your ability to remember.

Work at Being Involved

It would be silly for us just to tell you to work harder at listening, so we offer these suggestions that we think will help you to listen more effectively.

Use the speech/thought speed differential to your advantage. The average speaker talks at a rate of about 125 to 150 words per minute. Yet, as a listener you are capable of thinking at about five hundred words per minute. Consequently you tend to think awhile about what is being said, then you take a little vacation and think about something else. We've pointed out that this is often a contributing factor to attending problems.

Ralph Nichols suggested that listening can be improved by making use of wasted time.[7] His suggestion is to mentally review the point and supporting ideas the speaker has said. Pretend you are taking notes in your head. Further, take some "marginal notes." When you take notes, write additional notes to yourself in the margin. These are connections you make between ideas. Bring your experience with the topic into the current context. Anticipate the speaker's next idea. This kind of deliberate concentration will help you to work harder at listening. It will help you to focus more fully on what is happening. It will help you to be more interested because you will be more involved. It should, therefore, produce better understanding.

Participative concentration combats a common listening problem—how to overcome noise. You may recall that we defined noise as anything that disrupts or distorts the communication. By focusing your attention on what is being said, you pay less attention to other stimuli competing for your attention.

Say the main idea to yourself, then attach significant details. Try to separate the main ideas from the supporting materials. Focus all your effort, first, on the main ideas. Even if you have a very good memory, you will not likely be able to remember long lists of items and details. But that's okay because the point or points a person is trying to make are the most important parts for you to remember.

You will find it easier to spot the central concepts if you are able to identify the purpose of the communication quickly. Such questions as: What is this person after? What does this person want from me? and What is this person's most important idea? should reveal the main idea of the message and should help you know when you hear a central concept. You will then be able to link central concepts and main ideas to each other.

We think that studying the nonverbal elements of a message will sometimes help you know when you are hearing a main point. Main points are usually accompanied by changes in voice rate, volume, and pitch; gestures, body movement, and eye contact. Most speakers will stress ideas by slowing slightly. They may also increase volume, elevate or lower pitch, and gesture or lean forward slightly to reinforce. Indeed, we suspect that you already know these things very well, although you might not have been able to state them to anyone.

Consider this. You are reading this text, so it is reasonable to suppose that you are a college student. By definition, a college student is a professional listener. Now, consider the last lecture you heard. Did you use the differences in rate, pitch and force, volume, and physical behavior to cue you about the professor's ideas? If you didn't, why not? Next time you hear a lecture, pay attention to your own listening behavior.

Listen for the specific details. Details help to clarify a main idea. For instance, details often reveal the context of the remark and the person's special perspective. So details allow you to gain important understanding that cannot be achieved if you take mental "vacations" when the details are being presented. And while you may not remember the details very well, they still enhance your understanding and retention of main ideas.

Ask yourself questions about the content and feelings. Recall that we presented an agenda for talking about relationships in chapter 1 (fig. 1.5). That agenda is shown again in figure 4.4. Several of the items in this agenda can help you think more fully about what the other person is saying. Here are questions that will be useful.

1. What observations are being reported?
2. What inferences are being made?
3. What feelings are being expressed?
4. What wants and expectations does this person seem to have?
5. What intentions does this person have for you with respect to what is being said?
6. What degree of acceptance for the ideas and for him personally does the person expect from you?

This list is long, but useful. Try especially to consider feelings, wants, expectations, and intentions.

Figure 4.4 Agenda for Talking about Relationships

Task Dimension	Social Dimension
	Observations
	Inferences
	Feelings
	Wants and Expectations
	Intentions
	Latitudes of Acceptance
	Images
	Check Out

Keep an Open Mind

If you want to hear what another person is saying—if you want to avoid perceptual errors—then you must make a special effort to keep an open mind about what's being said. Easy advice to give, but often difficult to follow! Everyone has biases. In fact, you probably don't think of your beliefs and attitudes as biases at all. Rather, you think of them as the "correct" way of viewing a situation. You apply these beliefs and attitudes quite automatically. This unconscious application is why it is often difficult to keep an open mind.

Bringing biases to a conscious level will take some effort on your part, but the payoff will be worth it. One particularly helpful technique is to ask yourself this series of questions as soon as you discover the speaker's topic:

What is the topic of conversation? (Topic)
What is the speaker's position on the topic? (Position)
Do I agree or disagree with this position? (Agreement)
How strongly do I agree or disagree? (Strength)
Do I consider this an important issue? (Importance)

This series of questions can help you to discover not only your position, but also the extent to which you may be closed-minded. For example, if you disagree strongly, and, if it is an important issue, your bias may be messing up your communication. Perhaps you've heard the joke that ends, "Don't confuse me with the facts. My mind's made up."

Listen with Empathy

Empathy allows you to move from your perspective to the perspective of the other person. Empathy enables you to understand the other person's frame of reference. There is a difference between understanding what has been said and understanding what a person has said *from the speaker's perspective.* An understanding from the other person's perspective is a deeper and more reliable kind of understanding.

Charles Kelley expressed this distinction when he contrasted *empathic listening* and *evaluative listening.*[8] He said that empathic listening does not impose your own frame of reference on a situation. Evaluative listening does. Kelley expressed this difference clearly.

> The difference between empathic listening and deliberative listening is primarily motivational. Both listeners seek the same objective: accurate understanding of communication from another. . . . The empathic listener lets his understanding of the speaker determine his modes of evaluation, which are automatic; the deliberative listener's understanding of the speaker is filtered through his predetermined modes of selective listening, and he actually spends less time as a communication receiver. The empathic listener is more apt to be a consistent listener, and is less prone to his own or other distractions.[9]

In other words, you should withhold evaluation long enough to discover and understand the other's point of view. You'll hear the communication more clearly, understand it better, and respond to it more appropriately if you do.

But it is difficult to empathize if the partner in the relationship hasn't given you enough detail. It is usually easier to understand the other person's position if it is clearly stated. There are several response skills you can develop to encourage the person to explain more fully.

Verbally indicate your interest in knowing more. You can encourage the person to explain more fully by interjecting phrases and questions. You might say What else happened? Tell me more, What else were you feeling?, or Yes, I see. These probing statements and questions are illustrated in the following short conversation.

Tim: I nearly got fired at work today!

Mary Ann: What happened?

Tim: You know I was just hired at the Soft Serve Ice Cream Shoppe. New employees are supposed to practice using the ice cream machine. There is a rule, though, about eating ice cream and not paying for it. I ate an ice cream cone that one of the other new people made. The boss really flew off. I thought I was gone!

Mary Ann: I can tell you were surprised. How else were you feeling?

Tim: Sort of scared at first. It was like being a kid, caught with his hand in the cookie jar. Then I got really mad. I wasn't really doing anything wrong!

Mary Ann: Do you believe the boss wasn't being fair?

Tim: No, he was fair. I was warned. I just think it's petty!

Notice that the questions Mary Ann asked motivated Tim to say more.

Second, be sure that any response you give is nonjudgmental. Judgmental statements are those that reveal evaluation—good or bad, worthwhile or not. Often these statements reveal disapproval which often arouses defensive behavior in the other person. Suppose that Mary Ann said to Tim, "That was a really crazy thing to do," instead of, "I can tell you were surprised." This evaluative statement might lead to defensive behavior, which in turn could lead to the withholding of information and feelings for protection.

Finally, recognize and affirm the other's feelings. Give a supportive response. Some of the most successful supportive responses are those that recognize the other person's feelings. Responding to other aspects of the situation may not be received as well. For example, telling the other person, "Don't worry. Things are not really that bad," might be received as a put-down. It is in effect saying, "You shouldn't be thinking what you are believing." Recognizing the other's feelings and empathizing with the person avoids this potential problem. Here you will need to pay attention to the nonverbal cues you receive from the other person, as these often carry the feelings. In Mary Ann's dialogue with Tim, for example, she said, "I can tell you were surprised. How else were you feeling?" Such questions allow the speaker to know you, the listener, are with him emotionally. They reveal your interest in the person and in what is said. The person is likely to feel supported.

Use Active Listening

Active listening is the technique of responding to a message you have received. The listener paraphrases the content of what he hears—gives his own version of what the speaker said. Often the listener will want to "check out" the feelings of the speaker too. Suppose Cheryl engaged Elizabeth in this conversation on the way to class one day.

Cheryl: I met this really neat guy at Rick's last night. He seemed very interested.

Elizabeth: So, you met a super guy that you really like and you feel very excited?

Cheryl: Yes!

Elizabeth: Tell me more.

Elizabeth uses active listening to feed back both the content and her guess about Cheryl's feelings. Clearly, if the conversation were more involved and complex, this couldn't be done skillfully unless you are actively involved in listening.

There are three listener benefits that are the result of active listening. First, you are forced to listen more carefully so that you will be able to repeat what you have heard. Clearly, when you are going to repeat, you must listen carefully and you must try to remember.

Second, you will also know whether you understand the person to whom you are listening. If you don't understand, there is an opportunity for the speaker to correct your understanding.

Paraphrasing is not parroting. You certainly have had an experience in rote memorization where you were able to repeat but did not necessarily understand what the words meant. One professor has a vivid recollection of learning to say the Latin responses in the Roman Catholic Mass. He did not have the foggiest notion of what the words meant, but he can still, after more than thirty years, repeat most of the phrases he committed to memory by rote. Certainly, this was not active listening behavior when he learned to mouth Latin phrases. Paraphrasing allows you to discover if you do understand by making you explain the meaning in your own words.

A third benefit of active listening is that it allows you to show the other person you understand. The other person discovers that you are interested enough to pay this kind of close attention. Such commitment seems unusual and flattering and ultimately strengthens your relationship.

There are some specific behaviors that can help you be a better active listener. Skill in these areas will undoubtedly result in these three listener benefits.

Give the speaker cues that you are listening. These cues can be both nonverbal and verbal. You can use such movements as nodding approval or disapproval, leaning forward to show interest, displaying an open body posture, or maintaining direct eye contact to show involvement. Verbally, you might insert comments such as Yes, What else? Tell me more. Be sure you use a variety of cues. (Imagine how Yes, Yes, Yes might be received by another person.)

Paraphrase both content and feelings. This is important because there are both content and feelings associated with most communication. Clearly, the content is the easier part for most people to understand. Thus, you may focus mostly, or perhaps entirely, on content. But be sure to recognize the feelings and feed these back, too.

After you restate, clarify the areas of uncertainty. Mary Ann might have said to Tim "I understand your boss was angry when you helped yourself to ice cream. But why was it such a big deal for him?" Or, Elizabeth might have replied to Cheryl, "I can tell that you are really excited about this new guy. When do you think you'll see him again?"

Overcoming Difficulties with Active Listening

You are well aware of the child's game of imitating another person in order to irritate. Likewise, paraphrasing can be annoying if it is used continually. So we want you to understand some general rules about its use.

First, use it in situations in which the information is particularly important.
Second, use it if the information is particularly complicated or involves a
    series of hard-to-remember steps.
Third, use it when you are helping another person solve a problem. The
    person will want you to pay careful attention and to provide this kind of
    feedback.

There is something else you can do to make active listening easier. Learn
a variety of ways of leading into paraphrasing what you have heard. Many
people who use active listening for the first time will adopt a "lead-in" phrase
and use it every time. You will hear "What I heard you say is . . ." Think of a
variety of ways of saying this and your use of active listening will seem less
artificial. Here are just a few of the many possible lead-ins that you might learn.
"I think you just said . . ." "Do you mean . . . ?" "Are you saying, in other
words . . . ?" "Would it be accurate for me to repeat that this way: . . . ?"
"I'm wondering if you mean . . ." "So you think that . . ." "I'm not sure I hear
you. Did you say . . . ?" "I'm surprised (shocked, pleased, etc.)." "I think I
heard you say . . ."

Check Out Your Conclusions

Sometimes people expect you to understand more about what they are saying
than the actual words convey. They expect that you will make the "normal
assumptions" about what they are saying, even though they are not explicitly
stating them. Sometimes this involves game playing, but other times it is an
innocent omission.

Consider, for example, a conversation that Cheryl had with Tim. Tim was
beginning to be attracted to Cheryl. He had considered asking her for a date,
but decided against this because he knew she was very busy with studying.
He decided that maybe she would be willing to spend some time getting to
know him if he asked her for a "study" date. She heard him correctly when he
asked to go studying. He *assumed* that she *understood* that a study date would
include a certain amount of horsing around. He was wrong. Examine their communication briefly.

"Cheryl, I'm going to the library to study tonight. Would you like to go
along with me?"

Cheryl replied with a note of skepticism in her voice. "Well, I am really
snowed with course work, but I guess I'd be willing to go study. In fact, that'd
give us a chance to talk about the interpersonal project."

Tim said, "I'm glad. I'll pick you up at about six?"

"Great!" Cheryl replied.

You might guess from the conversation that both Tim and Cheryl were
making private conclusions about what the other meant. You might also suppose that their inferences about the message didn't quite match. But neither
was listening carefully enough to pick up the cues that might have signaled

the differences. Also they did not check out their conclusions. Consequently, the "study" date was an unpleasant experience for both. If they had checked out their conclusions, they might have avoided the problem.

Sometimes this clarification might be prompted by an *interpreting response*. An interpreting response clarifies communication by posing an interpretation of what a person has said. This allows the person to confirm your understanding.

The three skills complement each other. If you want to listen with empathy, you will find that active listening will help. If you use active listening and listen with empathy, you will find that you are paying closer attention. This may cause you to pick up cues about the inferences the other person is making. When you discover these cues, you may check them out. This is particularly true if you are aware of the problems created by not checking out unspoken inferences. Being aware of the problem may lead you to use more care. When used together, these skills can dramatically affect your listening skill. We urge you to practice these skills and to see if they make a difference in your personal listening effectiveness.

Increase Your Ability to Remember

We painted a rather sobering picture of the difficulty most people experience with remembering. Recall that there is a dramatic drop in a person's ability to remember within a short period of time after hearing a message. We also said that it is possible to retard that memory loss. Memory experts suggest three principles that should help: (1) organize the information, (2) associate what you are trying to remember with things or concepts you know, and (3) incorporate ways of adding repetition.[10] We have found that one of the best sources of easy-to-use memory techniques is the work of Tony Buzan. His suggestions are designed to interrupt the forgetting curve.

Look again at the forgetting curve Buzan plotted, shown in figure 4.5. If you examine the curve, you will notice that the remembering process peaks after the initial input of information. Buzan found that this happens about ten minutes after the information has been received. After this, forgetting sets in.

Buzan suggests that you should attempt to intervene at the onset of forgetting. You can do this in several ways. For example, you can sit down and write some notes about your communication, causing you to organize your ideas. Organizing the ideas in some systematic way will help you to remember them.

Another way to improve your memory is to force yourself to review, point-by-point, everything you can recall from a conversation. When you do this, try to put information into categories, but be careful not to include too many categories. The categories serve as focal points that can later be recalled, so you need to keep the number limited.

Or your memory will improve if you try to associate what a person has said with experiences you have had. Recall the example of the counselor, Ms.

Figure 4.5 Spacing, Organizing, and Practice Sessions to Aid Memory

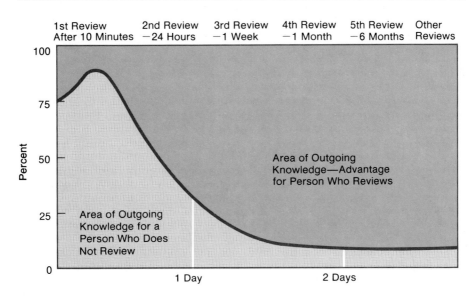

Phillips, discussing with Elizabeth and Tim the constituents of a healthy inter-personal relationship. Suppose Ms. Phillips said that one important aspect of a healthy relationship was commitment to the relationship. Elizabeth might be better able to remember this if she associates it with her mother, a person with a real sense of commitment to relationships. Similarly, you can increase your ability to remember by making associations to your real world.

You need to associate carefully if the method is really going to work for you. Suppose for a moment that Elizabeth's mother possesses other charac-teristics that overshadow and draw more attention than the commitment char-acteristic. Then the association would not work as Elizabeth had intended since the association should be a clearly straightforward connection. It also must be similar in relevant characteristics.

Finally, build in some system of reviewing the information you are trying to remember. If you want to retain some information for a long time, you need to review it. You already understand this principle, of course, since you are probably using it in studying for your classes. You may also understand that review sessions need to be spaced apart from each other, rather than con-nected. The term for this principle is *distributed practice*. Teachers know that if you space out your practice over a period of time, practicing a little bit each time, you will learn more and remember longer than if you study the same amount of time in one sitting. This is why, incidentally, cramming for exams usually doesn't help you much. Perhaps you can pass the test if you cram, but you will be unlikely to remember what you learned, say, five weeks after the exam.

Review sessions should be apart from your initial study and organizing time. You should compare and relearn if you have taken notes. If you have not taken any notes, then the best you can do is to recall the key organizational words and try to fill in as much detail as possible. Buzan recommends that you space these sessions at twenty-four hours, one week, one month, six months, and so on (if necessary). You interrupt the forgetting curve with these spaced review sessions.

There is an additional advantage to remembering and storing information for future use. Buzan suggests that doing so aids your memory by making stored ideas available for future associations.[11]

> Failure to review is equally as bad for general memory. If each new piece of information is neglected, it will not remain at a conscious level, and will not be available to form new memory connections. As memory is a process that is based on linking and associations, the fewer items there are in the recall store, the less the possibility for new items to be registered and connected.
>
> On the opposite side of this coin, the advantages for the person who *does* review are enormous. The more he maintains his current body of knowledge, the more he will be able to absorb and handle. When he studies, the expanding amount of knowledge at his command will enable him to digest new knowledge far more easily, each new piece of information being absorbed in the context of his existing store of relevant information.[12]

We hope you will work with these memory techniques because memory can be improved if you spend some time working at it. Details such as names of new people as well as other information these individuals are willing to reveal are important to the development of the relationship you are establishing. These memory techniques will help you remember and form useful habits in either situation.

Summary

Listening can be a problem in interpersonal communication for several reasons: (1) listening takes effort; (2) noise is distracting; (3) attention wanders; (4) assumptions are made about the speaker's message; (5) ideas that are contrary to values and beliefs are resisted; (6) or sensing mechanisms may be faulty. Any one of these factors may impede interpersonal communication.

Listening involves sensing, attending, understanding, and remembering. Sensing is not listening; it is receiving stimuli through the senses. Listening, on the other hand, is more than receiving stimuli. It also includes *attending* (selecting one of the many stimuli and allowing it to register in the brain); *understanding* (interpretation and evaluation of that which is sensed); and *remembering* (recalling the understood message). Both attending and remembering are selective processes.

Sensing problems are created by defective sensing mechanisms and noise. Attending problems are caused by selectivity, poor attending habits, attitudes and needs, low intensity messages, and message length. Problems with understanding result from confusion created by agreement, experience differences, lack of empathy, coordination, and closed-mindedness. Remembering problems develop without intervention in the forgetting process.

You can improve your listening through the understanding and use of six techniques. These include (1) work at being involved; (2) keep an open mind; (3) listen with empathy; (4) use active listening; (5) check out your conclusions; and (6) work to increase your ability to remember. These techniques can be easily implemented so that your listening is more effective.

Discussion Questions

1. Identify a person you would like to get to know better. Ask the person how his or her day is going. Engage in active listening as a part of this experience. Then report to your class.
    How did the person respond?
    How did you feel when actively listening?
    What nonverbal cues did you get?
    What were your images of the other?
    What image did you project to the other?

2. Try this experience and be prepared to discuss it in class. Turn on the television set and sit with your back to it. Listen for the cues, other than words, that are intended to help you interpret the program. These may include sound effects, the laugh track, or music. Identify as many of these auditory cues as possible and report your findings in class. How did the inability to see the program influence your ability to understand?

3. It is reasonable to suppose that a person with a hearing impairment will have greater difficulty in listening than a person who is not hearing-impaired. In what ways might a person with normal hearing impair his or her own ability to listen?

4. Suppose that you were to seek the advice of a counselor concerning some personal problem. What would you do to help yourself listen better and to pick up the information you need? How would you help the counselor to understand your problem?

5. Suppose you receive a low grade on a midterm project. You believe the grade has been unfairly assigned, so you make an appointment to confront the instructor with the problem. Identify attitudes and other factors that might make listening difficult for both you and the instructor in this context.

Endnotes

1. R. Nichols and L. Stevens, *Are You Listening?* (New York: McGraw-Hill, Inc., 1957).
2. L. Thayer, *Communication and Communication Systems* (Homewood, IL: Richard D. Irwin, Inc., 1968), 51–53.
3. D. Campbell, "Systematic Error on the Part of Human Links in Communication Systems," *Information Control* 1 (1958): 334–69.
4. T. Buzan, *Use Both Sides of Your Brain* (New York: E. P. Dutton, 1976), 49–50.
5. Ibid, 55.
6. H. Ebbinghaus, *Uber das Gedachtnis: Untersuchungen zur Experimentelen Psychologie* (Leipzig: Dancker und Humbolt, 1885).
7. Nichols and Stevens, *Are You Listening?*
8. C. Kelley, "Empathic Listening," in *Small Group Communication,* ed. R. Cathcart and L. Samovar (Dubuque, IA: William C. Brown Publishers, 1984), 297.
9. Ibid.
10. J. Deese, *The Psychology of Learning,* 2d ed. (New York: McGraw-Hill, Inc., 1958), 237–48.
11. Buzan, *Use Both Sides,* 55.
12. Ibid, 57.

Talking about Feelings

Preview

Every relationship can be characterized by its range of feelings and emotional experiences. But most people are not very good at talking about their feelings. It is hard to talk clearly about them, and this difficulty often increases as the need to discuss them becomes more important.

   The ability to talk about feelings is a necessary skill if you are to grow in your relationships and to mature as a person. This ability allows you and others to know who you are and where you stand in a relationship. This chapter introduces a system for talking about feelings that is both easy to learn and enormously helpful.

Objectives

After reading this chapter you should be able to complete the following:
1. Explain these basic arguments:
    a. It is useful to make a distinction between feelings and emotions.
    b. Feelings exist as physical experience; emotions exist in the language you use to talk to yourself and others about the feelings you are experiencing.
    c. Emotions are—or can be—under cognitive control.
    d. Language flexibility is a key to emotional control.
    e. Emotions have behavioral consequences.
2. Define affiliation, dependency, and attachment, and explain how they are interrelated.
3. Recall and explain five common strategies used to deny feelings.
4. Distinguish between feelings and emotions.
5. Identify and explain four behavioral alternatives you can choose when you discover a "block" in your goal path.
6. Compare and contrast the two possible directions that interpersonal, goal-directed behavior can take.
7. Explain how emotions are metaphorical, and why this aspect of interpersonal growth is so important.
8. Explain the negative impact your limited language ability can have on your emotional health.
9. Identify, define, and explain the following terms: generalization, distortion, and deletion. How can knowledge of these concepts help you to talk more accurately and flexibly about feelings?

5

Y ou can imagine how Tim must have felt when, after he'd worked all weekend and after Mary Ann had helped him to proof his term paper, he got
it back with the following note:

> Dear Tim:
>
> I'm sorry to have to assign a "D"
> to your paper. While the grammar
> and spelling are perfect, the ideas
> you present don't warrant a higher
> mark. I'd be willing to talk to you
> about this if you want.

Tim couldn't believe his eyes. He'd worked day and night on that paper.
And not only did he need at least a ''B,'' he had a strong emotional need for
that paper to be appreciated, too. He had given it birth; it was his baby. He
wanted it to breathe.

''Get a grip on yourself, Tim,'' he thought. ''Calm down!'' But by now he
was imagining an argument with the professor. ''You only like your ideas! Mine
are just as good as yours!'' The blood in Tim's veins boiled over. He picked up
the phone and called the professor—a big mistake.

Communication and Emotional Control

Communicating while not in emotional control is a common mistake. How you
handle a moment of emotional arousal can be enormously important, both for
you and for other people. You need to learn to manage the emotional moment
carefully by identifying feelings, separating feelings from emotions, and talking
with greater fluency about your feelings.

The behavior that is examined in this chapter is interpersonal and goal-oriented, and can be divided into two categories. Some behavior tends to push people away from each other. Other behavior tends to pull people together.

Attachment

Behavior that pulls people together includes any that stems from an attachment motive. This motivation is to make and keep a relationship.

Dependency is one variation of the attachment motive. This is demonstrated by great submissiveness; seeking help, support, or reassurance from others; conforming to the expectations or norms of associates; or attempting to gain someone's approval or disapproval. Dependency can be either useful and positive, or of no use, depending upon the context and nature of the relationships. Thus, the term "dependency behavior" does not make a judgment. It only suggests that such behavior is always the result of *choices*. Learning to make these choices wisely is a useful communication skill.

The things you do to cultivate your friendships are classified as *affiliation,* a form of dependency. Expressions of affection and love are also classified as affiliation. Marriage and sexual behavior, for instance, belong in this category.

Affiliation, dependency, and attachment are, then, very closely related terms. You can see that these things are *affective;* they are fundamental to an individual's emotional self. If you have a need to affiliate, you act. If you have a need to be, for a time, dependent, you act. If you love another, you act.

Thus, your emotions have behavioral consequences. These behavioral consequences can be of enormous significance to you. Your friendships may be at risk; your family relationships may be at risk; your professional, or work place, relationships may be at risk (with potentially dire consequences for your entire working life); and, even your most casual social relationships may be at risk. Sadly, however, you do not always have the language skills and fluency to talk effectively to yourself and others about your emotions.

Controlling your emotional and relational self can be more easily achieved by learning some basic language skills. For example, it requires skill to expand the vocabulary you use during emotionally intense moments. If you term an emotional experience "anger," your physical response will correspond to the ways you have learned to be angry, which might be a very unwise choice. On the other hand, you might call that same experience "frustration." Your physical response to frustration is quite different from your physical response to anger. Now, add another person to the equation. If you respond to another in anger, instead of frustration, will that make a difference in the way that individual feels and acts toward you? Would not your *choice* involve a risk to your friendship?

Learning to talk about feelings means learning to cut across the teachings of culture. You have to start—everyone does—by overhauling some very strong and very subtle cultural learning.

More effective communication about feelings begins with recognizing those feelings in the first place. Feelings are physical and present-tense phenomena. People turn these feelings into emotions with language used to identify and catalog feelings. Thus, better talk about feelings implies that you need to expand the vocabulary you use to describe them. It also implies that you need to become more aware of the completeness and accuracy—or incompleteness and inaccuracy—of your verbal statements about the world. (You can learn to become more aware by practicing some fairly simple questioning techniques.) Finally, better talk about feelings implies learning to avoid the culturally based strategies used to deny your feelings.

Denial Strategies

There are five very common strategies that people in American culture use to deny their feelings. Children learn early to explain rather than to describe their feelings. ("I feel that you're mad at me." "I feel you've pulled away from me.") This strategy allows people to hide from themselves! Second, people learn to substitute statements about their feelings with statements about their wants and interpretations. ("I feel rejected." "I feel like you don't pay any attention to me.") Similarly, individuals learn to describe cognitive activity as though that cognitive activity were their feelings. ("I feel confused." "I feel very interested.") Fourth, metaphors are made instead of talking about feelings. ("I feel like going to a movie." "I feel like a car was taken off my shoulders.") Finally, a common strategy for denial of feelings is to cast them into the past. "I felt this yesterday" seems to be more acceptable in a relationship than "I feel this right now."

Each of these common strategies for denying feelings can sometimes create relationship problems for people. If you are to have a happy and growth-producing relationship with another, then learning to talk about feelings is a basic skill. What you feel, and how you express your feelings in words, is one of the basic components of all relationships.

Methods for improving your expression of feelings and emotions are presented here. Learning to talk fluently and appropriately about feelings will help you to become more mature, more self-aware, and more self-accepting. Moreover, relationships become more satisfying and more intimate as you learn to show yourself to another.

Expressing Emotions

Emotions Exist in Language

A definite distinction exists between feelings and emotions. Feelings are physical experiences, but emotions exist in the language you use to talk to yourself and to others about the feelings you are experiencing.

What you feel is a physical experience. You feel the condition of parts of your body at some moment in time and space. The feelings exist as tiny firings in nerve endings in the tissues of your body. You feel tense muscles; you feel aching joints; you feel the linings of your stomach signaling you that you are hungry; you feel the sharp pain "behind the eyes" that sometimes occurs when you have eaten too much ice cream too fast. Feeling is a physical experience.

What you tell yourself about your feelings constitutes your emotions. While your feelings are physical, your emotions exist only in the world of words.

Experience: Feelings and Emotions

To illustrate this difference between feelings and emotions, try the following experience. Induce some pain in your hand by slapping it against a table top. Now try to describe the ongoing experience of the pain. Does this description square with your experience?

Although your experience of pain is dynamic—constantly changing and continually in the present tense, a global experience of your entire hand—your language fails you. The language you use must flow out in a single line. It must focus upon one aspect of the dynamic experience at a time. Much of the experience is deleted. Much more is distorted. The rest is generalized. And, by the time that you have described your experience, the description is already obsolete.

A second interesting discovery is that while the experience is always in the present tense, the language you use to describe the feeling tends to be in the past tense. Students we ask to do this focus upon, say, the first joint of the right thumb. "It hurts," they say. "The experience is like a burning sensation. It was very hot, but now it's cooling off some. It was like someone was tapping a hot wire there at the joint. . . ."

Speakers go to past tense to "catch up" with experience in language. Notice, also, that the language sample focused only upon the heat sensation of the first joint of the thumb. What of the rest of the speaker's experience? What was the rest of his hand telling him?

"It hurts" applies not only to the feeling, the experience of physical pain, but also to the emotions that surround your physical experience, as well. For example, you might suddenly experience a loud noise while walking across the campus after dark. A barking dog jumps out from under an azalea bush. You will have a physical experience—a sudden, electrochemical, very real, physical experience. The blood will rush away from your skin. Your endocrine system will instantly infuse your blood with certain chemicals. Your heartbeat will increase. Your muscles, now strengthened by the dramatically heightened adrenaline levels in your bloodstream, will tense. Your stomach will feel like it is knotting up. And, finally, the hair on the back of your neck will "stand up" and, chances are, you will begin to tremble.

Under these circumstances—in that particular moment on the campus when confronted by a barking dog—you are experiencing a set of physical feelings. What will you call them? Will you call them fear? Will you call them something more self-confirming? Will you call them "startled"? Would it be correct to say that you were surprised? And would it be correct to say that you experienced anger? Anger at what? At the dog? At your own inability to control the fight-or-flight reaction? Will you call that experience cowardice? Will you call it embarrassment? What appropriately describes that physical condition in that moment in time and space? What you choose to call it is most important, indeed, since so much depends on it! Your self-concept is at issue in your choice of words.

Emotions exist, not in physical feelings, but in words. You *feel* your body but you experience emotions in quite another way, with language. *Because you experience emotions with language, what you experience as emotions contains cognitive information.* You take meanings directly from what you say to yourself about your feelings, and what you take—the information you derive from your emotions—influences arousal and the way you experience and express those emotions. Thus the emotional condition is very complex. This complexity is directly related to interpersonal communication. Notice how it affects interaction in the following situation.

Tim might have said on the phone to his professor: "Professor, you so-and-so, you made me mad!" Like most people, Tim thinks of his emotional self as aroused by *causes* outside himself, and that the emotions he experiences leads him to behavior.

To further illustrate this point, here are some typical examples of common beliefs about how emotions occur:

1. A dog barks while jumping out from behind a bush. This makes you fearful so you jump back to get out of the way.
2. Someone you love dies. This makes you sad and so you grieve.
3. The car breaks down. This frustrates you so you take out your frustrations on the car.

Far more accurate than such common beliefs, however, is that people do not respond directly to an actual event. People usually take information from the event, make the information meaningful, then respond to the cognitive structure of the event they, themselves, have created. Thus it is not accurate to say you "make me mad," or for a barking dog to "make me fearful." Rather, you observe the event, invest the event with some significance of your own design, then choose (or at least allow) the emotional response and the consequent behavior.

Of course, this sequence of events happens very rapidly—almost simultaneously. Indeed, in a startling situation, such as being taken by surprise by the loud report of a firecracker nearby, you may experience a knee-jerk response, or a flinching response, automatically, and then go to work processing your experience in your head. But much can be learned from a step-by-step analysis of this sequence.

Look again at the three examples of how emotions occur.

1. A dog barks while jumping out from behind a bush. You perceive the situation as threatening, immediate, and urgent. You also perceive the situation as dangerous. You *choose to jump away in fear.*
2. Someone you love dies. You perceive your loss. You understand that you will miss that person greatly. You realize that there were many things you didn't say to the person, and regret that you did not work through some of the kinks in your relationship. Facing all that, you *choose the emotional response* of sharp distress or sorrow.
3. The car breaks down. You see that you are going to be late. You begin to recall choices you made earlier to put off having the car worked on, perhaps because you were too busy. You anticipate that dire consequences will result, both from being late and from having to expose your earlier, faulty choices. You then *choose to respond emotionally.*

In each of these examples, the response is not to the event per se, but to the particular way you look at the event. You respond to the information you have drawn from the moment and the connections you have made between that information and your own prior experiences. Those connections always exist as words. How you talk to yourself about the event shapes your responses. Could you have chosen other responses if you'd chosen to talk about the event differently?

This fact, that people are responsible for choosing their emotional responses, is an important idea. You learn habitual responses to situations that seem to fall into similar categories. You seem to program yourself to respond to certain events in certain ways. And once the program is stabilized, you come to believe (at least, many people do) that you have little choice but to follow through with the programmed behaviors.

But it is possible to rewrite the program! It is possible to make alternative choices of behavior. The key lies deeply embedded in the language you use.

When you perceive danger, you do not have to choose fear if you have alternative language for describing your feelings. You can, and sometimes do, choose excitement, for example. The fun in climbing a mountain exists partly in confronting your own fear response. Ask a mountain climber why he or she climbs, and you are likely to get the cliché "Because the mountain is there." The climber accepts the challenge to test his skill as climber, betting that he can overcome the danger—just for the fun of it.

Tim loves to float down white-water rivers in a canoe or raft. The activity is dangerous, but it does not produce fear in him. It produces, instead, exhilaration. He *expects* the event to be exhilarating (that's cerebral, cognitive).

Tim's friend once agreed reluctantly to join a white-water float down part of the Arkansas River in Colorado. The river was raging and full with the spring runoff. The friend perceived a threat, rather than a challenge, when he saw that river, so he chose to remain in camp while the rest of the party made the float trip. Clearly, it was the perception and not the phenomenon that aroused his emotions. The perceptual system is always involved, not only in the arousal of emotions, but also in the choice of behavior that follows. That perceptual system is based in your language fluency. You need greater language fluency in order to talk about your emotions better.

Emotions Are Cognitively Controlled

Emotions are under cognitive control if you have sufficient language flexibility. If the language you have is limited (English is very limited), then so is your mind, yourself, and the society in which you live! It is also true that you construct your behavior out of your own definitions of situations in which you find yourself—clearly a symbolic process. Who you are as a person, and who you are in your interactions with others, exists in definitions you have inherited or that you have generated. If your definitions are limited by your own limited ability to use language, then your lack of fluency limits who you are.

To illustrate this idea, suppose a person could use only the following pairs of words, and no others, to describe himself. He might say, "I am . . ."

good	bad
pleasant	unpleasant
beautiful	ugly
strong	weak
passive	active
sharp	dull
small	large
heavy	light
smart	dumb
talented	incapable

Without any other language, (if these words were all that he could say about himself) the person's self-concept would be impoverished. Similarly, this person might have only the following pairs of words to describe his feelings. Again, his lack of language flexibility would impoverish his emotional range. He might say, "I feel. . . ."

aroused	calm
cheerful	unhappy
joyful	sad
happy	unhappy
interested	bored
free	bound

Clearly, the person's language is a cognitive control system for his emotional range and his self-concept. His lack of fluency limits who he is.

Joshua Weinstein and his associates, in 1968, found that the way people express their emotions is more dependent on their personality style than upon their state of emotional arousal.[1] For example, some people deny their strong emotions and suppress any show of arousal, while others are quick to reveal very high levels of physical arousal, even though they may not be experiencing a very strong emotion.

Elizabeth provides a good illustration of Weinstein's findings. You remember that Elizabeth is the group member who is a bit unsure of herself, but still fairly competent. Elizabeth also experiences very great levels of emotion, such as fear, anger, and affection. Elizabeth has developed a personality style that makes it difficult for people to know what is going on inside her. She told Tim about this style one afternoon.

"People are different in how they handle their emotional problems. I try to center. I try, especially when I'm angry, to move down—to get calm. Of course, I'm not always able to stuff things, but usually I can control my body so that what I'm feeling doesn't show."

"Why do you do that?"

"Because . . . well, because . . . uh. When people are angry, they usually do some very predictable things. Like they move from specific to general. They move from the concrete up the ladder of abstraction very quickly. They begin to talk louder and to move about more rapidly. When they do this they turn on some automatic systems that pump natural drugs into their blood. That gets them more excited. . . ."

At this point it was clear that Elizabeth was giving a lecture to Tim, and not disclosing herself. Tim, thinking that she might be talking about him, came out with one of his typical responses. "That's just bunk, Elizabeth. I didn't ask for a lecture. I asked for an answer to why *you* do what you do. How come you play such a poker face when you're ticked off?"

"Because I'm afraid that the other guy will win."

There it was. A clear, frank statement, in both cognitive and affective terms, of a personality style that Ross Buck would call *internalizers*.[2]

Buck found that there are different personality styles, and that these differences manifest themselves in different ways of showing emotions, based upon and as a result of selective attention to information. People who repress their emotions, and who verbally deny their fear, tend to experience higher physiological arousal. They adapt to emotional situations by playing down any expression of their arousal. On the other hand, some people who verbally admit their fear and who, for example, show their fear in facial expressions, tend to experience lower levels of physiological arousal. It is not known why these people behave in these ways, but *how they respond* to stimuli is dependent upon the cognitions of the individual.

Of course, there are other variables that influence emotional arousal. These include an individual's health; the physical state of arousal (perhaps based upon an earlier stimulus situation); whether or not the individual is satisfied or deprived of a particular need; and the importance or significance assigned to a situation. Any of these will influence the way in which an individual experiences emotional arousal and, to some extent, the expression of that arousal. The bottom line is that emotions are aroused by information processing. The information can come from outside or inside of oneself. Thus, emotions can be under cognitive control.

Emotions Have Behavioral Consequences

Emotions have behavioral consequences because they are motivators. The behavior that your emotions produce may be interpersonal, goal-directed behavior, a fundamental idea in Aristotle's discussion of *pathos* in his *Rhetoric*. And even into the first decade of this century, scientists were still arguing that a person's performance is related to the degree of his arousal.[3]

You may already be aware that when an individual is not aroused at all, he or she probably will perform at a low level. This is why, for example, athletic coaches in high schools are eager to have pep rallies in the school gym, where the sound of choral screaming can echo back to the screamers. The noise pumps up the student body and the players. An aroused individual outperforms an individual who is not aroused, so it is hoped the enthused players will win the game.

On the other hand, you may be surprised to know that when a person's arousal is too high, he or she also is likely to experience a very low level of performance. If you listen closely and watch carefully, during the game you may notice the coach trying to calm his players. "Settle down, Chuck. Bill, pull back a little. Count to ten before you take a shot. Jim, you keep reminding them to stay cool."

There appears, then, to be a curvilinear relationship between the level of arousal of emotions on the one hand and the level of performance on the other. This idea is the Yerkes-Dodson Law (fig. 5.1).

Throughout this century, scholars have been studying the relationship between what people feel and what they do. At the same time, much evidence has been collected to support the idea that emotional conditions motivate people. From a communication perspective, these two research approaches are joined by language. What we'd like you to understand is that emotions are, at least among adults, often controllable, and that the key to successful control is communication.

Figure 5.1 The Yerkes-Dodson Law

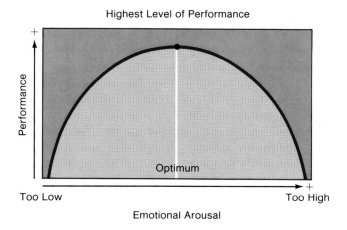

To better understand this important point, consider figure 5.2. It shows that individuals are driven (motivated?) to achieve certain goals, which may be almost anything. If that drive is blocked in some way, frustration occurs. The frustration is experienced most strongly if the individual is very committed to achieving that goal. Under such circumstances, frustration leads to emotional arousal. The arousal is often signaled by increased effort to achieve the goal (Do it harder!); by persistence of the effort (If, at first, you don't succeed, try and try again); by aggression (individual slams a door or bangs down the hood of a car); by withdrawal of interest (Ho, hum, I guess I'll try something else); and by joining up with others against the frustration or the source of frustration (Strike!). Whatever the individual chooses to do is called *coping behavior.* Coping behavior is motivated by an individual's emotional arousal.

Sometimes, of course, an individual's emotional arousal can be counterproductive. For instance, children (and adults who behave like children) sometimes get caught up in a cycle of aggressive behaviors. Aggressiveness leads to aggressive behavior in the other person. This is called *blocking* because the individual attempts to block the aggressive behavior. (Mother punishes the child.) Now doubly frustrated, the child responds with additional aggression and meets another punishment, as in figure 5.3.

A more appropriate response to the frustration would be to reevaluate the situation and try another goal path. Of course, such an alternative assumes that the individual is able to exercise some control over his or her emotional arousal. This control is one of the measures used to judge the emotional maturity of friends, neighbors, and colleagues.

This alternative response is sometimes called *displacement,* and occurs when you run into a block in one goal path and so choose another path to the goal. You will notice immediately that *this control is the result of how you talk to yourself about your experience.*

Figure 5.2 Responses to Frustration

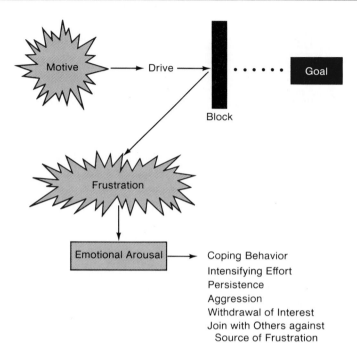

Two additional responses to a block in the goal path exist. One of these, *substitution,* occurs when you change the goal as a result of finding a block in the original goal path. For example, you have had a bad day at school, but ''blow up'' when your best friend does some small thing that irritates you. Your frustration with school was redirected to your friend.

Substitution can have very serious consequences in a relationship. For example, Mary Ann confided in Cheryl one day about a work problem. She has a part-time job at a large bank. Her relationships with her fellow workers seem to her to be strong and trusting, and she feels, generally, quite comfortable in the free-wheeling give-and-take that goes on in a mostly male environment. But on the day she spoke to Cheryl, she was quite depressed.

''What's the matter, Mary Ann?''

''I'm not sure,'' she replied.

''Tell me about that, will you?''

''Well, I'm not sure where to begin. Today, for no apparent reason, Bill was very ugly with me about the department, and how we were trying to run the show, and how we never take him into account about the decisions we make.'' Then the tears came. ''I didn't even know what he was talking about, and he just stood there and chewed me out.''

Figure 5.3 Blocking Goal Achievement

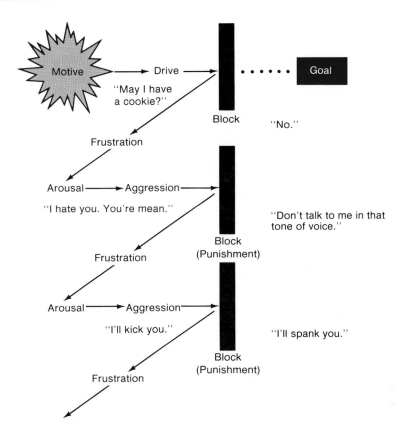

Although the man later apologized for his behavior, the damage was already done to his relationship with Mary Ann. He had apparently experienced some block in his own goal path, and because he was angry, and because Mary Ann was present at the time, the man shifted his anger to her. This, then, is a classic example of substitution.

The other alternative response is called *rationalization,* which occurs when you, having discovered a block in your goal path, convince yourself that the goal wasn't worth achieving anyway. For example, one individual dreamed for years of becoming a jet pilot. When he applied for pilot training as a young Navy recruit, he discovered that his eyesight wasn't good enough to meet Navy standards. Thus blocked, the man began to say to himself and to his friends such things as: "It's probably a good thing. Jets glide like a stone," or "Well, this means that I won't have to spend six to nine months at a time trying to land an engine with wings on a floating postage stamp." Again, this kind of

Figure 5.4 Four Possible Responses to a Block

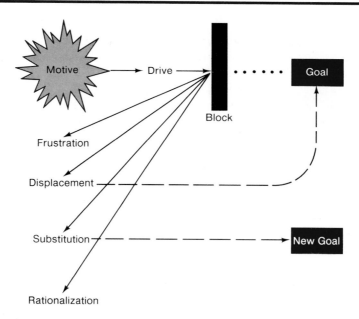

behavior is cognitive control resulting from talk. Figure 5.4 exhibits these four possible responses to blocking: frustration, displacement, substitution, and rationalization.

Anxiety Has Behavioral Consequences

Just as frustration has behavioral consequences, so does anxiety. Anxiety is a state of psychic tension and apprehension that results from anticipation of danger, usually from some unknown source. Most often, anxiety leads to avoidance behavior, although people respond in other ways, too.

Anxiety is an emotion that gives rise to some very predictable, and perhaps, counterproductive behaviors. One of these behaviors, *selective perception,* is picking out which parts of the real world that will conform to, support, and confirm your image of reality. Selective behavior is a way to lie to yourself, and is a function of how you talk to yourself about the world.

A second predictable response to anxiety is *withdrawal.* Like putting your head into the sand, withdrawal can help you feel better, but it won't solve or resolve the problem that produced the anxiety. As a young child, frightened at night by a noise outside your window that you couldn't identify, did you crawl under the covers in order to withdraw from the perceived threat? Were you saying to yourself "I will hide from whatever is out there"?

A third response to anxiety is *controlling.* Again a matter of selective behavior, people tend to look for ways to lie to themselves. This occurs when you, by talking to yourself, form some disconfirming stereotype so that your own personal reality can be held intact. For example, suppose a group of students, all members of the Young Democrats on campus, are talking about the activities of a similar group, the Young Republicans. One of the Young Democrats begins to deride the members of the other group. "They're all right-wing reactionaries, anyway," he says. "They couldn't possibly understand the politics of this situation."

This negative stereotype (right-wing reactionaries) gives the speaker permission to ignore what the Young Republicans really think. Moreover, the stereotype also gives the speaker permission to create feelings of hostility toward the Young Republicans. Such communication behaviors strengthen group members' perceptions of the speaker's loyalty, which may convince them that the individual is sincere—another source of persuasive clout.

Recall that anxiety often results when you anticipate danger from some unknown source. If you are uncertain, especially about the timing and severity of some unpleasant consequence, you'll have a pretty strong motivation to get information. So anxiety, like frustration, generates behavior. Sometimes, that behavior is interpersonal and goal-directed, as for example, when you approach another with your questions. You might ask that person to tell you what's going on between her and Helen if you think her relationship with Helen might jeopardize your own.

Interpersonal, goal-directed behavior can only work in one of two possible directions. You can pursue a goal that will push you apart from another or you can pursue a goal that will pull you together. Aggression and anxiety usually produce behaviors that push people away from one another.

Communicating Feelings

Behavior that pulls people together springs from an attachment, or affiliation, motive. Its most common variations are (1) friendship behavior; (2) love and marriage behavior; (3) sexual behavior; and (4) professional, work place behavior.

If you look at these four categories more closely, you will discover that they are all emotionally loaded, and that neither the categories nor the behaviors implied in them can exist independent of some form of communication about individual feelings. Your success in these four contexts are dependent upon your ability to talk clearly and accurately about your relationships.

Recognize Feelings

In order to talk about feelings, you must first recognize them. When you are frustrated, do you experience a "pain in the neck"? Have you ever told someone to "get off your back" when you felt that they were "putting you down"? Notice that each of these statements is a metaphor that ties the physical feelings you are having to the situations in which you are involved.

Suppose you only have one metaphor for feelings of depression. Would you say "I'm feeling really down"? Can you imagine how limiting it would be if you could only describe your depression with that one metaphor, "down"? We suspect, however, that you don't have very many metaphors to describe your feelings of depression.

One professor asked four intelligent adults, two of whom had doctorate degrees, to name, in three minutes, as many metaphors as they could to describe their feelings of depression. You will find their list interesting. After three minutes, these four individuals were able to develop only eight metaphors to describe depression:

deep	not okay
numb	overworked
out of it	overloaded
blue	dumb

This brief list constitutes a poverty of language to describe something as potentially important as the experience of depression. But we don't think such a poverty of language is uncommon. It occurs in relation to all feelings and emotions because feelings aren't words. They are physical sensations. Your metaphors are limited to symbolic locaters of those physical sensations.

Just as language about feeling often reflects the physical location of the feeling, it also can blind you from locating the feeling. Language is very vague. The more vague and nonspecific it is, the more likely it is to keep you from being aware of your physical experiences. This vagueness will cause you to filter and blunt your sharp and unpleasant emotional experiences. Sometimes this behavior is called "stuffing" an emotion.

One woman lost both of her parents to cancer during a three-year period. The sharp pain of the double loss was just too much for her to bear, and so, after the second death, rather than experience the pain directly, she blunted it by rationalizing the experience in language. "She's better off. She was so lonely without Daddy," she said. She also said, "I know that she is happy now in heaven with Daddy so I'm not sad." The problem with this choice to "stuff" her grief was that, while it was possible for a time for her to put the pain out of her conscious awareness, it was not possible for her to make the pain go away. Soon it began to manifest itself in short-tempered behavior, an upset stomach, nervousness, and sudden, inexplicable outbursts of rage and sorrow.

Clearly these behaviors were counterproductive, both to the woman and to her relationships with her colleagues, her children, and her friends.

According to Marcel Kinbourne, who is director of the Department of Behavioral Neurology at the Eunice Kennedy Shriver Center for Mental Retardation, this behavior may be explained by the so-called *"split brain" research.* "It is now becoming increasingly clear," he says, "that each hemisphere [of the brain] supports a different emotional state . . . the right hemisphere is involved in negative feelings and their expression, while the left is associated with positive feelings and their expression."[4]

This idea is closely related to the now widely accepted notion that the two hemispheres of the brain are specialized for different functions.[5] The left side controls language, sequential skills, and rational thinking. The right side controls spatial relationships and global perspective. Kinbourne continues: ". . . the right half is apt to react with angry irritation at matters that bother the left half not at all. What is more, depressed people have abnormal brain waves over the right side."[6] But quite the opposite occurs when the left half of the brain is in control. One form of epilepsy, for example, produces abnormally increased amounts of electrical activity in the left hemisphere. People with this affliction "laugh without the intention or cause to do so."[7]

If this research is correct—and Kinbourne makes clear that the observations are controversial—then what may have been happening to the aggrieved woman was that she was sending her feelings into her head. She talked to herself (left-hemisphere function) in ways that allowed her to blunt and avoid the experience of grief over the loss of her mother and father. But those feelings were there, lurking in the right hemisphere, and finding no outlet for expression in the conscious world, they began to manifest themselves in dysfunctional ways.

The woman could have taken a better approach. She could have gotten in touch with her feelings and then discovered a wide range of emotion language to describe her feeling state. This ability to talk about feelings will release these feelings and emotions when they are working against you, and allow you to choose more functional emotional responses to your perceptions of the world.

Sound advice, however, is far easier to offer than it is to accept.

How might you go about getting in touch with your feelings? We believe that there are two thinking habits to develop. First, remember that the feelings you have are physical experiences. Second, remember that the feelings you have are present-tense phenomena. (You can only live in the present.)

Emotions: The Expression of Physical Feelings

Our point—don't lose sight of it—is that human feelings are physical, and that you turn those feelings into emotions when you put them into language categories. How you attach language to your physical experiences is often a function of the culture into which you're born.

Clearly, culture passes on to you some very strict application rules for talking about your feelings. Perhaps you've heard your parents or "significant others" say one of the following phrases:

"She's a cold fish."
"Have a heart."
"Don't feel bad; it's going to be all right."
"You'll feel better tomorrow, don't worry."
"Keep your chin up."
"Every cloud has a silver lining."

Each of these phrases, and hundreds like them that you could name, outlines the cultural rules you're to follow when expressing your feelings. Sometimes you're supposed to show your feelings. Sometimes you're not supposed to show your feelings. And the situations under which you're allowed to show or not allowed to show them are acquired just as people acquire any concept—by experiencing a large number of positive and negative examples and situations.

Interestingly, in the growing body of research on brain hemisphere functioning, one of the most exciting, and perhaps one of the most controversial scholars, Tadanobu Tsunoda, has theorized that Japanese brains function quite differently from other peoples'. Tsunoda's theory states that this difference is not inherited, but rather, is a function of the peculiarities of the Japanese language.[8] He argues that language shapes the neurophysiological pathways of the brain, that the language learned as a child influences the way the brain hemispheres develop and so the special talents the individual possesses! Could it be that you can learn new language habits to replace those that cause you emotional trouble? Although this may be possible, it seems clear to us that you cannot merely "break" a habit of thinking. You have to replace the habit with the new one. Doing so takes rote practice, and it begins with recognizing feelings.

Limited Language Ability

Improved talk about feelings requires learning more feeling words. It also necessitates an increased awareness of the completeness and accuracy of your verbal models of the world. It is also true that you construct your behavior out of your own definitions of situations in which you find yourself—clearly a symbolic process.

Incomplete Language
Just as the educators could only discover eight ways in three minutes to develop a metaphor about depression, which denoted a poverty of language, there exists a poverty of language for most feelings. To illustrate this, we often ask our students to fill in the blanks shown in figure 5.5. What words would you put in the blank spaces provided?

Figure 5.5 Can You State in Words Your Degrees of Feeling?

Angry				Calm
Happy				Sad
Bored				Excited
Hateful				Loving
Hot				Cold
Bad				Good
Strong				Weak

If your experience is like ours, you had some difficulty filling in the spaces. Since language tends to be two-valued (since you don't have words between poles, you take on a two-word system), you may also find that you have used a number of nonfeeling words for spaces in the middle of the continuum, such as "average" and "moderate" and "medium."

The greater the number of available options for turning feeling into emotions, the greater the emotional range of feeling, and the greater the accuracy of the real world. Although not an original idea, we think it is very important because of its potential to help people grow.

Limited Accuracy

Richard Bandler and John Grinder identified three "constraints" that limit the accuracy of an individual's model.[9] These are neurological constraints, social constraints, and individual constraints.

Neurological Constraints "Our nervous system systematically distorts and deletes whole portions of the real world. This has the effect of reducing the range of possible human experience as well as introducing differences between what is actually going on in the world and our experience of it."[10] Thus, perceptions are limited.

Social Constraints The second category of constraint includes any filtering effect that is the result of membership in a particular society. Language, accepted ways of perceiving, and all culturally based assumptions are included in this category.

Bandler and Grinder illustrate this type of constraint by comparing Maidu, the language of an American Indian group in Northern California, to English. The terms for the color spectrum were compared (fig. 5.6). Maidu has only three words to describe the color spectrum, whereas English has eight words. Both languages are impoverished, clearly, since the human eye can distinguish an estimated 7.5 million color variations.

Figure 5.6 Maidu Color Words

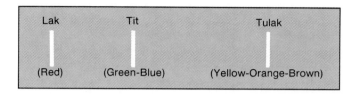

Lak	Tit	Tulak
(Red)	(Green-Blue)	(Yellow-Orange-Brown)

Since people who speak Maidu have only three words in their color vocabulary, they group their color experience into the three language categories. Native speakers of English, with an eight-word selection, group their color experiences into the eight categories supplied by their language. Thus the native speaker of English is "permitted" by the language to perceive a greater number of colors than the native speaker of Maidu.

Glance across the room in which you're now sitting. You may see before you two different books, one blue and one green. You experience them as different based upon the color choices you have in your language. To you, they *are* different. But the Maidu speaker tends to ignore what you believe to be a significant difference. To him the books are both "tit" in color. He does not experience them as different. Look further. Do you see a yellow book? How about one that has a brown cover? Both are "tulak" to the Maidu speaker, who does not experience them as different because he is limited to only one color word.

The neurological filters are similar in all people, but the social filters separate members of speech communities. Because you are a member of a separate speech community, you don't share the same models of reality, the same maps, with people of different speech communities. Fortunately, you can easily overcome the limitations imposed upon you by your social filters.

Individual Constraints The third constraining category is very complex. All of the representations and connections you have made personally, as a unique human being, based upon your personal and unique history, constitute the *individual constraints* category. No two personal histories are ever alike, and your personal history guarantees that you have a unique world of words—a model of reality unlike any other. If this model of reality is too limited, problems are almost certain to occur. As Bandler and Grinder put it:

> Our experience has been that, when people come to us in therapy, they typically come with pain, feeling themselves paralyzed, experiencing no choices or freedom of action in their lives. What we have found is not that the world is too limited or that there are no choices, but that these people block themselves from seeing those options and possibilities that are open to them since they are not available in their models of their world.[11]

Figure 5.7 A Typical Life Drawing Studio

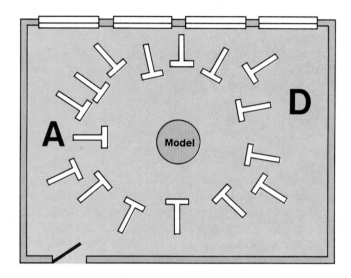

This problem may be similar to a common experience in sketching and drawing classes. Imagine that you are a student in a course in life drawing, where you and other students, seated around a central stage, draw sketches of models who are posed upon the stage. Figure 5.7 may help you to imagine this situation. Suppose you are the student located in position *A.*

After about two hours of drawing, the professor suggests that you move slowly around the room, examining every other drawing, and making a comparison between it and your own. The twenty students in the drawing class have looked at and worked at the same reality from unique perspectives. Each student's sketch suggests that the artist was blocked from seeing those options and possibilities that would be available to them if they had been located in different positions in the room. If you, now at position *A,* had, instead, been located at position *D,* you would certainly have created a different drawing of the same physical reality.

This illustration, however, breaks down quickly because it makes reference to point of view, or perspective, in the physical sense. Bandler and Grinder are talking about language limitations. You use language to represent your world to yourself—thus your language is a reasoning, imagining, thinking, model-of-reality-making phenomenon. You also use language to present your reality to others; to communicate, to talk, to write, to listen, to read.

Solving the Problem of Expressing Emotions

Structural linguists, scholars who study language-related components of perception, may hold the key to solving the problem of limited and incomplete verbal expression of emotions. In essence, the linguists are saying that languages are divided into two levels, *deep structures* and *surface structures.* The deep structure of language is a full and complete linguistic model, or map, from which you draw your fluent, surface structure discourse. Surface structures are characterized by the actual words and sentences you speak. This natural flow of fluent language usage is full of gaps, repetitions, incompletenesses, and unspoken presumptions. And because you're a native, fluent speaker of the language, you can and do assume others can understand the complete, underlying sentences represented by the incomplete ones you have uttered. This assumption is based on your faith that those to whom you usually speak have a fairly complete grasp of the deep structures of your language. In other words, they have had experience with fragmenting of this type, do it themselves, and are able to supply the underlying sentence from the deep structure.

You're usually able to close the gaps, fill in the omitted material, and test the unspoken presumptions of the deep structure. Because you're a native speaker, you make two intuitive assumptions: (1) if you want to, you can form your sentences completely and correctly, and (2) each native speaker "knows" what parts of each sentence go together. Because these two assumptions generally hold true, you know how to understand the following sentence: Young John hit the winning run.

At the level of the *surface structure* (fig. 5.8), you intuitively know that these words go together.

At the level of *deep structure,* you intuitively know that there is much more to be gleaned from the sentence. Figure 5.9 suggests only a small fragment of that rich potential.

Moreover, as a native speaker of English, you can examine two different surface structures and glean the same deep structure. For example, you know that the following two sentences mean the same thing; only the surface structure has been transformed.

A. Young John hit the winning run.
B. The winning run was hit by Young John.

You presume the name of the game and that the game is *played,* not fought. And you can even break up the elements of the surface structure and still understand the deep structure of the sentence, as you often do in a conversation. For example:

Figure 5.8 The Surface Structure of a Sentence

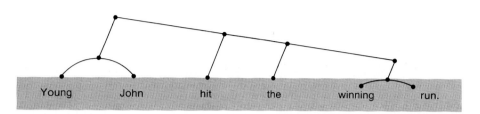

Figure 5.9 A Fragment of the Deep Structure of a Sentence

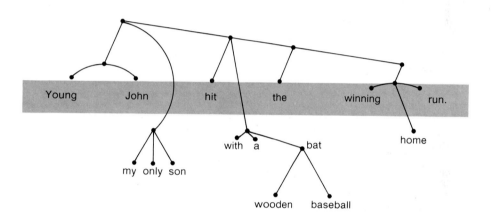

Parent 1: Who hit the winning run?
Parent 2: John.
Parent 1: Which John?
Parent 2: Young John.

Such things are possible so long as your verbal models of reality are complete. They are complete only if you are aware, at some level, of the deletions, distortions, and presuppositions you make when you move from the deep structure to the surface structure. But so what? What has all this to do with talking about feelings?

Consider the possibility that two individuals are involved in the following conversation. They have been seeing each other for some months, and each has considered that the relationship could lead to marriage. Their evening has just begun when he says "What would you like to do tonight, Suellen?"

"I don't know, Don. Why don't you choose?"

"Well . . . we have lots of possibilities. . . ."

Figure 5.10 Comparison of Suellen's Words and Thoughts

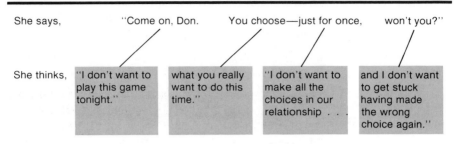

Figure 5.11 Private Understanding Can Quickly Lead to Trouble

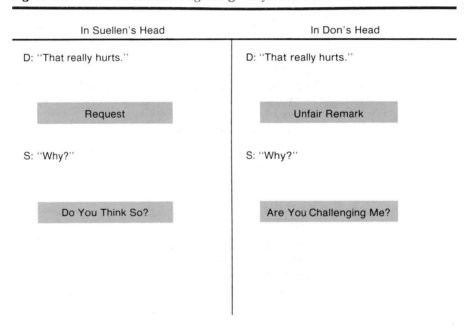

There is nothing notable in this conversation. But something notable might exist in their ways of understanding what the conversation is about in what they don't say.

Suellen frowns. Her voice hardens, then pleads. "Come on, Don. You choose just for once, won't you?" What Suellen may be thinking, however, as she says this is shown in figure 5.10.

Such silent, private understandings could quickly lead to important differences between Suellen and Don—differences buried deep in the structural assumptions of the language they use. Figure 5.11 illustrates this problem. The left-hand column shows Suellen's use of the language, both at the surface and beneath. The right-hand column shows Don's use of the same language at both levels. It won't take long to discover how divergent the deep structures can be, and how important they are in evolving relationships.

Up to this point, we have been saying that there is a big difference between experiencing and talking about experiencing. We're saying that feeling may very well be inhibited by the way we use language to think and talk about the feeling. You talk about your feelings in habitual, sometimes highly distorted and dysfunctional ways. It is possible to learn more effective ways to talk about those feelings when doing so would be productive.

Learning More Feeling Words

As a means to help you learn more feeling words, we have provided a list of such terms (table 5.1). Herb Hess and Charles Tucker, both of Northern Illinois University, published this list in *Talking About Relationships*.[12]

Table 5.1 Feeling Words

Positive

absorbed	eager	good-humored	pleasant/ure
adventurous	ecstatic	grateful	proud
affection	effervescent	gratification	quiet
alert	elated	happy	radiant
alive	electrified	helpful	rapturous
amazed	encouraged	hopeful	refreshed
amused	engrossed	inquisitive	relief/ved
appreciate	enjoyment	inspired	satisfied/faction
aroused	enlivened	intense	secure
astonished	enthusiastic	interested	sensitive
blissful	exalted	intrigued	spellbound
breathless	excited	invigorated	splendid
buoyant	exhilarated	involved	stimulated
calm	expansive	joy/ful/ous	surprised
carefree	expectant	jubilant	tender/ness
cheerful	exuberant	keyed-up	thankful
comfortable	fascinated	love/ing	thrilled
complacent	free	mellow	touched
composed	friendly	merry	tranquil
concerned	fulfilled	mirthful	trust
confident	gay	moved	warm
contented	glad	optimism/tic	wide-awake
curious	gleeful	overwhelmed	zest/ful
dazzled	glorious	overjoyed	
delighted	glowing	peaceful	

Table 5.1—*Continued*

Negative

afraid	disinterested	humdrum	reluctant/ance
aggravated	dislike	hurt	repelled
agitation	dismayed	impatient	resentful
alarm	displeased	indifferent	restless
angry	disquieted	inert	sad
anguish	dissatisfied	infuriated	scared
animosity	distressed	inquisitive	shaky
annoyance	disturbed	insecure	shocked
anxious	downcast	insensitive	skeptical
apathetic	downhearted	intense	sleepy
apprehensive	dread	irate	sorrowful
aroused	dull	irked	sorry
aversion	edgy	irritated	sour
beat	embarrassed	jealous	spiritless
bitter	embittered	jittery	startled
blue	exasperated	keyed-up	surprised
bored	exhausted	lazy	suspicion
breathless	fear/ful	let-down	terrified
brokenhearted	fidgety	lethargy	tired
chagrined	forlorn	listless	troubled
cold	frightened	lonely	uncomfortable
concerned	frustrated	mad	uneasy
confused	furious	mean	unglued
cross	gloomy	melancholy	unhappy
dejected	grief	miserable	unnerved
depressed	guilty	nervous	unsteady
despair	hate	nettled	upset
despondent	heavy	overwhelmed	uptight
detached	helpless	passive	withdrawn
disappointed	hesitant	perplexed	woeful
discouraged	horrified	pessimism/tic	worried
disgruntled	horrible	provoked	wretched
disgusted	hostile	puzzled	
disheartened	hot	rancorous	

Source: Herbert J. Hess and Charles O. Tucker, *Talking about Relationships* (Prospect Heights, Illinois: Waveland Press, Inc., 1980), 37–39.

Spend a good deal of time with the list if possible. Do you know all the words? Can you create a sentence using each one? Can you imagine how each of these feels? Can you feel each one? Can you add to the list? By spending time with the word list, you can stretch your feeling vocabulary. If you knew more words to describe the feeling you usually call "angry," you'd experience less anger.

Table 5.2

Surface Structure	Deletion of Definition	Deletion of Identification
1. I'm afraid.	Of what?	Of whom?
2. I'm just full of hatred.	What do you hate?	Who do you hate?
3. That irritates my soul.	What's "that"?	
4. I'm miserable.	How does miserable feel? What is causing you to feel miserable? Are you ill? Have an upset stomach?	
5. I'm really feeling up.	What do you mean "up"?	
6. I'm proud, really proud.	Of what are you proud?	Of whom are you proud?

Completing the Verbal Message

Whenever you talk with another, you're using words that you draw from your verbal models of sentences, the deep structures, to present your messages to that person. When you build verbal messages that are designed to express the emotions you're experiencing, you frequently pare them down, simplify them, change and twist them in some way, and make generalizations about them. Indeed, deletion, distortion, and generalization are the three means by which you create verbal representations of your experience.

Deletion

Deletion is the process of leaving chunks out of the verbal message, something you do all the time. For example, you might say "I'm afraid to walk in the park by myself after dark." You might also say: "I'm afraid of George Johnson." But what you're most likely to say, if you express your feelings of fear at all, will be the much simpler sentence "I'm afraid." These examples illustrate the two kinds of deletion: deletion of indefinite elements and deletion of identities. We have listed some examples of deletion (table 5.2).

Distortion

Distortion occurs when someone turns an ongoing process into a fixed event using language. Look at table 5.3 for some examples of distortion.

Table 5.3

Said	Meant
1. I love you.	I feel really deep affection for you right now (but I may not later).
2. That's a boring book.	I was bored (most of the time) when I was reading the book.
3. She is mean and spiteful.	Her behavior (that I noticed and stored in my memory) at dinner seemed mean and spiteful.
4. He's a hothead.	He sometimes loses his temper in conflict situations.
5. I'm dissatisfied with my decision, but I'm stuck with it.	I'm dissatisfied that I can't see a personally acceptable way to choose another alternative.

When distortion occurs, you must work at translating the sentence from what you hear about the idea or event, a fixed idea or event, into a process. This won't be easy, but there is a technique that may work for you. It is based on the idea that your distortions are under your control, and that you can choose another alternative. You simply ask about the control mechanism in the deep structure.

1. I hate you.	Do you always hate me? Did you hate me yesterday? Will you hate me tomorrow?
2. That's a boring book.	Every page? What did you find boring?
3. She is mean and spiteful.	What did she do? Under what circumstances? When?
4. He's a hothead.	What do you mean? How did he behave? When? Under what circumstances?
5. I'm dissatisfied with my decision, but I'm stuck with it.	What would you prefer? Can you choose differently? Is your decision permanent? Aren't you continually choosing? What alternatives are available?

Generalization

A generalization is a statement in the underlying language, either directly made or presupposed, usually containing the word "all." The statement must be true if a sentence in the language you hear is to be accepted.

Table 5.4 Allness Rules

Child	Parent	Possible Lesson
1. I hate you!	Don't say that! I'm your parent!	Expressions of anger toward significant others are taboo.
2. I'd like to kill (my sibling)!	You naughty, awful child! Don't you dare say that again!	Expressions of anger toward equals are taboo. I'm not okay.
3. These potatoes stink and taste yucky.	Don't talk to me in that tone of voice. Shut up and eat your potatoes.	Expressions of preference, especially if emotionally loaded, are taboo. They are not productive. I am not okay.
4. School is boring.	Too bad. You have to do your homework anyway.	Expressions of opinion about social institutions accomplish nothing. I'm not okay.
5. God is mean for letting Fido get run over. I hate God.	Get down on your knees and beg forgiveness.	If expressions of anger toward significant others are taboo, expressions of anger toward God are even worse. I'm not okay.

Most of the time the allness assumptions of the language don't get you into trouble, but there are many times when what you believe, based upon an allness assumption, is inaccurate. If it is also harmful, it can be confronted merely by remembering to consider the presupposition. For example, a very young child might hear the following instructions from mother.

"Always go to the corner of the block to cross the street. Never, never walk across the street in the middle of the block. You're a bad girl to walk across this street in the middle of the block. Now, let's go down to the corner and cross with the light."

Mother, clearly concerned about her child's safety and operating out of well-intended motives, may have implanted an allness assumption that will not be appropriate in the child's adult life. Twenty-five years after the event, the young woman may still be requiring herself to walk to the corner of every block in order to cross the street, whether or not there is any traffic or if the risk to her is greater by walking there than by crossing in the middle.

Similar allness rules are frequently placed upon you as you're learning to express your feelings (table 5.4).

So thorough is your training in expression of feeling that you learn some very subtle ways of denying them, even to yourself. When it becomes necessary to talk about them, you often find that you're unable to do so. American culture discourages expression of feelings, so denial strategies are common.

Table 5.5 Five Ways Feelings are Denied

1. Explain, rather than describe.	I feel this is really important. I feel really successful this morning.
2. Substitute wants, interpretations.	I feel you're pulling away from me. I'm feeling betrayed. I feel like you don't spend enough time with me.
3. Describe thinking as though it were feelings.	I feel set up for a fall. I feel that you've betrayed me. I feel really stupid. I feel that's wrong.
4. Substitute metaphor for feeling.	I feel like a little girl. I feel like someone has lifted a car off me. I feel like you've poured cold water on my idea.
5. Denying the present tense.	I felt angry when you did that. If you do that, I'll be really hurt.

Avoiding Denial Strategies

You must avoid culturally based denial strategies in order to talk about your feelings. There are five very common strategies in American culture that are used to avoid or to deny feelings:

1. Explain feelings rather than describe them
2. Substitute wants and interpretations for feelings
3. Describe thinking as though it were feelings
4. Substitute a metaphor for a feeling
5. Deny feelings by denying the present tense

Each of these five strategies can work independently or in context with the others. So your defense mechanisms—your strategies for denying your feeling—can be very complex and subtle.

To illustrate each of these strategies, we have created table 5.5. An example or two is included for each strategy. Perhaps you have heard, or used, some of these strategies yourself.

In every case, the solution to the problem expressed here is to describe the feeling directly.

Experience: **Identifying Statements of Feelings**

To help you practice this, we suggest that you study each of the following statements. Some are feeling statements and some are not; in some of the statements speakers have elected to use a strategy for denying their feelings rather than stating them directly. Which of these statement seems to be a clear and direct statement of feelings?

1. I feel like a tramp when you look at me that way.
2. I feel used.
3. I feel excited.
4. I feel tremendously involved.
5. I'm really glad you're here.
6. I'm feeling curious about your motives.
7. I feel like you're lying to me.
8. I'm experiencing very intense joy right now.
9. I feel real bad about that.
10. I feel wonderful.

Statements 3, 5, and 8 are fairly direct statements of feeling. The others reflect one or more of the five strategies for denying feeling. Can you identify why? Look at the following for help.

1. How does a tramp feel? (Presents a metaphor)
2. How does used feel? (Substitutes interpretation for feeling)
3. (A fairly direct feeling statement)
4. How does "tremendously involved" feel? (Substitution of cognitive activity for feelings)
5. (Direct statement about the speaker's feelings)
6. How does curious feel? (Curious is a cognitive matter)
7. How does this feel? (Substitute interpretation or want for feelings)
8. (Direct feeling statement)
9. How does "real bad" feel? (Explains the feeling rather than expresses it)
10. Again, more an explanation of feeling than description of it. Wonder is a cognitive activity. (Describes thinking as though it were a feeling)

Summary

You need to learn to manage your communication during moments when you're emotionally aroused. Learning to do this involves learning how to identify your feelings and how to separate those feelings from the words you use to describe them. Because your emotional reality is a function of the words you use to describe your feelings, fluency is a major factor in the emotional ranges you experience and express. Moreover, emotions always have behavioral consequences, some of which are productive and some of which are not. Unless you learn to talk about your feelings intelligently and productively, you are seriously limiting your potential for growth and your potential to establish and maintain satisfying relationships with others.

We described ways in which people in our culture deny their feelings, and what that denial does to them. You explain your feelings. You substitute your wants or your interpretations for them. You describe your thinking as though it were feelings. You substitute metaphor for feeling. And you deny your feelings by denying the present tense. In doing these things, you risk interpersonal honesty and accuracy, and your own emotional health. There is always a cognitive element in the experience of emotions because your emotions are based in language. People do not respond to an actual event; they respond to the cognitive structure they create around the event as a result of their fluency with language.

You can control the emotions you experience by learning to talk to yourself and to each other with a broader range of language and a broader understanding of how your emotional responses work. Since emotions always have behavioral consequences, learning to control these emotional experiences will help you to handle your interpersonal behavior more intelligently. In turn, learning to handle interpersonal behavior is important because such behavior, always goal-directed, can only work in one of two directions. You can pursue goals that will push you apart, or you can pursue goals that will pull you together.

There are several ways that people can learn to communicate their feelings more accurately and successfully. The first suggestion is to learn to recognize those feelings. The next suggestion is to learn a far broader range of words—both positive and negative—to describe your feelings. The third suggestion is to learn to identify the incompleteness of most of your sentences, and to test the assumptions you usually make concerning the other person's ability to fill in your gaps, and your ability to fill in the gaps in other peoples' sentences. Especially in emotionally loaded sentences, such confidence is rarely warranted.

But talking about feelings is not easy. There are three categories of constraints that keep people from creating complete and accurate verbal models of their worlds. Neurological constraints result in serious distortion and deletions in your world model. The filtering effects of belonging to a particular speech community constrain you from perceiving and interpreting the world accurately. Finally, you learn how to interact in a complex evolutionary history of experiences, so everyone has learned to filter incoming information in unique ways. Since no two people's experiences are alike, their perceptions and understandings of the world cannot be alike.

An awareness of the deep structure and the surface structure of a sentence will assist you in making the verbal models you use, and hear others use, more complete. These ideas constitute a powerful set of skills that should help you to communicate far more effectively. We firmly believe that the result for you, personally, and for your relationships will be interpersonal growth.

Discussion Questions

1. It is a common assumption that every human being loves at least one other human being with some level of intensity. Identify such a relationship in your experience. In what particular ways are you dependent upon that person? In what ways does your dependency

influence your ability to talk about your feelings with him or her? Does the other person depend upon you?

2. Pretend it is time for an important examination. Attempt to identify the physical experience you would be feeling under this stress-producing situation. Can you describe that experience to others without labeling the emotion?

3. Write down as rapidly as you can ten words you would use to describe the emotion you would experience in the testing situation described in question 2. Now, share your list with your classmates and discuss the implications of your list. Does the language you use influence the experience you have?

4. Everybody is an actor at heart. Experiment by role playing the following emotions: anxiety, fear, affection, curiosity, and joy. What physical experiences did you have as you role played the emotion? What memory did you have in producing the emotion?

5. Can you think of any situations in which your attitudes control your physical experience? Can you think of any situations in which your physical experience controls your attitudes?

Endnotes

1. J. Weinstein et al. "Defensive Style and Discrepancy between Self-Report and Physiological Indices of Stress." *Journal of Personality and Social Psychology* 10 (1968):405–13.

2. R. Buck, *Human Motivation and Emotion* (New York: Wiley, 1976).

3. R. M. Yerkes and G. D. Dodson, "The Relation of Strength of Stimulus to Rapidity of Habit Formation," *Journal of Comparative Neurological Psychology* 18 (1908):459–82.

4. M. Kinbourne, "The Brain: Sad Hemisphere, Happy Hemisphere," *Psychology Today* (May, 1981):92.

5. See, for example, S. P. Springer and G. Deutsch, *Left Brain, Right Brain* (San Francisco: W. H. Freeman and Company, 1981).

6. Kinbourne, "The Brain," 92.

7. Ibid.

8. A. Sibatani, "It May Turn Out that the Language We Learn Alters the Physical Operation of Our Brains," *Science* 80 (December, 1980):24–26.

9. R. Bandler and J. Grinder, *The Structure of Magic: I* (Palo Alto, CA: Science and Behavior Books, Inc., 1975).

10. Ibid., 9.

11. Ibid., 13.

12. H. J. Hess and C. O. Tucker, *Talking About Relationships,* 2d ed. (Prospect Heights, IL: Waveland Press, Inc., 1980), 37–39.

Language and Interpersonal Relationships

Preview

You live in a world of words, not in a world of observations, phenomena, and events. If your use of language is impoverished, then your world is equally impoverished, and your relationships and personal growth are diminished. Better understanding of and facility in using language are the most important interpersonal skills that you can develop. This chapter addresses those significant relational skills.

Objectives

After reading this chapter you should be able to complete the following:
1. Discuss the interrelationship among events, thoughts, and language using the Triangle of Meaning.
2. Explain abstraction, and how this process functions during interpersonal communication.
3. Discuss the ways that culture, society, and relationships have influenced your language habits.
4. Identify denotative and connotative meanings.
5. Identify symmetrical and complementary language.
6. Explain how language, and naming in particular, affects the expression of the self-concept.
7. Provide personal examples of the problems of rigidity and overdiscrimination.
8. Present personal experiences with nonassertive, assertive, and aggressive communication.
9. Explain and recall an example of stereotyping from an interpersonal encounter.
10. Explain self-fulfilling prophesy. Provide an example from personal experience.
11. Discuss the way that reification contributes to problems in interpersonal relationships.
12. Recall an experience in which polarization, or the two-valued orientation, created interference in the communication process.
13. Describe the impact of stress on orientation in interpersonal relationships.

6

Cheryl and Mary Ann were sitting in the lounge of the student center, talking about the term paper assignment for their interpersonal communication class. Mary Ann, her paper well under way, was listening to Cheryl relate her difficulties in getting started on the assignment when Tim approached.

"Hey, Cheryl," he called, "you look awful. What's the matter with you anyway?"

"Thanks a lot, Tim. That's just what I needed to hear," replied Cheryl.

Tim seemed surprised at Cheryl's quick reply. "Well, I don't mean you look awful, I mean people like you never look this upset. What's bothering you?"

Cheryl turned bright red. "What do you mean, people like me?" she shouted.

Tim stammered, saying, "Well, you know, uh, people who are, uh, sort of . . . heavy."

As Mary Ann listened to this exchange, her eyes opened wide. "Tim!" she interjected, "Cheryl and I are working on ideas for the interpersonal paper. If you want to work with us, that's okay. If not, will you let us get back to it, please?"

Tim, looking embarrassed, started to back away. "No problem, I'm sorry I interrupted. I'm sorry, Cheryl, I didn't mean to hurt your feelings."

Cheryl gave him a sharp look and said, "Just leave us alone, will you Tim?"

As Tim wandered off, Cheryl looked at Mary Ann and said, "That Tim is such a turkey!"

Mary Ann nodded and said, "Well, sometimes he just doesn't think before he talks. Let's get back to work."

Cheryl started shuffling through her papers and moaned. "I always go through this when I have to start a paper. I'm just not a writer. Remember what happened in Hotchkin's class? I had A's on all the tests, then blew my grade on the paper assignment. I just know the same thing is going to happen to me this term. I can feel it."

Mary Ann reached over and touched Cheryl's arm, saying, "Forget last term for now. Concentrate on what you have to do for this assignment, make a plan, and carry it out."

Cheryl sighed, "I don't know, Mary Ann. The bottom line is I just can't write papers. If I don't get an idea right now for this assignment, I'll just have to drop the class."

"I don't think you need to drop the class because of this problem," Mary Ann replied. "Besides, dropping out won't solve the real problem anyway, will it? Let's make a list of your ideas for possible topics, then you can get an appointment to go over them with our instructor. I bet he'd be glad to explore them with you."

Cheryl, looking through her papers, said, "Well, I've got some notes here already. Maybe we could start with them."

Anyone who listened to this conversation would realize what is going on without much difficulty. The language of the conversation reveals much about the participants, their points of view, and their relationship.

Up to this point, we've shown you a number of ways to look at what happens when people talk, and in this chapter, we're going to provide yet another focus. This chapter is about the language you use in your relationships. Language represents a principal means for conveying your wants, feelings, and intentions to another person. After working through this chapter, you will have an understanding that provides for more appropriate self-expression and more accurate self-disclosure. You will know how to effectively use language in making interpersonal contacts, and you will be more capable in creating and maintaining interpersonal agreements. Finally, upon completing this chapter, you will understand the ways that language contributes to variation in the intimacy of relationships.

Three major ideas about language are conveyed in this chapter. First, you use language to relate your ideas to events in the world around you. Second, you use language to disclose yourself, to express yourself, and to connect yourself to others. Third, your use of language sometimes results in problems which, with careful attention, you can solve. Overall, we want you to understand that careful attention to the language that you use can assist you in facing interpersonal difficulties and so lead to interpersonal growth.

The Nature of Language

According to George A. Miller, you could give three different answers to the question "What is language?" (1) You might answer in a way that emphasizes the *structure* of language; (2) you could answer in terms of the process of *uttering the sounds* associated with spoken languages; or (3) you might also respond in terms of the *social conventions* associated with using language; that is, in terms of the relationship between the language and the world around you.[1] Winifred P. Lehmann identified these three definitions respectively, as the "syntactic," "phonological" and "semantic" components of language. The semantic aspect of relationships is the component that relates most directly to the process of interpersonal communication.[2]

Howard R. Pollio provided a useful definition of language. He said language is a system of symbols, governed by rules, that describes what combinations of symbols are acceptable for use in communicating. These symbols, along with the governing rules, are abstract; the symbols are separate from the tangible objects and experiences that they are meant to describe.[3]

Several important characteristics of language are suggested in this definition. First, language is composed of symbols—that is, words. Second, the words you use have no necessary relationship with the objects, events, persons, and feelings they represent. Third, the use of any language is rule-governed. The rules that govern your use of language come, in part, from your culture. Other rules represent agreements you have made in particular relationships.

Language and Experience

Language is the principal means of conveying your experiences to others. It is related to experience in two important ways. First, language is the tool that you use to communicate your perceptions of experience to others. Second, you use your language to perceive and interpret the messages of others. Of course, the messages another sends are tied to that individual's own experience.

In reading the chapter on perception, you became aware of the many variables that affect your intake of information. For example, the frame of reference, or the view you hold of the world, is a composite of ideas that you have about images received through your senses. You also know now that perception is filtered in a number of ways. Filtering also takes place as you attempt to relate your view to others. Language serves both as a tool for conveying meaning and as a filter through which messages must pass as you receive them.

The Triangle of Meaning

C. K. Ogden and I. A. Richards depicted the way language works in communication as a triangular relationship among events, thoughts, and symbols (fig. 6.1).[4]

The *referent* in the lower right corner of the triangle is what your communication is about. The referent may be a person or object, an event, or a want or a feeling. The referent is the object of your perception and that to which your message refers.

The top of the triangle displays the word *thought*. This represents your perception and interpretation of the referent. It includes all the attributes you assign to your image of the referent. Additionally, your feelings about the referent, past experiences related to it, and other perception variables may be included. In other words, the thought is a mental approximation of the referent.

The lower left corner of the Triangle of Meaning is labeled *symbol*. A symbol is something that stands for something else. In language, words, phrases, and sentences stand for thoughts. You cannot communicate your thoughts directly, so you must translate them into a medium that you have in common with the other person in the relationship. Language provides this common medium.

The lines in figure 6.1 indicate the relationships among the elements of the Triangle of Meaning. A solid line connects the referent with the thought.

Figure 6.1 The Triangle of Meaning

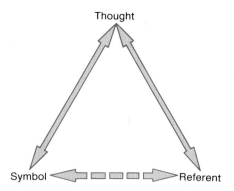

The referent acts as a stimulus for the thought. You have a thought because you perceive a referent. Frequently, your thought is *about* the referent, but it may also be an association with something quite apart from what is taking place around you. (This situation was discussed in chapter three, the study of perception.)

The reason a relationship exists between the thought and the symbol you use to convey that thought is similar to the reason for the relationship between thought and referent. You use the symbol because you had the thought. The symbol, however, does not express all of the thought, nor does it necessarily represent the thought accurately. You select your symbols from those that are available to you in order to approximate as closely as possible that which you intend to communicate.

The dashed line connecting the symbol with the referent indicates that there need be no correspondence whatsoever between these two elements. The word is not the thing. The symbol is not the referent.

What are your reasons for studying interpersonal communication? Examine your answers to this in terms of the Triangle of Meaning. The language of your reasons is emitted as *symbols*. Some examples of these answers are in the following:

"To get four credits in an interesting subject."
"Because it's a required course."
"I heard the teacher was good."
"I want to improve my communication skills."

You know that none of these statements tells the entire reason for enrolling in the class. This language only symbolizes your reasons; puts them in a form everyone can understand.

The *thought* aspect of the Triangle of Meaning includes everything that goes on in your head when you hear the question. This includes assumptions, feelings, reflections about past experiences, physical sensations, and other mental activity. All of these relate to your answer because your answer is designed to represent some or all of these thoughts. Your thoughts also relate to the referent, which in this case is interpersonal communication. You have these thoughts because we gave you the topic "interpersonal communication" to think about. Your thoughts, then, refer to interpersonal communication.

Remember that there is no causal relationship between the symbol and the referent. You can see that your reasons for studying interpersonal communication do not come from interpersonal communication by itself. Your words about it are not the same as the experience of it. The thought aspect of the Triangle of Meaning is the critical connector between symbol and referent. If we show you the *word* "chair," you will think about it and then point to a referent chair. If we show you a *chair,* you will think about it and then utter the word "chair." You cannot get from symbol to referent or from referent to symbol without first passing through thought.

The Abstraction Process

The term *abstraction* describes the role of perception in helping to translate experience to thought, and then into language. Condon explained abstraction in terms of selectivity.[5] He said that in order to create language that will convey your experience of events, you must ignore some aspects of the events *(selective exposure)*; you must focus on particular aspects of the event *(selective attention)*; and you may even distort aspects of the event *(selective perception)*.

Levels of Abstraction

Hayakawa offered a useful explanation of the way you abstract and how that abstraction process relates to language.[6] His treatment of the subject suggests how the event, your experience, and the context work together. He said that abstracting is like climbing a ladder. As you climb higher up the ladder, your view of the event changes in several important ways that affect the language you use to describe your experience of the event. The higher you climb a ladder, the further you get from the ground, so the less detail you can see. You can also see more territory from higher up on a ladder. As you climb the abstraction ladder, your ability to relate experience through language is affected similarly. First, the more abstract your perception of the event, the farther you are from your direct experience of the event. Also, your perception includes more of the context surrounding the event when viewed from a higher level of abstraction. Finally, your perception contains much less detail about the event itself as you move higher on the abstraction ladder.

Experience: **Understanding Abstraction**

You can gain a real sense of abstraction by working through the following brief experience. What do you see in figure 6.2? Write down some words that describe what you see. Now arrange these four or five words from least abstract to most abstract.

Figure 6.3 lists some language people have used to describe the object pictured in figure 6.2. The language is arranged so that a reduction of figure 6.2 appears at the bottom, and higher and higher levels of abstraction appear toward the top. How do your levels of abstraction compare to these?

Suppose that you used language similar to that in figure 6.3. The car that you perceive in the picture at level one is not a word or a thing, but rather a referent, an object of experience. It is not the whole car or even the whole picture. It is your experience of the picture based on aspects selected through your senses. At the next level up, you may have recognized this object as a Mercedes Benz. The name characterizes the object, stands for it, and distinguishes it from other vehicles. However, the name also omits many of the unique characteristics of this particular Mercedes Benz. At level three, the word "car" summarizes the characteristics of this and similar objects. Notice here that you are moving farther from the actual object as you use this more abstract language. Characteristics peculiar to this type of "car" are omitted. When the Mercedes is referred to as "transportation," as in level four, more of its functional context is included. This

Figure 6.2 Abstraction

Figure 6.3 Levels of Abstraction

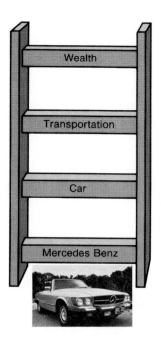

way of looking at the object does not distinguish it from other objects that perform similar functions, like a train or a bus. You might use the language of the fifth level, "wealth," if you were experiencing the value context surrounding the object. For many people, a Mercedes Benz is a symbol of status and wealth. Specific aspects of the object are almost completely missing at this high level of abstraction.

Levels of abstraction are important to relationships in three ways. First, the abstraction level of the language identifies the characteristics of the relationship that you see. This includes not only ways of talking about the relationship, but also behaviors that are viewed as, to some degree, appropriate to the relationship. Second, the abstractness of the language used in describing a relationship indicates your view of the depth of involvement people have in the relationship. The intensity with which you experience the relationship may also be indicated by the abstractness of the language. Third, the language used by one partner to talk about a relationship is similar to some degree to that used by the other partner in the relationship. The more the two descriptions reflect similar levels of abstraction, the better able are the partners to sensibly talk with one another about the relationship.

Experience: Describing Relationships

These three points are illustrated by the following experience. Here is a list of words that people sometimes use to describe their relationships with others.

Friend
Associate
Companion
Acquaintance
Colleague

Now write the answers to each of the following questions. Writing the answers will help you to think more thoroughly about the three points.

1. Arrange the words in order of increasing abstraction, with the highest level abstraction at the top of your list.
2. Now examine each level of abstraction and create a list of adjectives that characterize the relationships represented by that level. What behaviors are included at each level? In what ways do the characteristics and behaviors you named differ from level to level?
3. Do these levels represent different intensities in relationships? How? Does involvement vary from level to level? How?
4. Evaluate these different levels on a continuum from impersonal to interpersonal. What do you find?
5. How would communication between two people be characterized at each of these levels of abstraction?
6. What if the two people involved used different levels of abstraction in defining the relationship? How would communication between them be affected?
7. What words could you add to this list of relationship descriptions? Where would each fit in the abstraction ladder? What effect do they have on the way a relationship grows?

You can see that language provides a set of symbols that you use to transmit your thoughts to others. Experiences of people, events, and objects are reconstructed in symbolic form, which becomes talk about those experiences. In using language, you choose words (symbols) that represent the idea you intended to communicate. Try to analyze the conversation between Mary Ann and Cheryl at the beginning of the chapter in terms of levels of abstraction. At what levels do they respond to Tim? What about their images of the writing problem?

The words you use vary in terms of abstraction level. The more abstract your language, the further you are from direct experience, the more territory

Figure 6.4

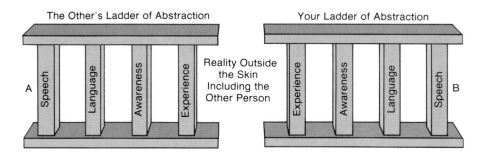

your language covers, and the less specific detail about the characteristics of the experience are included in your message. Now compound the problem— as it is compounded in every relationship in which you are involved. If such a process as abstracting is going on inside you, it is also going on inside the other person with whom you're talking. Thus, when you interact, you are truly living in a world of words. Figure 6.4 makes this problem clear. We have turned the abstraction ladders of two people sideways to show their interaction. Notice how far each individual is from their mutual experience when operating at the speaking level.

The Bases of Language

From where does your language come? How does it shape your frame of reference? As you will see, your range of available symbols is determined and limited by culture, society, and the particular rules of the relationship.

Language and Culture

The particular set of symbols available to people for use in conveying ideas seems to reflect those things that are important in that culture. J. Dan Rothwell noted several striking differences among the languages of different cultures.[7] For example, how many names do you have for that white stuff that falls from the sky in winter? The Eskimos have at least nine different words for snow. What about the animal that provides most milk? In Africa, the Masai language uses seventeen different terms for a cow. How many words would it take you to describe a camel? In Arabic, there are about six thousand words that relate directly to this animal. The point is that each language carries with it a particular frame of reference, and culture represents a major contributor to that world view. Jerome Bruner, Jacqueline Goodnow, and George Austin summarized this idea when they wrote:

> The speakers of a language are partners to an agreement to see and think of the world in a certain way—not the only possible way. The world can be structured in many ways, and the language we learn as children directs the formation of our particular structure.[8]

This idea, that language influences your experience of the world at a cultural level, also directly applies to the way relationships are defined in a culture. G. P. Murdock studied the language used to describe family relationships in 250 different cultures and found important differences among them in how relationships and rules for behavior toward them are defined.[9] For example, in several of the cultures, a hierarchy of "aunts" was noted, with the importance of each determined by which side of the family she was on, whether her connection was biological or marital, and other conditions.

It is important to realize that your frame of reference is colored at a cultural level for three reasons. As technological advances bring various cultures into more frequent contact, you will find yourself communicating with people from those other cultures more regularly. Knowing that they hold a view of the world that may involve different priorities will help you to get along with them. Secondly, the American culture is composed of a variety of subcultures—black, Hispanic, and native American, for example. These subcultures frequently have different views of their experiences and use different language to describe them. Finally, it is useful to remember that the frame of reference provided by your language is only one of many that are available. Realizing this can help you look for alternatives for interpreting your experiences.

Language and Society

The effect of society on the language you use is similar to the effect of culture. Your view of events and relationships is shaped by the language that you have available to describe your experiences with them. Social influences on your language, however, may be more temporary. Social rules about your language change over time in ways that are more directly observable.

Social differences in language use include those based upon geography or region, ethnic identification, and subgroup slang. Although these language differences come in and out of fashion, while in use they help to shape the way you interpret your experiences and relate to others.

Experience: Comparing Terms

Slang expressions have an interesting effect on language and frame of reference. Consider the list of definitions that follows.[10] Provide a word that best describes each of the items. Then compare your terms with those of your classmates.

Table 6.1 Select a Term to Describe Each of These

1. An easy college course
2. To be drunk
3. A difficult college course
4. What a person with special influence is said to have
5. A poor social evening, a wasted night
6. To study very diligently for an examination
7. To fail an examination
8. To go alone to a social function
9. A particularly rough and noisy party
10. One who puts a damper on a party

What message do you get from the language used by others to describe these situations? Look up each of the terms you used in a current dictionary. How does the dictionary definition compare with your usage?

Newsweek magazine listed some terms and their definitions that represent the language of certain American subgroups of the 1960s (table 6.2). You can understand the changing nature of language usage by examining the list. How many of these terms are still in use now? How many of them still mean the same thing? What new language has developed to take the place of those terms which have gone out of fashion?

Just as some language is peculiar to a particular generation, other language may be useful only in the social context of an occupation or activity. People who work with computers may recognize the following terms compiled by Lance Morrow.

> In the Hacker's Dictionary, one finds "gronk" (a verb that means to become unusable, as in "the monitor gronked"), "gweep" (one who spends unusually long periods of time hacking), "cuspy" (anything that is exceptionally good or performs its functions exceptionally well), "dink" (to modify in some small way so as to produce large or catastrophic results), "bagbiter" (equipment or program that fails, usually intermittently), and "deadlock" (a situation wherein two or more processes are unable to proceed because each is waiting for the other to do something).[11]

What conversational language is unique to *your* hobby or occupation? The language that you use to describe your experiences includes much from your culture and your social milieu. These forces help to shape not only your frame of reference, but also your style of communicating that point of view.

Table 6.2 Terms Adopted by Subgroups in the 1960s

groove, n. & v. (also groovy, adj., grooving on, pr. part.). Ecstasy, a good thing ("Life I love you. All is groovy."—Simon & Garfunkel, "The 59th Street Bridge Song").

hang-up, n. Quirk, problem, difficulty. Hang-up, v. Causing the like, "hanging someone up." See Hassle. Hung-up, Hung-up on, p.part., obsessed with, preoccupied by, in mental anguish over.

nitty-gritty, n. Unvarnished essence, the heart of the matter, as in "getting down to the nitty-gritty."

together, adj. Composed, rational, reconciled, e.g., get your head together, keep it together, he was very together (Beatles, "Coming Together").

up front, adj. Open uninhibited, e.g., "he was up front about his hang-ups." adv. Summons to the head of the line of march in a radical demonstration, as in "chicks up front."

up tight, adj. 1. Tense 2. Copacetic 3. Close to, intimate, as in up tight with.

zap, v. Destroy, obliterate, take sudden aggressive action against ("Zap the Cong," i.e., kill Viet Cong)

Language and Relationships

Your relationships influence your language in three important ways. (1) Your pool of available symbols is mediated by the roles you take in relationships. (2) Different kinds of meaning may be assigned across relationships. (3) Your language reflects the view you hold about the relationship.

Experience: **Using Language in Relationships**

Try this experience. For each of the situations listed in table 6.3, imagine that you are involved in the situation and want to explain it to each person listed in the second column. Create an explanation for each situation for each relationship listed.

How would you characterize the language you used in each of these situations/relationships? What is it about the relationships that makes using some language appropriate?

You can monitor the way your language habits shift as you move from one relationship to another. In some relationships, you feel the need to use more "proper" language than in others. For example, your explanation of failing courses might be less formal with your best friend than it would be with your academic advisor. In other relationships, you might explain at a lower level of abstraction than others. For example, your discussion about your failing grades might be carried out with vivid detail for your best friend, but in much more general language for your parents, and in even higher abstraction for your academic advisor.

Table 6.3

Situation	Relationship
You want to study overseas for six months.	Best friend
You are failing all of your courses this term.	Spouse or lover
You have met and fallen in love with someone new.	Parent Academic advisor

Language is also a part of each *role* you take. In every relationship, there are agreements about what language is appropriate and what is not. In order to keep these relationships working, always attempt to use language that is recognized as a part of the relationship you have.

Denotative and Connotative Meanings in Relationships

Dictionaries do not provide all the definitions that are useful in communicating; they only represent the denotative meanings of words. Denotative meanings are what words are "supposed" to mean, usually aside from any particular context of the communication and the relationship between the communicators. Denotative meanings are used in all messages, even in those that do not have words.

There are times when you want to stress the denotative meaning, such as when you are giving *instructions* to a subordinate in the work setting. You want to be as clear and specific as possible to be sure that the task is done in the way that you want. Denotative meaning may also be important when you are *reporting* an event to someone, again perhaps at work to your boss. In both these instances, you want to be as clear as possible, so you use specific, unambiguous language. You describe at the lowest level of abstraction that you can.

In some cases denotation simply does not exist at all. If people do live in a language world of their own construction, then their understandings of the symbol-referent relationship are unique. Thus, if I use the word "dog," you will attach your own understanding, and you will do it *inevitably.* In that sense, there is no way that a term can "mean the same thing" to everyone in a speech community.

There is another kind of meaning that takes the listener beyond the denotational level. It is called connotative meaning. *Connotative meaning* is your personal meaning for a word. It is influenced by what is said, and by the person talking, the subject of the conversation, and even the environment in which the conversation takes place. Consider the example shown in table 6.4.

The meanings in the connotative column represent what each individual might have been hearing at the connotative level. These are, of course, only some of the possible meanings that might have been assigned in this conversation. What judgments do you see implied here? What does each seem to

Table 6.4 Denotative and Connotative Meanings

Said (Denotative)	Other's Thought (Connotative)
Teacher: You know, a course in statistics might be really helpful for you, especially if you're planning on graduate school.	He wants to see me enroll in a stat course. He thinks everyone who goes to graduate school should have stat.
	He thinks I should go to graduate school.
Student: Well, I really hadn't thought about it, but I will now that you mention it. Maybe I'll catch a statistics course next term.	He just wants to finish school and land a good job. He's not taking any statistics.
Teacher: Drop by and see me around registration time so we can talk about it more. You know, a graduate degree can be quite marketable.	He wants to convince me to take statistics and go on to graduate school.
Student: Okay, I'll get in to see you sometime when we're both free. I know you're busy a lot, but I'll catch you.	He's changing advisors.

believe about the subject of the conversation? What about their views of one another? What difference would environment have made? What if the conversation took place in the classroom? What if it took place in the teacher's office?

It is very important to be aware of the potential in the connotative level of meaning because people do not always say what they intend in a way that you can understand. You can help yourself become better at listening for the intended meaning by practicing the skills presented in the chapter on listening.

Symmetrical and Complementary Language

Another aspect of relationships that is important to your selection of language is your view of the relationship. Dennis R. Smith and Keith Williamson explained that each individual has a view of every relationship that suggests a perceived status of the other person [12] The view is *symmetrical* if you see yourself as an equal partner in the relationship. The view is *complementary* if you see yourself "one up" or "one down" in status from the other person.

The language that you employ reflects your view, either complementary or symmetrical, of the relationship. When your view is symmetrical, your language might be more "we" oriented, with clear indications that control of the relationship is shared. Your relationships with friends and classmates are typically symmetrical. Classmates are usually all "in the same boat" as far as responsibilities in the course and to one another are concerned. Thus you share a common and equal basis for your relationship. Your relationship with friends will also be symmetrical when there is an expectation that each partner will contribute equally to the success of the relationship.

Relationships between parents and children are frequently viewed as complementary. Teacher-student relationships also may be viewed in this way. In such relationships, the language of the conversations will indicate that one of the participants has more responsibility for determining the direction and goals of the relationship than the other.

Problems can arise between people when their language reflects different views of the relationship. For example, how would you characterize the communication taking place between two classmates, one of whom views the relationship as symmetrical while the other views it as complementary? Or, how do you think communication between a husband and wife would sound if they both viewed the relationship as complementary, with each other as "one down"?

In both of these instances, as well as in other combinations of the two views, a third party listening to the conversation might get the impression that the two people talking do not know one another very well, or that they do not like one another very much. Listen for language that tells you about the other's view of your relationship. If you hear images that are different from your own, you know that you need to talk with your partner about the relationship. You need to clarify your own view; to work to understand that of the other person; and to work out language that expresses some agreement between you.

Language and the Self

You use language to express who you are in relationships and in situations. You reveal yourself and make contact with others through the language that you use. *Naming* is the major language process involved in this self-expression.

Language Expresses the Self

Using communication to reveal yourself to others is called *self-disclosure*. As you talk with others, your language contains clues about how you see yourself and about how you would like others to see you. Some of these language clues are used intentionally. For instance, a child wanting your attention may scream as though hurt just to let you know that she is feeling alone. The intentional aspects of self-expression include both what you say about yourself, to yourself, as well as what you say to others. Athos and Gabarro theorized that the language you use in conversation reveals something about all aspects of the self-concept.[13]

Consider, for example, this list of statements.

"I can't do math."
"I like going out on the town."
"If I were you, I'd lay it on the line."

These are all direct statements about a person's view of herself. They may have been made to the self or to someone else. What images of this person do you get from these few statements? You use statements like these about yourself to define boundaries about what you are and are not willing to do. As you will discover later in this chapter, you sometimes allow these statements to become laws that you feel obligated to defend and use to limit the range of your experiences. But even when this happens, statements such as these still represent intentional messages about how you see yourself and how you would like to be seen.

Figurative Language Reveals the Self

Some of your language reveals information about your self-concept in more subtle ways. Listeners may draw inferences about the way you see yourself from the frequency with which you talk about certain things. People may also come to learn about your self-concept by noticing the metaphors you use in describing your experience. Both of these ways of communicating the self-concept are largely conducted unawares.

If you listen carefully, you will notice that a person brings certain ideas or topics into conversations more frequently than others. Usually these ideas or topics are of special importance to this person. (You need to be careful about this, though, as not everyone realizes that they are conveying these priorities; they might respond defensively if it were called to their attention.) Having an idea about what the person deems important should help you to select language that conveys your intended meaning.

One individual's language is a good example of this. He tends to respond to conversations in monetary terms. Upon seeing a new car, he might speculate about its value. After spending an inordinate amount of time waiting to see a customer service representative at a local utility office, he conveyed his irritation by sending the company a bill for his time. If others want to be sure he hears them, all they have to do is listen for a money-oriented response, or put their point in financial language. Then they know they have his attention.

If you listen carefully to the language people use to describe their experiences, you may see some consistency among the metaphors they use. Consistent use of similar metaphors is a clue to what the individual holds as important, and to his frame of reference.

If, for example, promptness is something that you value a great deal, you may include references to time into your conversation without even realizing that you are doing so. You frequently use figurative language that has at its base things that are important to you that may be otherwise unknown to the people with whom you are talking.

Another man, a local businessman, is a true football fan. He never discusses his passion for the sport or the sport itself as a subject because he believes in doing business during business hours. But when you hear him speak, it is easy to read that this is an important part of his life outside the office. He uses the language of the sport to communicate about his work. Here are some examples:

His company is the "home team."
When he makes a big sale, he walks into the office smiling and says,
        "Touchdown!"
When he wants to discuss a business matter, he meets in his office for a
        "huddle."
Losing a customer is called a "fumble."
Traveling out-of-state on business is called "going long."

This person's language is, perhaps, an extreme example of metaphor use. It is not hard at all to predict that in his off-hours, he is a season ticket holder for the local professional football team, that he videotapes all televised football games, and that he generously supports the athletic program of the college he attended. Thus, the figurative language that you or people in your relationships use may reveal some consistencies that tell you something about what is important to you or to them.

The language you use in everyday conversation also reveals much about you. You sometimes intentionally choose language in order to create certain impressions about yourself. At other times, people learn things about your goals, priorities, and assumptions by listening to the style of your communication. Even aspects of your self-concept that do not relate to your current situation may be revealed in the language that you use. Figurative language is especially disclosing of these facets of your self-concept.

Naming the Self and Relationships

Another personal use that language serves for you is *naming*. John Lyons discussed naming in detail, and observed that names are used for two purposes.[14] You name people and things so that you can talk about them. This is called the *referential function* of naming. Second, you sometimes name people and things so that they will talk to you. This is called the *vocative function* of naming. The difference between these two functions of naming is your intentions. If your intent is to call attention to someone or something, then you are using the name referentially. If your intent is to get the attention of someone or something, then you are using the name vocatively. Tim used the vocative function in the episode at the beginning of this chapter when he called, "Hey, Cheryl." Examine the names that you use when referring to people in your relationships, as well as those that you use in communicating with those individuals directly. The differences that exist will tell you something about your view of the person and of the relationship.

Figure 6.5 Naming and Perception

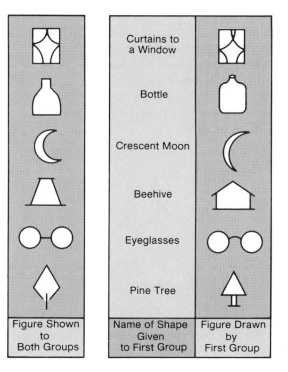

Figure Shown to Both Groups	Name of Shape Given to First Group	Figure Drawn by First Group	Name of Shape Given to Second Group	Figure Drawn by Second Group
	Curtains to a Window		Diamond in a Rectangle	
	Bottle		Stirrup	
	Crescent Moon		Letter "C"	
	Beehive		Hat	
	Eyeglasses		Dumbbells	
	Pine Tree		Trowel	

No matter which way you are using names at a given moment, they affect both your perception of things and others' perception of you. L. Carmichael, H. P. Hogan, and A. A. Walter conducted an experiment about the effect of naming on perception.[15] Two groups of people were shown the same drawing. The two groups were given different names for the figures depicted in the drawing and then were asked to reproduce the drawings. As you can see from the results depicted in figure 6.5, the members of each group "improved" the drawings to make them better resemble their names.

John C. Condon, Jr. observed that people tend to notice those things for which they have names.[16] Thus, they also tend not to see those things for which they have no names. Your relationships exemplify this. You tend to notice, recognize, and acknowledge those people whose names you know more than those whose names you do not know. This is also largely true of certain aspects of your self-concept. You usually act on those qualities for which you have names, and tend to disregard those for which you do not have names.

Experience: "I Am" Statements

You name yourself in terms of both qualities and your group affiliations. In chapter 2, you were asked to identify some of these qualities and to check them against the perceptions of others. Instead of providing the qualities for you, we might have asked you to supply them by filling in the blanks in a group of "I am . . ." statements. Try this now. Complete ten "I am" statements below on a piece of paper with the language of your choice. Do not use the same answer more than once. If you get stuck, think about some of the roles you've taken over the past few days.

I am _____
I am _____
I am _____
I am _____
I am _____
I am _____
I am _____
I am _____
I am _____
I am _____

As discussed before, such statements reveal aspects of your self-concept. In reviewing your list, you might find qualities, behaviors, and group identifications included. For example:
I am *generous.*
I am *a procrastinator.*
I am *a Boy Scout troop leader.*

It is important that you recognize the ways you name yourself. Awareness of these names can help you to know who you are and help you in conveying that knowledge to others. Certainly, naming yourself in this way is limiting, and it is essential to remember that you are in charge of these boundaries. You placed them, but you can remove them at any time if you choose to do so. You also "name" relationships so as to set limits or boundaries on the range of behaviors that are appropriate in them. Sometimes the language used in such definitions are similar to the following:
"We're just good friends."
"I know him casually."
"My one true love."

Remember, the views you have—the images you have—of a relationship constitute one of the components of that relationship. You will recall that images are also included as part of the suggested agenda for talking about the relationship. Your view of the relationship is part of that image. Your view of someone else—your guesses about what may be happening inside of that person, and of how he defines himself—are also part of that image.

Jot down the names of three individuals with whom you share relationships of varying intensity. Next to each, write the language that you use to name that relationship. Which behaviors are appropriate for each of these? What messages can and cannot be exchanged because of your definition of the relationship? How does your image influence your choices and the other individual's choices about the relationship?

Rigidity in Naming

As interpersonal relationships grow, your definitions of them must keep pace. Hayakawa pointed out that this may cause you some problems.[17] The names that you choose for yourself and for a relationship may "harden" or become fixed. You may come to believe that the name you have selected is the "right" one, which carries with it the belief that (1) other definitions must be "wrong," and (2) the self must be protected from experiences that challenge this rigid definition. The results of this problem can seriously affect both your relationships and your own mental health, as Hayakawa explained.

> When the self-concept is thus rigidified, it may remain unchanged for a while. Trouble arises from the fact that the *self* will not stay put. The self slips away from the self-concept; the individual's ideas about himself become less and less real as time goes on. In other words, it may originally have been true that the man was the best salesman in the company, but as time goes on and the facts of life change, it will require more and more self-delusion on his part to maintain his self-concept.[18]

This phenomenon of rigidity may also operate in relationships. One couple remained married for at least five years after the relationship was actually over. Their need to adhere to a definition of the relationship led them to pretend that the relationship was working and to communicate as though things were OK. There might have been a way to salvage things if they had recognized the problem early and, perhaps with professional help, addressed the problem. The relationship met a tragic end because they recognized only one definition for it, and failed to see it in light of other definitions that might have been more useful or appropriate.

Overdiscrimination through Naming

Condon identified another problem that results from naming.[19] He said that once you have names, you fail to see some things. In explaining this idea, Condon presented the example of the night sky. When you look up into the night sky, you see points of light that you call stars. Then you take a course in astronomy and learn to identify the various points of light as galaxies, nebulas, red giants, white dwarfs, and other stellar phenomena. You didn't notice these before because you did not know what to look for. The names help you to discriminate.

Suppose, though, that you had taken the astronomy course before you ever looked up into the night sky. When you looked up for the first time, you automatically saw all the different stellar bodies; you would never see stars. Once you would have names that lead you to discriminate among events, it is difficult to see the similarities among them.

This aspect of naming also functions in the language you use about yourself and your relationships. It is possible to create so many names for yourself that you may begin to lose the overall sense of self that unites the diverse roles you have created. When this happens, you may feel lost and unmotivated, in spite of having many specific goals that relate to the various aspects of the self-concept. You can spread yourself too thin just through naming.

Overdiscrimination among relationships can have negative effects. When you find that you have a different name for each and every relationship, and correspondingly different boundaries for each, you sometimes lose the sense of commonality that exists among them. You fail to treat them as different in terms of abstraction levels because you are too busy keeping them separate from one another in your mind. This can be very confusing. You may feel confused about your priorities and your goals for many of the relationships, which will make it difficult for you to communicate about them; difficult to make them grow.

The solution to this problem of overclassifying your experience is to remain flexible in your thinking and in your communication. It is important to move among levels of abstraction when describing yourself and your relationships. At times it will be appropriate to create messages that depict a very specific, low level of abstraction in talking about yourself and your relationships. At other times, it is useful to identify the common themes that run through your roles and relationships by creating messages about them at a very high level of abstraction. The only way to maintain the necessary flexibility is to practice by listening to yourself and to others and asking questions about the levels of abstraction presented in the messages you hear. You might also experiment by attempting to convey messages at various levels of abstraction, seeking the level that works the best for you and for the other person.

Naming helps you to perceive, but at the same time, hinders your perception. You use language to tell yourself and others who you are, and to set the boundaries within which you are willing to act. Sometimes naming results in overdiscrimination, where you fail to see the whole because you are too busy dealing with all the parts you have named. You can understand, then, the importance of the language you use to describe yourself and your relationships. It reveals much about you. Careful use of language can result in your presenting yourself in appropriate ways at the correct times.

Modes of Expression: Assertive, Nonassertive, and Aggressive

Appropriate self-expression must include a consideration of the way language influences others' perception of your manner and style. The words that you choose, along with your manner of articulating them, may result in you being perceived as *assertive, nonassertive,* or *aggressive.* In the conversation that began this chapter, Mary Ann wanted to work with Cheryl when Tim started to distract them. Mary Ann dealt with Tim's interruption quickly and assertively by telling him "Cheryl and I are working on ideas for the interpersonal paper. If you want to work with us, that's okay. If not, will you let us get back to it, please?" Mary Ann might have responded aggressively, with "Get lost, you jerk!" Or a nonassertive response would be "Gee Tim, we're working, but you're not interrupting anything." Notice that with the aggressive response, Mary Ann will get what she wants, but at the possible expense of Tim's friendship. She commands and rebukes Tim in communicating what she wants. In the nonassertive example, Mary Ann gives up what she wants and places Tim's desire to interrupt ahead of her own desire to work. In this case, she may give in, but resent Tim because of it.

According to Robert Alberti and Michael Emmons, assertive behavior is the desirable mode since nonassertive and aggressive behaviors are normally anxiety-based.[20] Nonassertive language has the following characteristics:

- It generally denies (or ignores) the self.
- It can sound hurt, anxious, or inhibited.
- It allows or encourages others to choose.
- It does not achieve the desired goal.

Note that each of these could result in resentment because the individual has forfeited so much in the relationship.

Aggressive behavior exists at the other end of the spectrum. Aggressive language exhibits the following characteristics:

- It is self-enhancing, but at the expense of another.
- It is expressive, but depreciates others.
- It assumes control of the choices of others.
- It achieves its desired goals, but does so by hurting others.

Assertive expression lies between the extremes of nonassertive and aggressive modes of expression. Usually, the most appropriate language, it is characterized by the following:

- It is self-enhancing.
- It is expressive, but in a positive way.
- It indicates choices made by the self, for the self.
- It may achieve the desired goal.

The following situation provides examples of nonassertive, assertive, and aggressive responses. Study these carefully, then see if you can recall situations in which you have responded similarly.

You are a member of a group working on a class project. Susan, one of the group members, has missed several group meetings. She arrives late for the current meeting and without the library materials she had agreed to bring.

Nonassertive: "Don't worry about it Susan, I'll go to the library on my lunch hour and get the materials."

Assertive: "Susan, would you go to the library now? We have set aside this time to work on our project and must have those materials before we can proceed."

Aggressive: "Susan, you have been lazy and irresponsible throughout our work on this project. If you don't get over to the library right now and bring back those materials in an hour, we're going to kick you out of the group and never speak to you again."

Sharon and Gordon Bower summarized the importance of assertive behavior, stating, "Above all, as an assertive person you can learn to negotiate mutually satisfactory solutions to a variety of interpersonal problems—from dealing with your neighbor whose dog likes to march over your marigolds to adjusting an unsatisfactory relationship with a friend or relative."[21]

There may be times when the nonassertive alternative is seen by you as appropriate, and is so. Alberti and Emmons pointed out that there may be times when, after examining the possible consequences of assertive behavior, you decide that another response mode is more desirable.[22] They wrote: "If an individual *can* act assertively under given conditions, but *chooses* not to, our purpose is accomplished. If he is *unable* to act assertively (i.e., cannot choose for himself how he will behave, but is cowed in nonassertiveness or triggered into aggressiveness), his life will be governed by others and his mental health will suffer."[23]

Generally, you will find the assertive mode of expression the most productive. Using language to assert who you are and what you want will help you to know yourself better, and help you to present yourself to others in a better light.

Problems with Using Language

The individual most responsible for the attention and concern given language in interpersonal relationships is Alfred Korzybski.[24] He said that the degree to which you use language in an appropriate way is a measure of your sanity. Hayakawa summarized Korzybski's definition of "sanity" as follows:

> The sane individual, he said, does not confuse levels of abstraction; he does not treat the map as if it were the territory; he does not copy

animals in their reactions, and therefore is not a *dog*matist, or a *cat*egorist (the pun is Korzybski's not mine); he does not treat as identical all things that have the same name; he does not exhibit a two-valued orientation in which absolute good is pitted against absolute evil; . . .[25]

This definition clearly identifies several areas of language competence that Korzybski and Hayakawa believe are important. Problems with these areas of competence include treating all things with the same name as though they are the same, confusing maps and territories, and the two-valued orientation.

Stereotyping and Self-Fulfilling Prophesy

Wendell Johnson is often quoted as saying, "To a mouse, cheese is cheese, and that's why mousetraps work."[26] You may have heard this same concept applied to people or relationships:

"Women are women."
"Hey, what can I do, business is business."
"You men are all alike."
"What do you expect, he's a (*fill in the ethnic descriptor of your choice*).

The failure to view people and relationships as separate from the classes in which you have placed them can be a major obstacle to effective communication in your relationships. Others are affected when you behave on the basis of stereotyping. You are affected when your failure to see yourself as more than a class results in self-fulfilling prophesies.

Stereotyping is the application of fixed judgments about a class of people to an individual representative of that class. You are probably familiar with this term and are aware of the problems that result from racial and ethnic stereotyping. You may even be aware of the stereotyping of women and the aged, and the societal problems that have resulted.

But think of stereotyping in more personal terms. When you communicate through a frame of reference dominated and colored by a stereotype, you are missing out on the experience of dealing with someone who might affect your life in a positive way. Tim's reference to "heavy people" elicited a response that caused him to leave. Had he not stereotyped Cheryl, he might have been able to help her deal with her problem.

Stereotyping, however, is a useful process in the early stages of relationships. It helps you to infer characteristics about people you meet in order to direct conversation. It becomes a problem, however, when you use the stereotype as sufficient information about a person, create expectations of the person on the basis of that stereotype, and behave toward the person solely on that basis. Therefore it is important to separate the individual from the stereotype as soon as you can. This is accomplished by putting aside the group perceptions that you have of the individual, and seeking to get to know that person as an individual.

Earlier in this chapter, we explained that naming yourself can help to identify you for yourself and for others. We said that naming can result in problems for you when your names for yourself become fixed and unchangeable. A related problem is creating labels for yourself and then attempting to live up to them. When you use language to predict what might happen to you, your prediction may cause it to happen. This act of predicting your own future, and then carrying out your own predictions, is called a *self-fulfilling prophesy*. It is the outcome of forgetting that the language you use to define who you are is under your control. Telling yourself, for example, that you're not good at writing papers, as Cheryl did at the opening of this chapter, may lead you to devote more energy to rationalizing a poor job on the paper than to the actual writing of it. This self-deception can reinforce the label because you frequently do not notice that you devoted more of your time to creating language that explains your failure. You may believe you were spending that time trying to write the paper. Thus, the next time you get a writing assignment, you still have the negative label, and, even more detrimental, have had a recent experience to support that label.

The solution to the self-fulfilling prophesy begins with understanding its nature. A self-fulfilling prophesy can only involve something over which you have some control. If you say, "It will snow on Friday," your prediction may or may not come true, but there is nothing you can do to influence the outcome. In other words, in order for a self-fulfilling prophesy to happen, you have to make it happen.

Once you have realized that you are simply seeing all experiences as having the same negative outcome, you can choose not to participate in this fantasy. This is easy to see but difficult to carry out because you have comfort in the familiarity of failure from the self-fulfilling prophesy. Remember the discussion of the survival orientation in the chapter on self-concept? You have to create language that describes yourself in a new, more successful way, and work to carry out the behaviors outlined in that language. In the case of the paper writing example above, you must say something like, "I know that I did not do well on my last paper assignment, but I'm not going to let that get in the way. I know what I did wrong on that paper and I'm going to be careful when writing this paper to avoid making those same mistakes. I'm going to use my past mistake as a tool for improving myself, not as an excuse for another failure. And if I don't do well this time, it will be because of what I did this time, not because of who I am."

Confusing the Map and the Territory

A second major problem that results from the misuse of language is the confusion of the map and the territory. In such a situation, you forget a very basic rule of language, that the symbol only represents the thing, event, or person. You respond instead to the symbol as if it were the thing itself. The extreme form of this is called *reification*. When you engage in reification, you treat a symbol that has no referent as though it is an object to be manipulated. Ideas like democracy, friendship, and love have many associations, but are not things in and of themselves. When you manipulate the things associated with these ideas, and think that you are changing the ideas, you are only fooling yourself. Sometimes you get very emotionally attached to an object that you associate with a relationship. If something happens to the thing, you may believe that it has actually happened to the relationship.

For example, Mary is an "idea person." Mary gets many ideas about the way to deal with problems and issues that are of concern to her co-workers. She frequently puts her ideas in the form of a written proposal. At this point reification takes over. If anyone suggests a revision to the written proposal, Mary takes it as a rejection of the idea and, sometimes, of herself.

Another aspect of symbolizing that involves the problem of reification is that of *possessing the symbol*. You may believe that by owning something that symbolizes an idea, you become that idea. Phil is a jogger. He believes that owning all the equipment that joggers own makes him a jogger. He has acquired the language and collected the "symbols." This acquisition of language and symbols so as to be identified with an idea is quite common in American society. Some people own shelves of books about how to communicate more effectively, as though owning the books results in better communication. Such concepts as power, love, and sensuality are acquired but not experienced by the possession of such symbols as blue suits, automobiles, and engagement rings. These artifacts do have communicative significance, but you must constantly remind yourself that symbols are *not the things they represent and that possession of the thing is not the same* as possessing the quality for which the thing stands.

Polarization and the Two-Valued Orientation

The term *polarization* describes your tendency to use language that exists in the form of pairs of opposites. You describe your experiences as good or bad, old or new, black or white, and so on. The problem with the overuse of such language in describing experience is that it may create a mind-set in which there are only two options. You limit yourself greatly by thinking in this two-valued way because you fail to see options. Things are either *A* or they are not *A*. For example, if you want to use the family car Saturday night and so does your brother, the two-valued orientation presents the problem in only one light: either you get the car or you do not. This invariably leads to a discussion and possibly a conflict about such indeterminate issues as who *deserves* the car, who *needs* the car more, who used it last, and whether you should keep track of the car's use and take turns.

The two-valued orientation surfaces in polarized language. Problems, relationships, and feelings about the self are considered in extreme terms. The use of this language to define experience results in tunnel vision with respect to your ability to perceive. Your frame of reference is limited to two options, two views. And when you disagree with someone, and you're sure you're right, the two-valued orientation dictates that the other person must then be wrong.

The opposite of the two-valued orientation is called a *multivalued orientation*. This use of language presupposes that it is possible to have win-win relationships. It causes you to look between the extremes for language that will describe your wants, feelings, and experiences. In the situation involving the car, a multivalued orientation might prove useful in generating a creative and satisfying solution to the problem.

Originally, the problem was defined as you want the car and so does your brother. It is first necessary to redefine the problem, making it "our" problem as opposed to "yours" or "mine." It might be restated this way: "We both have somewhere important to go and there is only one car between us. How can we get there?"

Since your relationship means more to you than having the car, you might agree to seek other transportation. On the other hand, if that is impossible, you might offer to hire a limousine for your brother for the evening. This solution would be a pleasant one, adding a nice touch to his evening and at the same time allowing you to get the positive feeling of having done something nice for your brother, and still getting what you want. Can you think of some other solutions to this problem that use multivalued thinking?

Stress has an interesting impact on the problem of orientation. Condon reported that as the stress of a situation increases, the participants in the situation tend more and more toward a two-valued orientation.[27] In the conversation at the beginning of the chapter, you may have seen Cheryl falling into this trap. The stress surrounding her paper assignment mounted to the point that she saw only two options—come up with an idea *right now* or drop out of the class. This unrealistic limiting of options is characteristic of the two-valued orientation. You can see that the result of this forced choice is just more stress, and thus, an even narrower view.

If you think about interpersonal conflicts in which you have been involved, you may find that stress was a factor in them. As the emotions heightened in the conflict, you may have viewed the issue more and more in terms of having or not having the relationship, rather than in terms of whatever stimulated the conflict. This is a particularly unpleasant aspect of the two-valued orientation.

These three kinds of problems, stereotyping and self-fulfilling prophesy; confusing the map and the territory; and polarization and the two-valued orientation, can be quite troublesome because they can result in damage to important relationships. They can, however, be averted if you remain aware of your use of symbols to talk about ideas, remember that there are usually more than two options available to you, and work toward a frame of reference that is multivalued.

Summary

The focus of this chapter is the interrelationships among events, thoughts, and language. I. A. Richards' Triangle of Meaning illustrates the idea that thoughts and language are tied to one another, but that words are not necessarily related to the things they represent. Rather, words are abstractions that exist apart from experience, created to assist in conveying experiences to others.

The bases of your language are found in culture, in society, and in your relationships. Culture shapes the general frame of reference for the language user. Society gives identity to people who belong to particular subgroups and helps self-concept growth by providing language for group identification. Relationships add a special dimension of meaning that involves denotation and connotation, as well as ways for expressing your views about relationships.

Your view of a relationship might be symmetrical, which suggests equality in the relationship. On the other hand, you might view the relationship as structured, having an unequal relation to the other person. This view is a complementary view of relationships. The language that you use in talking to and about the people in your relationships reveals the nature of the view you hold of them.

You also express your view of yourself and of your relationships with naming. You engage in naming through both direct expression and figurative language. Sometimes you don't allow your perceptions of people and things to change as they should because of the rigid names you've assigned them. Another problem associated with naming, called overdiscrimination, occurs when you create so many names and categories in your life that you are unable to see things as a whole.

Three modes of expression are presented in this chapter: assertive, non-assertive, and aggressive. Generally, the assertive mode is the desirable manner of presentation. In this style, you express yourself in a positive, appropriate, and responsible fashion, without hurting others. The aggressive alternative is one in which you may get what you want, but may harm others in the process. The other alternative, nonassertiveness, uses language that denies the self and encourages others to be responsible for your choices.

There are many potential problems with the language you use to express yourself. Some of the major difficulties are stereotyping and the self-fulfilling prophesy, reification and possessing the symbol, and polarization and the two-valued orientation. Stereotyping occurs when you fail to see people as separate from the categories into which you've placed them. This includes the ideas you hold about yourself, which can become fixed and so result in unrealistic expectations of yourself, or even in self-deception. Reification is another form of deception that occurs when you confuse the map provided by language for the territory of experience. You must remind yourself that words are symbols and that possession of the symbol is not the same as possessing the thing. The problem of polarization stems from the human tendency to view things in terms of opposites: good/bad, or black/white. This point of view results in a failure to see many of the options for working through communication problems.

You are encouraged to give careful attention to your language habits. You can improve your ability to create messages that will accomplish your intent. You will be better able to express who you are, how you see others, and the way you view your relationships.

Discussion Questions

1. Using the active listening skills you studied in chapter four, interview a friend or close acquaintance about something of personal importance to that individual. If possible, and if it is acceptable to the other person, tape the interview.

   a. What does the language used to talk about the situation tell you about the way this individual views his or her self-concept?

   b. What does the language tell you about the way this person sees the situation?

   c. Do you find any patterns of language that suggest any consistent image of reality and frame of reference?

2. Secure permission from an old person to tape an interview in which the person recounts experiences from earlier years, then report your conclusions about these questions to the class.

   a. Are there any language patterns that suggest an attitude or opinion about technology? About progress? About politics? About religion?

   b. What image do you believe the older person has of you? What evidence in the language of this person do you find for your conclusions?

   c. Can you identify variations in age, educational level, political affiliation, religious affiliation, or ethnic affiliation in the language people use? How so?

3. Locate an advertisement that includes words. Bring the ad to class. How would you characterize the audience for whom the ad was designed, with regard to the following:

age	religious affiliation
sex	socioeconomic class
ethnic identification	geographical orientation
educational level	hobbies or interests
political affiliation	

   How did you decide?

Endnotes

1. G. A. Miller, *Language and Speech* (San Francisco: W. H. Freeman and Company, 1981).
2. W. P. Lehman, *Language, An Introduction* (New York: Random House, Inc., 1983).
3. H. R. Pollio, *The Psychology of Symbolic Activity* (Reading, MA: Addison-Wesley Publishing Co., Inc., 1974).
4. C. K. Ogden and I. A. Richards, *The Meaning of Meaning,* 3d ed., rev. (New York: Harcourt Brace Jovanovich, Inc., 1959).
5. J. C. Condon, Jr., *Semantics and Communication* (New York: Macmillan, 1975).
6. S. I. Hayakawa, *Language in Thought and Action* (New York: Harcourt Brace Jovanovich, Inc., 1978).
7. J. D. Rothwell, *Telling It Like It Isn't* (Englewood Cliffs, NJ: Prentice-Hall, Inc., 1982).
8. J. S. Bruner, J. J. Goodnow, and G. A. Austin, *A Study of Thinking* (New York: John Wiley and Sons, 1956).
9. G. P. Murdock, *Social Structure* (New York: Macmillan, Inc., 1949).
10. Lehmann, *Language,* 213.
11. L. Morrow, "If Slang Is Not a Sin," *Time* 120, no. 19 (November 8, 1982): 91.
12. D. R. Smith and L. K. Williamson, *Interpersonal Communication* (Dubuque, IA: Wm. C. Brown Publishers, 1977).
13. A. A. Athos and J. J. Gabarro, *Interpersonal Behavior* (Englewood Cliffs, NJ: Prentice-Hall, Inc., 1978).
14. J. Lyons, *Semantics,* vol. 1 (Cambridge, UK: Cambridge University Press, 1977).
15. L. Carmichael, H. P. Hogan, and A. A. Walter, "An Experimental Study of the Effect of Language on the Reproduction of Visually Perceived Form," *Journal of Experimental Psychology* 15 (1932): 73–86.
16. Condon, *Semantics,* 36.
17. S. I. Hayakawa, *Symbol, Status, and Personality* (New York: Harcourt, Brace and World, Inc., 1963).
18. Ibid., 41.
19. Condon, *Semantics,* 36.
20. R. E. Alberti and M. L. Emmons, *Your Perfect Right, A Guide to Assertive Behavior* (San Luis Obispo, CA: Impact Publishers, 1974).
21. S. A. Bowers and G. H. Bowers, *Asserting Yourself: A Practical Guide for Positive Change* (Reading, MA: Addison-Wesley Publishing Co., Inc., 1976).
22. Alberti and Emmons, *Your Perfect Right,* 11.
23. Ibid., 47–48.

24. A. Korzybski, *Science and Sanity: An Introduction to Non-Aristotelian Systems and General Semantics* (Lancaster, PA: Science Press Printing Co., 1933).
25. Hayakawa, *Symbol, Status, and Personality,* 9.
26. W. Johnson, *People in Quandaries* (New York: Harper and Row Publishers, Inc., 1946).
27. Condon, *Semantics,* 59.

Nonverbal Expression

Preview

Most Americans are not generally skillful in talking about their relationships. Instead, they send most of their messages about relationships through nonverbal means. Gestures, postures, facial expressions, time, artifacts—all of the nonverbal codes—bear directly on the success in relating to others. This chapter explores those message codes.

Objectives

After reading this chapter you should be able to complete the following:
1. Identify and explain four broad categories of nonverbal message codes.
2. Specify, within each broad category, the choices people can make in order to send signals to one another.
3. Explain the fundamental differences between verbal and nonverbal messages, and explain how those differences influence interpersonal communication.
4. Identify and analyze relevant nonverbal messages in your own interpersonal exchanges.
5. Specify how heightened awareness of each of the four broad categories of nonverbal messages can be helpful in interpersonal communication.

7

Perhaps you'll remember that Mary and Russ had met each other, had come to enjoy each other's company, and had become quite close before their relationship suddenly seemed to come apart at the seams. They had become close because they had a great deal in common, but despite these common interests, and for some unexplained reason, their time together eventually became less satisfying. In the first chapter we speculated that, had they had a system for talking about their relationships, they might have been able to sustain the good aspects of their partnership. Remember that we presented an agenda for talking about relationships that might have helped Russ and Mary—and you. Let's review that agenda once again.

Relationships exist in the present, inside you. They exist in the observations you make and the inferences you draw about those observations. They exist, primarily, in your feelings; your wants and expectations; your intentions; the latitude of acceptance you have for others and for their ideas; and in the many images you generate, maintain, and exchange. As a last part of that agenda, we emphasized the importance of checking out the accuracy of your guesses.

Though you know about this agenda, you are often unsuccessful in talking about your relationships. That is because in the American culture, you learn to delegate your relationship messages to certain nonverbal codes. You smile, wink, glance, and touch. You wear perfume and cologne, carefully selected clothes, and attractive (you hope) hairstyles. You use space and time, the artifacts of dress and habit, and an enormously complex combination of these nonverbal signals to communicate about your relationships.

Fortunately, there is a large and growing body of literature written by people who specialize in researching nonverbal communication. But the literature isn't very clear about what the messages from different cues mean when they're taken together. A complex classification of nonverbal message codes can be examined in isolation, but the elements of that classification all work as parts of a nonverbal message system. So, once again, we offer this caution: You cannot know what your observations mean unless you check out your guesses about them. You cannot know how others are interpreting your nonverbal cues, either, unless you and the others talk about them. So you need to check things out, and you need to help other people to check them out, too.

Nonverbal message codes can be divided into four broad categories: general body cues, particular body cues, environmental cues, and paraverbal cues (fig. 7.1).

Understanding these categories, however, guides you only part way down the path toward better communication about relationships. Still unresolved is the use of the nonverbal message system as a means of communicating about yourself and your relationships. It is still useful, though, to examine some of what is known about nonverbal messages. Applications for each category of nonverbal message are also suggested.

Figure 7.1 The Categories of Nonverbal Messages

1. General Body Cues
   A. Clothes and Artifacts
   B. Body Movements and Gestures
2. Particular Body Cues
   A. Face and Eye Behavior
   B. Touching Behavior
   C. Taste and Smell
3. Environmental Cues
   A. Space
   B. Personal Distancing
   C. Time
4. Paraverbal Cues
   A. Voice Quality
   B. Speech Characteristics
   C. Interpretation

General Body Cues

There is a large number of *general body cues* that individuals can use to send signals to one another. Four of these are especially important. These are clothing choices, artifact choices, bodily movements (the way of walking, for example), and habitual and cultural modes of gesture. You may not make your choices at the conscious level although you *can* choose to send nonverbal messages if you wish to do so. Moreover, you often send messages that are unintentionally received. Loretta Malandro and Larry Barker created a grid to describe the nonverbal communication possibilities of clothes and artifacts (fig. 7.2).[1]

Clothing

The clothing you wear says something about you. For example, you do not hesitate to "dress up" when the occasion calls for dressing up. You have a clear sense of those occasions for which dressing up is appropriate. Likewise, you do not hesitate to "dress down" under circumstances that call for it. And, if you are like most people, you have also not known for sure just what to wear for an occasion. Should you dress up? How much? Should you dress down? How much?

These questions and concerns suggest that you are aware of the messages that are sent by the clothes you wear. Figure 7.3 says a lot about the people in it. Look at the photo very carefully and consider the dress. Does the dress suggest anything about the relationships of the people? Can you infer

Figure 7.2 Communication Possibilities of Intentional and Unintentional Messages

	Intentionally Sent	Unintentionally Sent
Intentionally Received	1	2
Unintentionally Received	3	4

Figure 7.3

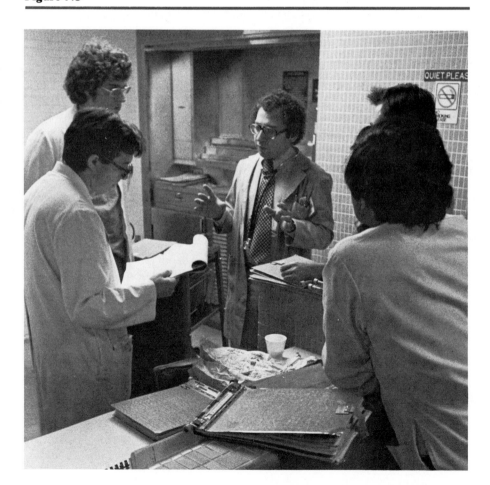

anything about the socioeconomic level of the individuals in the photo? Can you discover anything about the educational levels of the individuals? What, specifically, are you looking at that tells you these things?

If you could not see the faces, would you be able to tell anything about the ages of the people in the picture? Could you infer anything about the sex of the individuals in the photo? What signals are you picking up on?

You might find it interesting that nearly all of the research on the relationship between what people wear and the people themselves has focused upon personality and such characteristics as age, sex, socioeconomic status, and educational level. These demographic variables constitute stereotypes of people, and you probably are fairly sensitive to them.

Some of this research is over twenty years old. For example, M. L. Rosencranz conducted a fairly intensive study about clothes-conscious people in 1962.[2] He found that there was a relationship between married women who were clothes-conscious and where they stood socially: they were usually in the upper social classes; they were usually joiners—that is, they belonged to many organizations; and they usually were rather well-educated and more comfortable in intellectual conversations than were married women who didn't care much about clothes. Clothes-conscious women tended to have fairly high incomes and to be married to white-collar workers.

None of this is surprising, of course. Common experience tells you that dress is a first-class indicator of status. But if you look at the phenomenon from a somewhat different perspective, as Aiken did in 1963, you discover some interesting additional information.[3] Aiken wanted to know what kind of woman had an interest in clothing. He found that clothes-conscious women tended to be a bit insecure, quite conscientious, and stereotypical in their ways of thinking. Such women were also persistent and conventional, given to compliance in the face of authority, and rather tense and "uptight."

When Aiken asked, What kind of women are interested in and concerned about economy in relation to clothing? he found that such women were responsible, alert, efficient, precise, intelligent, conscientious, and controlled. Such women would probably spend time shopping for bargains, purchase quality clothing, and be concerned about the clothing budget. Aiken inferred that such care about clothing, reflected in what a woman wears, speaks about the personality of the woman herself.

Aiken had a third question to ask: What is a woman like who prefers elaborately detailed clothing and lots of jewelry—much more than normal? He found that women in this third category were not intellectual, and were rather conventional and stereotyped. They were also sympathetic, sociable, and conscientious. Moreover, they tended to be somewhat submissive.

On the other hand, women who conformed to popular norms of dress were found to be socially-conscientious and traditional. They were moral women, quite sociable, and they, too, were submissive. They tended to focus upon economic values, social and religious values, but not so much upon the more aesthetic values of the culture.

Finally, Aiken wanted to know what kind of women dressed primarily for comfort. You won't be surprised to know that such women were self-possessed and self-controlled, that they were socially-cooperative, and that they were very sociable. You might be surprised to learn, however, that they were considered to be thorough and deferential to authority.

In a later study, Rosenfeld discovered that clothes-conscious men were guarded, they deferred to authority, and believed that people were easy to manipulate.[4] On the other hand, men who were not very clothes-conscious were fairly independent and aggressive. They did not think people were easy to manipulate. Interestingly, men who were more interested in clothing for such practical reasons as warmth, rather than for aesthetic reasons, were somewhat inhibited and rebellious. Women in this category were clever and confident. Conversely, men who were interested in the aesthetics of dress were generally more success-oriented. They were seen as mature. Women in this category, however, were self-centered and detached.

Clearly, then, on the basis of common sense and these two examples, it can be concluded that the clothing choices you make communicate a great deal about you. Clothes can, and do, tell about your place of work (formal and informal dress codes), influence the social impression you make, tell people if you are likable or sexy, and say something about your age and social status. If clothes don't make the person, they certainly tell a lot about him.

For example, one man dressed in a fairly careful and conservative manner, sometimes wearing a tie and coat, but usually wearing a suit. His clothing was color-coordinated, and he made sure that his apparel was appropriate to his status as a professor who frequently met with business, industrial, and local government leaders. The man's dress, however, underwent a slow but steady change after he purchased a sailboat and became involved in the sailing subculture around Mobile Bay. His wing-tip shoes became topsiders. His suits were replaced by slacks and blazer. His ties, instead of diagonally striped, began to suggest nautical themes. Consciously or accidentally, the man's changing lifestyle was reflected in his clothes.

Artifacts

Look at figure 7.4, another picture of people. This time, though, don't concentrate on their clothing (although, that, too is sending messages), but look at the *artifacts* in the picture. Artifacts are the things people "collect" around themselves. What do the individuals do for a living? Where were they at the moment that the photo was taken? Do the artifacts tell you anything about the nature of their relationship? What, in particular, would you identify in this regard? Can you find any "markers"? Markers are artifacts that suggest that one of the individuals is claiming a territory. Who? What territory? How do you know?

Figure 7.4

Look more closely. Are there any artifacts that suggest relative wealth? What? Are there any artifacts that suggest the personality of the individuals? Any evidence of private life in the photo? Family? Hobbies? What do you know about the individual whose space this is? How do you know it?

Such personal artifacts as glasses, jewelry, and makeup, and such environmental and property artifacts as art objects, books, and desk tools, provide a good deal of information to a perceptive observer. Interestingly, the early studies in nonverbal message exchange that focused on these particular artifacts could not explicitly determine the communication! For example, near the end of World War II, people with glasses were perceived as more intelligent, more industrious, and more honest than those who did not wear them.[5] By 1968, women who wore glasses were seen as religious, conventional, and unimaginative.[6]

Similarly, it has been known for thirty years that whether or not a woman wears lipstick can have an important bearing on how she is perceived. A 1952 study examined the effects of lipstick on the perceptions men had of women.[7] In that study, a small group of men perceived women as more frivolous and more interested in males if they wore lipstick. Interestingly, the men were not able to identify the basis upon which they made their judgments!

The results of this thirty-year-old study are probably not surprising. Casual observation on any college campus suggests that women believe their facial appearance, including the decision to wear lipstick, can have an impact on how they are perceived. Moreover, advertisements in women's magazines throughout the past three decades reveal that lipstick and other makeup merchandisers have very consistently played to that perception.

Such artifacts as cigars, smoking pipes, cigarettes, briefcases and purses, books, and tools, all contribute to the impression people make as they move through their daily lives.

Experience: What Messages Are You Sending?

Check, right now, on the messages you are sending about yourself. First, notice the clothing you are wearing. Does the formality or informality of the clothing tell anything about you? Could an observer tell if you are male or female? Could an observer be able to infer, from your clothing or your artifacts, that you are a student? Could the observer tell anything about your age? About your socioeconomic level? Could your clothing or artifacts suggest anything about the nature of your relationships? Could an observer tell if you are attached or not? Could an observer tell if you are concerned about the time? Could an observer infer anything about your personal habits of grooming? Could an observer discover such personality traits as whether or not you are tidy and careful about your appearance and place? Could an observer make any discovery about your hobbies, attitudes, political preferences, or religious affiliation or orientation? How about your family status? Is there anything about dress and artifact that suggests geography? Would an observer be able to infer anything about what you read, or if you read at all? Would the observer be able to infer anything about your educational level and habits of reading? Do you write much? Looking at you in your present location, could an individual tell anything about your preferences when it comes to other people making contact with you? Are you a territorial person? Would an observer be able to infer this from anything about the clothing or artifacts you display? Are your strengths of character implied by your clothing and artifacts at this moment?

To put this self-examination into the context of the system for talking about relationships, could an observer infer anything from your clothing or artifacts about what you feel? How about what you felt when you got dressed? Could the observer tell anything about your wants, hopes, and dreams? About your expectations regarding other people? About your intentions? About your openness—your latitude of acceptance? About the image you have of yourself? About the image you have of some generalized other individual? You might discuss these questions with your classmates and your friends.

We think this self-analysis experience will assure you that your clothes and artifacts suggest something about you. Do they say what you would like them to say, and do you believe that you have choices about those messages? We think you do.

Body Movement and Gestures

Body movement and gesture—gross body movement and gesture, not the subtleties of facial expression—can have an enormous communicative impact, whether you intend them to or not. Of course, common sense makes this statement obvious, since our language is full of references to the communicative potential of gross body movement and gesture, as is obvious in the following statements:

You really look down.
Mary Ann is really wound up tight today.
He's so troubled that he looks like he's carrying the weight of his entire
    company on his back.
Perk up, Phil.

Have you thought about the messages you send out about yourself, just by the way you walk? Suppose, for instance, that you are in the city—perhaps Chicago, Los Angeles, New York, or Atlanta. You are walking alone down the street. After about six seconds of observation, a mugger could determine whether or not you would be an easy mark! Could you make the same determination?

In a study based on this question, Rubenstein videotaped sixty people walking alone in the late morning hours, then asked a panel of convicts to rate whether the individuals would be easy to mug.[8] The convicts were asked to rate each subject on a scale of one to ten: one meant "a very easy rip off," and ten meant "would avoid it, too big a situation, too heavy." Each videotaped sequence lasted from six to eight seconds. The expert judges had no difficulty in agreeing about which of the pedestrians would be easy marks! Their movements were awkward. They walked about as though in a daze. They seemed oblivious to what was going on around them. They appeared to be in conflict with themselves. On the other hand, pedestrians who were seen as "too heavy" walked in evenly paced, determined steps that rocked from heel to toe. They appeared goal-directed, determined, and confident about where they were going.

The study of body movement and gesture as communication is a relatively new discipline. Among the first individuals investigating the body's communication independent of voice was Ray Birdwhistle, whose most important work appeared in 1970. And, of course, you have heard about or read such books as *Body Language,* by Julius Fast. This book, a popularization of some of the research conducted in the early 1970s, was copyrighted in 1977.

Even though this is a relatively new area of study, a surprising amount of data has been collected. Nonverbal messages are quite different from verbal ones. For instance, there does not appear to be a nonverbal alphabet composed of discrete units. In contrast, English includes an alphabet having twenty-six letters, and a much more subtle set of base units, called *allophones,* which when combined, make words.

There is no system of rules in body communication. This is why, in part, body movement cannot be as readily understood as an English sentence. Even so, there is no doubt that people do take body movements into account and draw conclusions and inferences from them.[9] So it is worthwhile to study the communication potential of gross bodily movement.

Ekman and Friesen categorized gross bodily movements into *emblems, illustrators, regulators, affect displays,* and *adaptors.*[10] The definition and an illustration of each of these terms is shown in figure 7.5.

It is easy to see that a good deal of communicating is accomplished by gross body movements and gestures. If you are interested in pursuing the importance of these general bodily cues, we recommend that you do your own "field research." Begin to think about the gestures that are normally taken for granted. Try to imagine the last conversation in which you were involved that dealt with some strong emotion or controversial topic. Can you remember any gestures from the five categories?

Figure 7.5 Categories of Gross Body Movement

Term	Definition	Examples
Emblem	Deliberate movements that can be translated directly into words; discrete, categorical behaviors that are generally known and accepted.	
Illustrator	Deliberate movements used to reinforce and enrich verbal message.	
Regulator	Body movements that help us to interact; a gesture system that controls "taking turns" in the flow of communication.	
Affect Display	Any movement or gesture that reflects the intensity of our feelings.	
Adaptor	Any movement or gesture that is displayed as a means of alleviating psychological tension.	

Figure 7.6 Record of Movements and Gestures

Emblem: Deliberate movements that can be translated into words; discrete, categorical behaviors generally known and accepted.	*Your Notes*
Illustrator: Deliberate movements used to reinforce and enrich verbal messages.	
Regulator: Body movements that help us to interact; gesture system that controls "turn taking".	
Affect Display: Any movement or gesture that reflects the intensity of our feelings.	
Adaptor: Any movement or gesture that is displayed as a means of alleviating psychological tension.	

Experience: **Identifying Movements and Gestures**

After you have a pretty clear idea of the behaviors in each category, try carrying your textbook to a popular place on or near the campus. A local student hangout would be ideal, but so would a library or a popular patch of lawn. Be sure the place will allow you to sit with your book open on your lap or in front of you without being obvious. Then observe the behavior you see flowing around you, and make a record for a fixed period of time. You can use figure 7.6 to help you.

Posture

Even more subtle, perhaps, than gestures, *body posture* communicates an enormous amount of information about you. Even so, except for a few moments when you are conscious of posture, you don't think very carefully about how you stand or sit or slump or slouch around. But you send off a good many messages with posture, nevertheless.

Researchers have been able to develop an interesting and simple categorization for observing and recording bodily posture. There are basically only three categories of body posture: standing, bent-knee, and lying.[11] These postures occur along a continuum with *gesture* at one end, and *spatial behavior* at the other. Thus it is possible to observe posture as an extension of gesture. Likewise, it is possible to judge if a person's posture cues involve increasing or decreasing distance. This categorization is simple, yet very powerful, for as many as a thousand possibilities can be recorded using it.

Posture communicates information about your attitudes, status, and self-image. It communicates your sex, and whether or not you "conform" to the stereotypical gender cues of the American culture. Along with how you move from one place to another, posture communicates your personal and interpersonal style and image. And finally, posture communicates the emotions you're feeling. Because posture cues are very important communication cues, it is surprising that people appear to be so unconcerned about the bodily posture messages they send.

Imagine, if you can, that you are sitting on the beach in late afternoon. It is autumn, so there is a crispness in the air, and not many people on the beach are wearing swimsuits. Instead, the costume of the day is blue jeans and t-shirt, a sweater or light jacket, and bare feet. Some blue jeans are rolled up slightly so the walkers can wade in the water along the shoreline. As these people walk in front of you, they cast no shadow so that, for a moment, they are silhouetted against the sun path on the water.

What can you tell about the other individuals on the beach? Can you tell if they are male or female? Can you determine their approximate ages? Can you tell if they are attached somehow? Are they intimate? Can you tell if they have known each other for quite a while, or if their relationship is relatively new? Is one dominant; the other submissive? Is one person "showing off" for another? Can you tell how anyone is feeling? And perhaps more importantly, *how* can you tell these things? For if it is true that you can draw inferences about these questions just from the data available in the silhouettes of people who are paying no attention to you, it is reasonable to suppose that other people can draw such inferences about you from the way you present your body, too.[12]

Imagine again the people on the beach. Suppose that one woman leans forward toward a man. She allows herself to brush against him as she smiles into his face. He turns to face her, feet about eighteen inches apart, and smiles. He touches her eyebrow with his index finger and traces the line of her nose down to her mouth. She nibbles, then kisses, his finger. They clasp hands and amble down the beach, bumping and brushing into each other as they go. Shortly they stop and face each other again, now holding both hands.

These postural and touching cues suggest that these two individuals are nurturing a relationship. They apparently are attracted to each other. Each welcomes the other's proximity and touching behavior. To each other and to you, they have communicated an enormous amount of information. You and they could interpret the behaviors because each of you understands the norms of such behavior in the American culture. Such behavior is called *immediacy behavior,* one of two categories of behavior by which postural and other gross body cues can communicate attitudes, style, status, and emotions. The other category is *relaxation.*[13] Relaxation has to do with the degree, or extent, to which you are agitated or excited.

If you lean toward someone, smile, reach out, and open yourself to that person, you are expressing immediacy. If you lean away, pull back, withdraw

What Do You Think Their Attitudes Are toward Each Other?

from touch, and never touch; if you frown, glance away, avoid eye contact, and keep your distance, you are also expressing a dimension of immediacy. Thus, immediacy behavior exists along a continuum, in context with degrees of relaxation. Don't be confused; the terms are not opposites. Immediacy exists in degrees. Nonverbal behavior that decreases or increases the closeness between you and another, or that inhibits or improves visibility between you and another, are important relationship communication behaviors.

You observe these behaviors and base your guesses about the components of your relationships upon them. Unfortunately, you rarely talk about them. Instead, you believe that you "know" what they "mean." So you tend to fall into the dangerous habit of pretending that you can read others' minds by looking at others' behavior.

Particular Body Cues

Face and Eye Behavior

Just as gross body control and movement can communicate, so can *particular body cues,* such as facial expressions and eye movements. Indeed, the face and eyes are probably the most powerful generators of nonverbal messages.

So powerful are they that for centuries, they have been the subject of poetry and song, and the cause of very dramatic interpersonal and international episodes.

Perhaps you can hear Dr. Faustus (act 5, scene 7) as he says to the devil, who has taken the form of Helen of Troy:

Was this the face that launched a thousand ships
And burnt the topless towers of Ilium?
Sweet Helen, make me immortal with a kiss.

Or, imagine Cicero exclaim "The face is the image of the soul; and the eyes are its interpreter."

Recall John Lennon and Paul McCartney singing "Eleanor Rigby, wearing the face that she keeps in a jar by the door. Who is it for?"

Can you hear someone singing Burt Bacharach's "The look of love is in your eyes"?

Did you ever play the child's game of "Stare Down"? One individual captures and maintains eye contact with another, unsuspecting individual. The winner of the game is the one who is able to stare into this other person's eyes, without breaking contact and without blinking, for the longest period of time. The game is interesting because it always occurs in some public place such as a shopping mall or the school cafeteria. Since such behavior is a violation of social norms, the matches never last very long. And the game is always played by members of the same social group who know the rules of the game.

You can imagine how your actions would be received if you caught someone's glance in an attempt to play the game and he or she didn't know what you were doing! How long would the other individual be able to gaze into your face under those circumstances?

Perhaps you or someone you know uses makeup in order to improve facial appearance. Have you ever wondered why so many people spend so much money on powder, blush, lipstick, and eye shadow? Perhaps it is because the wearers do not think that their faces communicate what they want them to communicate! And why would so many men and women undergo plastic, cosmetic surgery or have hair transplanted? Again, they probably do this (at considerable cost in dollars and discomfort) because they want their faces to communicate something that they do not now communicate.

You draw inferences about many important things from faces. From the most obvious, the recognition of each other, to sex, race, age, and nationality, your face communicates messages. Most especially, you use your face to signal the kind and range of your emotional experiences. Your gross body movements tell the intensity of these emotions.

But, as we have said so often, learning to read the signals is far more difficult and complex than it at first appears. In effect, when you observe a facial expression, you relate what you are observing to your prior experiences with such expressions, and what you remember to have been the causes of them.

Can You Tell What This Person Is Feeling? How?

Thus, if someone looks at your face—or at the one in the following picture—and guesses about the emotional experience you are having, or the individual in the photo is having, he or she is presuming to read your mind. The fact is, that can't be done very well. For even though facial expressions of emotion are generally accepted as universal, there are some culture-specific variations in their causes and in the combinations of expressions people use and accept in certain contexts.

Because you cannot read another's mind, and because it is difficult to determine what your facial expressions mean, if you want to understand that person beyond a doubt, you need to check out the accuracy of your guesses. Put another way, you need to bring your guess about the individual's emotional state to the level of talk so that an incorrect guess can be corrected.

If your professor marks your paper lower than you would have marked it, and you feel some anger about it, we suspect that you, like many students, will try to minimize your facial expression of anger while you talk to the professor. To do otherwise would be contrary to a lifetime of training at home and in school.

As in this situation, you sometimes manage your facial expressions to *neutralize or mask* your emotions. You neutralize a facial expression of emotion when you try to eliminate it altogether. Perhaps you have heard of someone displaying a "poker face." This expression refers to the generally accepted wisdom that, if you are playing cards with an opponent who is a good observer, you should maintain rigid control of the facial and eye muscles to avoid telegraphing your hand.

Similarly, in the American culture, growing up male means, among other things, that it is not okay to express your strongest emotions—especially sentimental ones—with your face and eyes. Because of this, many young men have been embarrassed because they were moved to tears by a scene in a movie. The embarrassment undoubtedly arises from a conflict between experiencing an emotion and displaying that emotion. Men are not supposed to display visual expressions of fear and sadness except under extreme circumstances because these are considered feminine, not masculine, emotions.

Neutralizing emotions can be very risky and dangerous. Your entire nervous system could be damaged if you train yourself not to accept and express such emotions as fear and sadness.

Emotions are masked when you attempt to present a facial expression that is different from your experience. Thus, you often try to conceal strong or socially unacceptable feelings. For example, even though you may be feeling enraged, you will surely try to mask that emotion in public since it is unacceptable in most companies to "make a scene." And an employee would surely be unwilling to display disapproval of the boss' decision in public, although a conference might be held in private. Wouldn't you do the same?

Controlling Face and Eye Behavior

Interestingly, the range of emotions your eyes and face are capable of expressing is very great, but your ability to control and manage such expressions is limited. When you are being fluent—when you are thinking about your ideas or emotions, but not your facial muscles—your facial expressions are not under conscious control. When you are trying to manage the impressions you're making, you tend to use one of a very limited number of techniques for controlling facial and eye behavior.[14]

Sometimes you manage your facial expressions *to intensify or minimize* the emotion you are experiencing. Can you remember attending a surprise party, perhaps one thrown in your honor? Was the guest of honor really surprised? Or was the guest of honor intensifying the emotion? How do you know? *Intensifying,* in this sense, is nothing more than doing what is expected for the purpose of pleasing friends and maintaining relationships with them. If a friend gives you a present, you will register your pleasure with a facial expression. If she tries to surprise you, and you like her, you will register surprise with a facial expression (or, at least, you will try to do so), whether or not you are truly surprised. If a friend is experiencing sorrow, you will register your empathy in a facial expression because you care about him and about your relationship with him. If you show someone who you are emotionally, and it seems appropriate or necessary in that context that he reinforce your emotion, he will do so by intensifying.

But, of course, there are times when a facial expression of emotion is unwarranted and unacceptable. Under those circumstances, you will try to minimize your facial expression of that emotion. Everyone does this. For example, you may have viewed the final round of the Women's Singles at Wimbledon. If so, you might have noticed that the winner made an attempt to control her natural show of excitement in order to "save the face" of the loser.

But while as a general rule people are pretty good at displaying and communicating with bodily and facial behavior, they're not nearly as good at reading it. Moreover, they usually don't have these potent message systems under conscious control. So at least two kinds of problems can evolve. One is drawing inferences about other people that aren't correct. The other is sending off messages you don't want to send. In either case, where such errors begin to place your relationships at risk, you need a system for bringing your observations and guesses, your nonverbal messages, up to the level of talk.

Touching Behavior

There is little doubt that everyone needs and wants physical contact with others. If someone is deprived of this physical contact with others, this deprivation can be damaging. And it is equally clear that as you mature, much of what you know about conducting your affairs and managing your relationships is a function of the touching behavior you have experienced. Each of these statements has been developed and supported by research findings. But what does this mean to you, as a student of interpersonal communication?

The point is, touching behavior is completely a matter of choice. You can choose to touch or to withhold touch. You can choose to respond positively when touched, or to withdraw from the touching. And when you choose your touching behaviors, you are choosing to have a very powerful effect, both upon yourself and the other individual, and upon the nature of your relationship with that other person. So powerful a message as touching cannot be left to chance. Touching communicates your attitudes, your developmental needs, your body contact needs, your status, and your relationships. Touching also bears upon your health and growth.

Richard Heslin and his colleagues have been studying touching behavior for ten years, and have developed a category system that is a convenient way to organize the discussion of touching behavior (fig. 7.7).[15] (The display is Heslin's; he did not provide the definitions and examples presented in this figure.)

Figure 7.7 Heslin's Categories for Touching Behavior

Category	Definition	Example
Functional/Professional	Touch for the purpose of delivering some professional service	Example relationships: physician/patient; barber/ client; swimming instructor/ student; make-up artist/actor
Social/Polite	Ritual touching for the purpose of acknowledging someone's personhood or essential humanity, and/or for the purpose of acknowledging or neutralizing status differences	Examples: handshake; the kiss on the hand; the kiss on a Cardinal's ring; ritual greeting hugs
Friendship/Warmth	Casual and spontaneous touching that signals mutual acceptance and positive regard, but excluding love or sexual touching	Examples: asexual greeting hugs or kisses among friends or family; congratulatory shoulder- or back-patting; mock-violent behavior such as the playful shoulder punch
Love/Intimacy	Touching behavior that signals a special, or bonded, relationship, or that assumes or confirms intimate access to be appropriate to that relationship	Examples: hand holding, whether the couple are stationary or moving; mutual hand-on-hip postures; lap-sitting
Sexual Arousal	Touching that is pleasant because of the sexual meaning it conveys or because of the sexual stimulation it produces	Examples: prolonged kissing; petting; sexual foreplay; sexual intercourse

While this system is convenient, you cannot very comfortably use it to identify distinct sets of behaviors because communication events always occur within some context. It is the individual communicator's understanding of the context and the relationship within that context that govern the judgment about the appropriateness or inappropriateness of a touch. Moreover, touching behavior can rarely be isolated in just one category. Human relationships are more complex than this. Thus, two simple, but very powerful conclusions can be drawn:

1. Touching behavior suggests a bond between the people who do the touching and the people who are touched.

2. People respond to touching behavior according to their estimate of its appropriateness within that relationship and within that context.

Based upon these conclusions, it is reasonable to point out, once again, that a person who is concerned about improving his or her interpersonal communication must become sensitive to human touching behavior and to the cues that people send about their estimates of touching appropriateness. You will know that something is wrong if you feel some discomfort in response to touching. Similarly, you will know that nothing is wrong if you feel no discomfort in response to touching. But you will have to *infer* how the other person is experiencing your touch unless you are willing and able to *talk* about that experience when it seems appropriate to do so.

Touch only suggests a relationship—a bond—between the toucher and the touched. It does not explicitly tell you what only the other person can about his or her feelings, wants and expectations, intentions, latitude of acceptance, and the images he or she has of you, of himself or herself, and of the context. If you want to know these things, and if you want the other person to know these things about you, then you must bring them up to the level of talk.

Environmental Cues

Can you imagine yourself in the environment pictured in figure 7.8? You could probably draw many inferences about the people who occupy this space—about their personalities, about their relative socioeconomic status, and about their personalities and style of life—just by viewing this photo. You can also get a good sense of your own ability to be comfortable in such an environment from the *environmental cues.* Light and color, sound control, the physical layout and decor of the place, and its sheer dimension will all make a difference to you. Where would you be most likely to sit if you were a visitor in this space? Where would you be likely to sit if you were in the room all by yourself for a fairly long time? Would these seating decisions change if you owned this space? Would you rearrange the furniture in this room if it were yours? What image do you have of the status, warmth, stability, and privacy of the individuals who own this space? Are they friendly? Personable? Formal or casual in style? Do they have social clout?

How about the environment shown in figure 7.9? Would you find yourself comfortable in these rooms? Do you find the textures and the layout of space appealing? What about the light and shadow—do they contribute to the way you feel about this space? What can you infer about the people who own this space?

The utilization and arrangement of space, and the treatments you give to that space, communicate a great deal about you. Indeed, there is a large

Figure 7.8

Figure 7.9

and growing body of research collected from a broad variety of academic disciplines that focuses upon the impact of environmental factors upon the human condition and upon the transformation of spaces into reflections of the self.

You judge that a space is somewhere along a continuum from attractive to ugly. That judgment tends to generalize to all your related experiences. So, for example, if someone were put into a truly ugly room, the individual would be more likely to make negative judgments about the individuals whose photographs he viewed while in the room than he would if the experiment were conducted in a beautiful room.[16] Similarly, color and texture, lighting and decorative effects can all make an important difference on the people who occupy space, and upon the perceptions those people have of each other.

For example, colors are often termed "warm" or "cool" and are very carefully used to suggest such things as affection, vitality, calm, cheerfulness, sadness, or anxiety. Beyond this hesitation, you pick up on the moods that colors generate. Thus, if you paint your work rooms with bright red and yellow hues, before long you would find that your mood improved, but later became somewhat disturbed. You would likely be more productive and energetic in such a room than in one having walls painted in deep shades of blue and violet, a black floor and ceiling, and black velvet tapestry hangings.

Now look again at the Bernhardt room (fig. 7.8). Notice how the designers of that room have contrasted light and dark. The room seems pleasant, calm, and relaxing. It is dignified but welcoming. What feeling do you get from the Villeroy and Boch room (fig. 7.9)?

Experience: **Study on Environment**

Now study a room of your own. Use the form shown in figure 7.10 to help you examine the messages your own private space "give off" to those who enter it.

Space

People use space in a direct way. For example, there is some evidence that human beings are territorial creatures, and that the person-to-space ratio, or *density,* has an important bearing on interpersonal perception and communication. In addition, there appears to be a fairly well-tuned set of cultural norms about the appropriate interpersonal distance that guides individuals in interactions with others. Even the angle of interaction appears to be related to the quality and amount of interaction. Obviously, then, the dimensions of space can operate as communication.

Figure 7.10 Examining Your Space

	Messages	What Evidence Are You Observing?
Status:	_____	_____
	_____	_____
Warmth:	_____	_____
	_____	_____
Distance:	_____	_____
	_____	_____
Privacy:	_____	_____
	_____	_____
Intimacy:	_____	_____
	_____	_____
Constraint:	_____	_____
	_____	_____
Stability:	_____	_____
	_____	_____
Personality:	_____	_____
	_____	_____
Formality:	_____	_____
	_____	_____
Interests:	_____	_____
	_____	_____
Age:	_____	_____
	_____	_____
Sex:	_____	_____
Religious, Political, or Ethnic Origin:	_____	_____
	_____	_____

Territoriality

If you "own" space, it gives you a number of behavioral prerogatives that another individual cannot assume within that space. *Territoriality* is this tendency for individuals in American culture to claim and "own" space, and then to use it as an extension of their own personal space. Perhaps you have noticed that at the beginning of a new term, you and other individual students select the desk or chair in which you will sit, then "claim" that space. We have noticed that sometimes, our students will develop a solid claim on a chair in a classroom so that other students begin to refer to the chair as "Tim's" or "Elizabeth's chair." We have seen students express, both nonverbally and verbally, their irritation when, after a couple of weeks, someone else sits down in a chair that the student had claimed.

After a person has staked out, claimed, and begun to own a territory, that claim is very precisely defined—but not by the individual. It is also defined by the culture. The amount of space that any individual can "own" in this fashion varies from culture to culture.

Finally, it appears that the amount of space anyone can legitimately "own" in a culture is dependent upon cultural status. To illustrate, a secretary in the trust department of a local bank "owns" her desk and chair. She also "owns" the typewriter at her desk. But her desk and chair are placed in a large room with other desks and chairs of a similar kind. That large room also provides corridor space through which the trust officers and clients pass to get to the trust officers' enclosed spaces. The head of the department also owns an office. His office is in the corner of the building, and is about three times the size of any of the trust officers' smaller cubicles. Depending upon their status, these people own differing amounts of space.

But so what? What does this phenomenon of territoriality have to do with interpersonal communication? In at least two ways, territoriality can have an enormous impact on your life space. In superior-subordinate relationships, such as those that exist between physicians and patients; boss and employees; judge and citizens; professor and students; and dean and professors, territoriality can work to the advantage or disadvantage of each participant, depending upon the goals each has for the interaction.

Suppose, to illustrate, you call on a professor to challenge a final grade. If you go to her office, the professor has all the advantage of territoriality. You are in *her* office. She has arranged the desk and chairs, of course, and has put out all the markers that signal that the office is "hers." You are the invader. She may sit down behind a desk piled high with books and student papers. You must put your books on the floor or hold them in your lap. In such a bargaining process, whoever "owns" the space will have an advantage.

But say that you approach the professor in the corridor or a classroom and say, "Professor Jones, I would like to chat with you about my course mark from last quarter. May we meet sometime this afternoon?"

Professor Jones will almost certainly say, "Well, I guess you could come to my office this afternoon. I will be there from 1:30 until about 3:30."

You now must decide to give Professor Jones the territorial advantage or to challenge it immediately. Say you decide to challenge it. "Uh, I have an idea. Why don't we go to the center for lunch. I am really tied up this afternoon. I have two classes and I feel I must spend some time looking at the course materials for my second class, which meets at 3:00."

Suppose, now, that Professor Jones is aware of the effects of territorial advantage, but she also wants to do anything she can to equalize the power differences between herself and her students. Indeed, she might very well make the invitation herself and in doing so, have a dramatic effect on the ensuing

Figure 7.11 The Four Most Popular Seating Arrangements (Sommer)

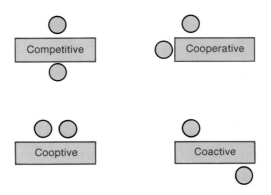

conversation. For one thing, the suggestion is far more likely to open up the conversation and to relax the participants. For another, the neutral location says something about the relative confidence each participant has in his or her own self and in the situation. And finally, the choice of the school cafeteria still permits some more subtle uses of space that each party might be able to apply as they work toward mutual understanding.

Angle of Interaction

Scholar Robert Sommer[17] conducted a series of studies in which he attempted to relate people's seating choices, or *angle of interaction,* to their perceptions of each other and of the situation. He was especially interested in whether the two-person subject groups of his study would perceive themselves as cooperating, competing, and coacting. Sommer asked people to report how they would seat themselves under the circumstances he wanted to study. His findings are both interesting and very useful (fig. 7.11).

When Sommer asked his subjects to show how they would locate themselves if they were going to compete with each other, the subjects typically took positions opposite each other. The large majority preferred positions across a table, face-to-face.

When Sommer asked the subjects to seat themselves in a cooperative situation, he found that the subjects took closer positions. One of the most common seating choices for this situation was diagonal seating, an arrangement across the corner of the table. Such an arrangement provides some security (the corner of the table intervenes between the participants) while at the same time, allows the participants to make close visual and tactile contact. They can work with each other at more intimate distances. This position allows the individuals to exchange personal and intimate information while maintaining their integrity and dignity, and without violating the personal and private space of the other.

Figure 7.12 Seating Preferences at Rectangular Tables

	1	2	3	4	5	6
Conversation						
U.S. sample (151 responses)	42%	46%	11%	0%	1%	0%
U.K. (univ.) sample (102 responses)	51	21	15	0	6	7
U.K. (nonuniv.) sample (42 responses)	42	42	9	2	5	0
Cooperation						
U.S. sample	19	25	51	0	5	0
U.K. (univ.) sample	11	11	23	20	22	13
U.K. (nonuniv.) sample	40	2	50	5	2	0
Co-action						
U.S. sample	3	3	7	13	43	33
U.K. (univ.) sample	9	8	10	31	28	14
U.K. (nonuniv.) sample	12	14	12	19	31	12
Competition						
U.S. sample	7	41	8	18	20	5
U.K. (univ.) sample	7	10	10	50	16	7
U.K. (nonuniv.) sample	4	13	3	53	20	7

Sommer asked his subjects to show where they would sit if they were in a situation in which they were working on the same task and trying to show mutual support. He called this arrangement *cooptive.* Most of his subjects agreed that they would sit side-by-side. Such an arrangement allows the participants to work together, to touch, to maintain personal distances, or to choose intimate distances. And at the same time, the position makes it possible for one subject to control—or "co-opt" the other. Interestingly, Sommer's subjects also found this position to be a fairly satisfying one for cooperation.

Sommer had still a fourth question. He wanted to know where his subjects would sit if they wanted to work privately, but on essentially the same task, where they could make contact and exchange views now and again, but where this would be more unusual than usual. The subjects chose to arrange themselves as far away from each other as they could at the table.

Recall that nonverbal communication can be related to the person's culture. Sommer's study was repeated with British subjects by Mark Cook.[18] Cook found some differences between the American and British arrangements. Figures 7.12 and 7.13 show Cook's findings.

Figure 7.13 Seating Preferences at Round Tables

Conversation			
U.S. sample			
(116 responses)	63%	17%	20%
U.K. (univ.) sample			
(102 responses)	58	37	5
U.K. (nonuniv.) sample			
(42 responses)	58	27	15
Cooperation			
U.S. sample	83	7	10
U.K. (univ.) sample	25	31	44
U.K. (nonuniv.) sample	97	0	3
Co-action			
U.S. sample	13	36	51
U.K. (univ.) sample	16	34	50
U.K. (nonuniv.) sample	24	26	50
Competition			
U.S. sample	2	25	63
U.K. (univ.) sample	15	22	63
U.K. (nonuniv.) sample	9	21	70

Now return to the luncheon you are about to have with Professor Jones. You and she have entered the school cafeteria and have selected your lunch from the serving line. You are moving to a table. Almost certainly, one of you will ask the other, "Where would you like to sit?" What will you do? Initiate? Wait for Professor Jones to initiate the question? Depending upon your own goals for the luncheon, we suggest that you initiate, and that you ask a different question. Suppose you really do wish to negotiate, but that you do not want to turn the affair into a competitive event. The best question might very well be, Would you like to sit at this table? rather than, Where would you like to sit? Can you determine why we prefer one question over the other? Where will you sit? Will you help the professor to a chair, or indicate one? And if she takes the initiative, will you submit to that without changing chairs once you have selected yours—assuming that you don't like the arrangement she has selected? Would you be willing to sit in a *booth* under these circumstances? You don't have to leave these matters to chance!

Personal Distancing

The angle of interaction is closely related to the *personal distancing* patterns of a culture. Personal space is used as a communication medium. Special space around you is reserved as private, and you don't let many people invade this private space.

You may have felt uncomfortable at one time when someone got too close to you. At other times, you were very pleased to have people get so close that actual contact was made. Thus, the private bubble of space is very flexible, shrinking and expanding according to the relationship you have with the other person. A prominent anthropologist, Edward T. Hall,[19] was interested in this use of private and personal space. He discovered that most Americans have what he called *intimate distance,* which extended from their skins to about eighteen inches. People reserve intimate distances for very close relationships or for telling secrets.

For normal, informal conversations Americans use what Hall called *personal-casual distance,* or a distance from about eighteen inches to about four feet away from the skin. However, business transactions and less personal business are conducted at a distance from four feet to about twelve feet—a distance which Hall termed *social-consultive distance.* The closer ranges in this bracket are typically used by people to present a more personal image in formal or business situations. The more distant space is typically used to keep people of lower power at a distance. If this were the case in the previous example, and you went to the professor's office, you might find that she has arranged her office so that she can put her desk between herself and her visitors.

Hall identified a *public distance,* too. Public distance extends from about twelve to about twenty-five feet in the near phase, and beyond twenty-five feet in the far phase. This public distance characterizes public address and communication situations outside of buildings. Figure 7.14 will give you an idea of Hall's categories for the use of space.

One of the variables of an environment, then, is space. How you use and arrange that space has a clear and direct bearing upon your communication in that space, as do such artifacts of the environment as texture, color and lighting, furniture layout, and design. But there is yet another component of environment that has an important impact upon your communication events. This component is time.

Time

Hall was concerned about more than space-related messages. He also was very interested in time as a communication system. He noted a number of interesting cultural differences in the way people use time. For instance, Hall described the Navajo Indians' belief that the time to start a ceremony is when all the necessary preparations are made. Such an understanding would defy

Figure 7.14 Hall's Categories for the Use of Space

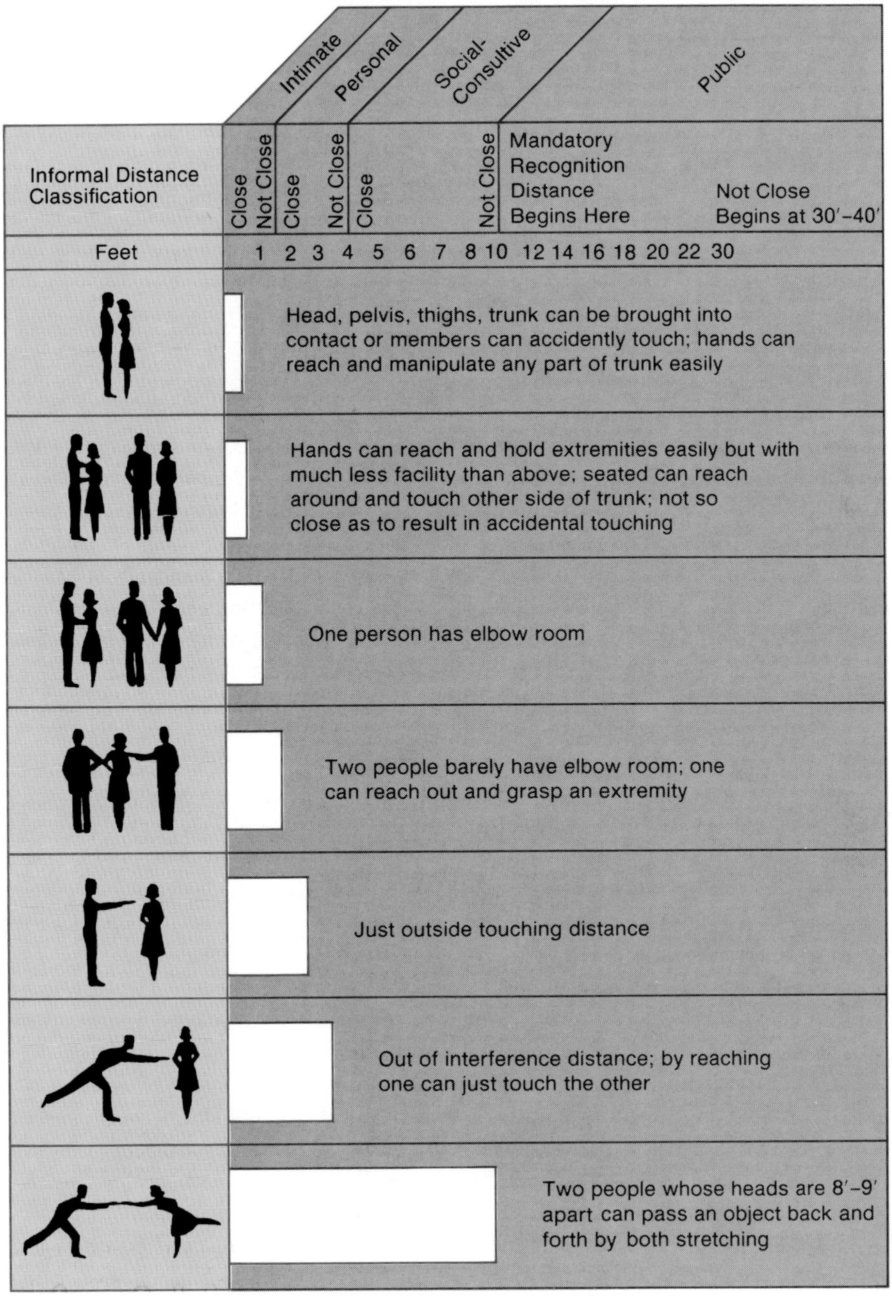

Informal Distance Classification	Intimate		Personal		Social-Consultive			Public	
	Close	Not Close	Close	Not Close	Close		Not Close	Mandatory Recognition Distance Begins Here	Not Close Begins at 30'–40'
Feet	1	2	3	4	5	6 7	8 10	12 14 16 18 20 22 30	

		Head, pelvis, thighs, trunk can be brought into contact or members can accidently touch; hands can reach and manipulate any part of trunk easily
		Hands can reach and hold extremities easily but with much less facility than above; seated can reach around and touch other side of trunk; not so close as to result in accidental touching
		One person has elbow room
		Two people barely have elbow room; one can reach out and grasp an extremity
		Just outside touching distance
		Out of interference distance; by reaching one can just touch the other
		Two people whose heads are 8'–9' apart can pass an object back and forth by both stretching

the expectations of certain North American industrialists. In the American culture, time is money. Time is spent; time is made; time is bought and sold as a commodity in advertising; time is saved and managed. Time is never approached casually unless special rules of some subculture allow it.

For example, a group of people who clock their workday activities with great precision may go on a weekend canoe trip with the understanding that all watches and clocks must be left at home. "There's no time on the river," says one. This statement verbalizes the subcultural rule that gives the group permission not to manage time.

Occasionally, you run into an individual whose notions about time are quite different from your ideas. If you are like most people in American society, time runs itself out in a line of predictable measure: 60 seconds to a minute; 60 minutes to an hour; 24 hours to a day; 365 days to a year. "Time marches on." But for Cheryl, time stops! In her lexicon of time, the key is not the relentless ticking of a clock. For her, time is a process of preparations and completions. She begins a project, such as writing a term paper, and time stops until she has finished that task or some identifiable portion of that task. Time then picks up its cultural rhythm until she begins another project. At the moment when she "loses herself" in the next project, time again stops. In this way she is more like the Navajos than she is like the industrialists.

Tim had an amusing realization of the communicative significance this difference in time orientations and understandings can have. He invited Cheryl to a dance. She accepted, and was determined to make a dress for the event. Since Tim's car was in the shop, they agreed that Cheryl would pick up Tim at 8:00 P.M. on the evening of the dance (he lives halfway between her home and the place where the dance was to be held).

This violation of the role expectations for Tim placed him in an unknown situation, a role reversal in which he was mildly uncomfortable and uncertain as to what he would do. When his clock indicated that it was 8:15, he began to worry because he lives by the clock. At 8:30, he was quite anxious, for it had started to rain. By 9:10, he decided that he would call Cheryl, notwithstanding the uncertainty about what rules applied to the situation. He reached for the phone just as it rang.

"Hello," he said.

"Hello," said Cheryl. "I just realized that I'm late. I started working on my dress and lost track of time. Anyway, I'll be there in just a few minutes. All I have to do is take a bath and dress."

Cheryl lives eight miles through the city traffic from Tim. It was pouring down rain. She had not had her bath nor had she dressed. It would *not* be "just a few minutes." Tim happened to have a bottle of wine. He put it on ice and built a fire in the fireplace. So what if they didn't go dancing?

You *can* make choices about how you will use time, and our guess is that you will make wiser choices if you stop to think about the implications those choices have. Does the way you treat time say something about you? Are you comfortable with what it says? Are you imposing an understanding of time upon other people? Is that imposition, if it occurs, appropriate? Are you wise enough to examine your own tempo, and to set your expectations aside if any are getting in the way? Would you have built a fire and chilled some wine? If not, you might have missed a beautiful evening!

Paraverbal Cues

So far, bodily and environmental cues that can have an important impact upon interpersonal relationships have been explored. Even so, those messages-without-words have not received nearly as much study over the years as the *paraverbal cues.* Indeed, the paraverbal cues may constitute the most important nonverbal message system in human communication. Certainly you will agree that they are vitally important, for *what* you say cannot exist independent of *how you say it.* Paraverbal cues are the "how" part of how you say something. Variations in rate, pitch, and force, and such particulars as how you articulate the suprasegmental elements of language, are included in this category. Also included are your particular ways of phrasing and pausing as you speak. Figure 7.15 illustrates the complexity of this message system.

There is a massive body of literature related to the paraverbal message system, including the entire study of speech pathology and audiology, oral interpretation, and a good part of the actor's art. Each of the variables in this figure is important to your interpersonal communication, and each is one that you can learn to control.

Turn Taking

One important variable is turn taking. How do you know when it is time for you to talk, and when it is time for the other to talk, during a conversation? How do you know whose turn it is when the talk turns into a fight or a squabble? Could you be making judgments about others, and they about you, because of turn-taking behavior?

You may know someone who sometimes seems rude. Perhaps this individual monopolizes the conversation; seems insensitive to your position in a conflict; runs over your sentences with his own; and doesn't appear to know how to put a period on his remarks. This individual is sometimes called a bore, and is rarely welcomed into groups. This individual could choose to change this situation, merely by becoming sensitive to the turn-taking behavior of others, and by learning to signal his interest in turns. As you see from figure 7.15, there are at least four categories of signals for taking turns in a conversation: yielding, refusing, maintaining, and requesting.

Figure 7.15 The Paraverbal Message System

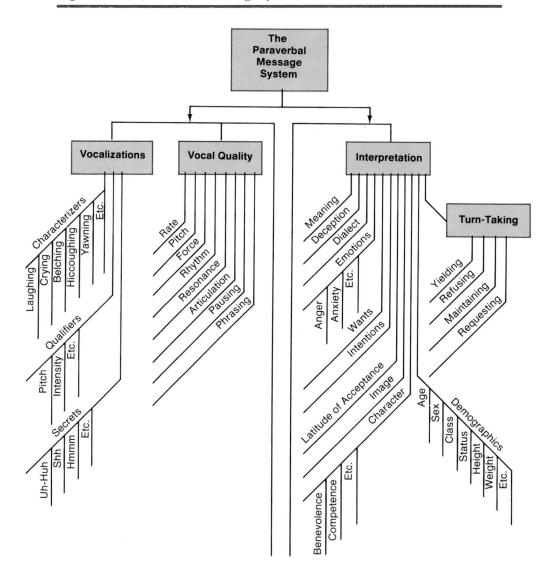

Interpretation

Recall from chapter six that meaning can be either denotative (the dictionary meaning), connotative (the personal meaning), or both. This lesson can be made more subtle and more significant by saying that the understandings you have of the world *is* the world for you. You live in a world of words, not of things.

The lesson about denotation and connotation is important when considering a second variable: *interpretation.* Figure 7.15 shows that you interpret paraverbal messages as you make guesses about such things as character, emotion, and deception. It is primarily by paraverbal cues that you learn to understand what others are telling you, although these cues never exist in isolation from the other nonverbal message systems. Was that sentence an insult? Was it meant to be? Did she intend her sentence to be an invitation? Is she playing it cool? Or did she mean it when she said she wasn't interested? Did mother's "no" mean "no"? Or, did it mean "maybe"?

Vocal Quality and Vocalizations

Think of the range of interpretations possible from vocal quality. We suspect that you could expand figure 7.15 under the heading "interpretation" with a little thought and effort. Even so, we have suggested some of the more obvious possibilities. You determine that someone is lying, for example, partly on the basis of her "tone of voice." You judge her emotional state. You guess about the individual's wants and expectations. You suppose her intentions and her latitude of acceptance. You guess about her character and about the image she has of you, partly based upon this important message system. You can tell how old an individual is, what his sex is, and something about his social class and status by listening to his vocal quality and his vocalizations. You can even judge a person's height and weight based upon the sound of his voice. But if you can make those guesses, so can he.

As mentioned before, guessing introduces the risk of being wrong. If you act upon your interpretations as though they were certainly true, but they turn out to be wrong, you may very well place your relationships at risk. That is why it is so important to learn to be sensitive to your processing of the nonverbal messages you send and receive, and to learn to bring your observations and guesses up to the level of talk when it seems like a good idea to do so. Since you can't get inside another's mind, you can't know what's going on in it unless you are told. Since the culture doesn't teach you to tell another—you use nonverbal message systems instead—you usually do not do so. But you can choose to do so, and you sometimes should.

Summary

Nonverbal message codes can be divided into four broad categories: general body cues; particular body cues; environmental cues; and paraverbal cues. When you communicate with others, these cues work together with the words you say in a communication system of considerable complexity. You can talk about yourself and the objects, phenomena, and events around you, of course, and you can also send and receive a very complex set of messages without words. You always do these at the same time, and you almost never use any particular code in isolation. Sometimes you are conscious of your communication but sometimes you are not. We tried in this chapter to point out the value of becoming more aware of the nonverbal messages you send and receive, and the relative difficulty human beings have in processing those nonverbal cues.

General body cues included two broad categories: clothes and artifacts, and body movements and gestures. We suggested something of the variety of inferences that people draw based upon such cues, and pointed out that even so, those inferences were fairly gross and general. Far more subtle and complex than the general body cues, we presented a second category, particular body cues. In this category we describe some of the findings from research into face and eye behavior and touching behavior. Here, again, we pointed out that no single nonverbal message can exist in isolation, and that, therefore, learning to read these subtle messages can be very difficult.

We presented three categories of environmental cues and showed how space and personal distancing behavior can have an impact on our communication, and how people use and relate to time differently. The fourth broad category of nonverbal messages, paraverbal cues, included voice quality and characterization on the one hand and interpretations on the other.

The point of all of this discussion was that the human communication systems we use, especially in interpersonal communication events, is comprised of a complex system of interacting cues and variables other than words, which accompany the language we speak. To become more sensitive to the subtlety and complexity of this system is to become a better communicator. And especially when trouble exists in our relationships it is useful to be able to identify what is being communicated nonverbally, and to talk about our interpretations. By doing this, and only by doing this, can we assure ourselves that our guesses really are shared meaning.

Discussion Questions

1. Suppose you are planning to entertain a very important person in your home. Describe how you would prepare for the date. What nonverbal messages would you choose to exhibit? For example, what clothes, setting, or furniture would you exhibit?

2. Assume you have scheduled a conference with a professor. What nonverbal messages would you choose to exhibit in this situation? How do nonverbal messages give clues about the relationship? About feelings, wants, expectations, intention, and latitudes of acceptance?

3. How do you nonverbally present yourself to your classmates and professors? What about your posture? Gesture? Space? Dress? Artifacts? Other?

4. Identify the four most important nonverbal messages you send about yourself. What kind of messages are they and why do they exist? What do you think they mean to the other person?

5. Recall the last time you participated in a large family gathering, perhaps at Christmas or Thanksgiving. Are there any nonverbal elements in this context that you might describe as ritualized? How do you and the others signal your membership status?

Endnotes

1. L. A. Malandro and L. L. Barker, *Nonverbal Communication* (Reading, MA: Addison-Wesley Publishing Co., Inc., 1983), 83.
2. M. L. Rosencranz, "Clothing Symbolism," *Journal of Home Economics* 54 (1962): 18–22.
3. L. Aiken, "Relationship of Dress to Selected Measures of Personality in Undergraduate Women," *Journal of Social Psychology* 59 (1963):121.
4. Reported in L. B. Rosenfeld and T. G. Plax, "Clothing as Communication," *Journal of Communication* 27 (1977):23–31.
5. G. Thornton, "The Effects of Wearing Glasses upon Judgments and Persons Seen Briefly," *Journal of Applied Psychology* 28 (1944):203–7.
6. P. N. Hamid, "Style of Dress as a Perceptual Cue in Impression Formation," *Perceptual and Motor Skills* 26 (1968):904–6.
7. W. McKeachie, "Lipstick as a Determiner of First Impressions of Personality: An Experiment for the General Psychology Course," *Journal of Social Psychology* 36 (1952):241–44.
8. C. Rubenstein, "Body Language that Speaks to Muggers," *Psychology Today* (August, 1980):20.
9. This is the basic argument in A. T. Dittmann, "The Role of Body Movement in Communication," in A. W. Siegman and S. Felstein, *Nonverbal Behavior and Communication* (Hillsdale, N.J.: Lawrence Erlbaum Associates, Publishers, 1978), 69–95.
10. P. Ekman and W. V. Friesen, "The Repertoire of Nonverbal Behavior: Categories, Origins, Usage, and Coding," *Semiotica* 1 (1969): 49–98.
11. M. Argyle, *Bodily Communication* (New York: International Universities Press, 1975).
12. We are assuming, in this discussion, that the individuals in our examples and discussions are from the same culture. There is some evidence that both the culture and general bodily configuration of an individual influence his or her ways of using and posing the body, and under what circumstances. For example, you may remember that the early Romans ate lying down. This position must have seemed as comfortable to them as sitting at table seems to us. Both of these examples are culturebound examples of posture control.
13. See A. Mehrabian, "Inference of Attitudes from Posture, Orientation, and Distance of a Communicator," *Journal of Consulting and Clinical Psychology* 32 (1968):296–308.

14. P. Eckman and W. V. Friesen, *Unmasking the Face* (Englewood Cliffs, NJ: Prentice-Hall, Inc., 1975).

15. N. R. Heslin and T. Alper, "Touch: A Bonding Gesture," in J. M. Wiemann and R. P. Harrison, eds., *Nonverbal Interaction* 2 (1983):47–75.

16. A. H. Maslow and N. L. Mintz, "Effects of Esthetic Surroundings: I. Initial Effects of Three Esthetic Conditions Upon Perceiving Energy and Well-Being in Faces," *Journal of Psychology* 41 (1956):247–254.

17. R. Sommer, *Personal Space: The Behavioral Basis of Design* (Englewood Cliffs, NJ: Prentice-Hall, Inc., 1969).

18. M. Cook, "Experimentation on Orientation and Proxemics," *Human Relations* 23 (1970):61–76.

19. E. T. Hall, *Silent Language* (Garden City, NY: Doubleday, 1959). This entire discussion of personal space is based upon this interesting book.

Defending and Supporting

Preview

The old saying, "We always hurt the ones we love," means that when you argue with those who are close to you, the arguments often end in lashing out or in some other hurtful behavior. Hurtful behavior is often chosen because there seems to be no way around communication that creates defensiveness. There is, however, an alternative: supportive behavior. This chapter examines specific, helpful suggestions on how and when to be more supportive.

Objectives

After reading this chapter you should be able to complete the following:
1. Discuss the major reasons people defend themselves in interpersonal communication situations.
2. Specify and explain the two basic strategies people use to defend themselves.
3. Identify the characteristics of a defensive interpersonal communication climate.
4. Suggest the two primary negative responses a person could make to another's definition of self.
5. Discuss the consequences of defensive communication behavior.
6. Identify the characteristics of a supportive interpersonal communication climate.
7. Explain the benefits of supportive communication behavior in an interpersonal relationship.
8. Specify how you can help yourself choose to remain supportive.

8

The group decided to go out after class one Thursday night to relax after a really tough week. Midterm exams were finally over and this was a chance to let down. After they had reassembled at Stan's Pizza House and had ordered a round of beverages, Cheryl noticed that something seemed to be bothering Tim. She chose to ignore Tim's sullenness for a few minutes, but finally decided that she could no longer endure the pained expressions and negativism he was radiating. "Tim," she said, "you're being pretty hard to get along with. What's your problem?"

What happened next was a surprise to all. Tim picked up his drink, stormed off to another table, downed the drink in less than ten seconds, then returned only long enough to say, "Cheryl, you'd be a decent human being if you'd learn how to talk to people!" Then he hurried out before anyone could reply.

As you can imagine, this scene created a great deal of commotion. Elizabeth ran to intercept Tim and the others tried to calm Cheryl. Tim would not stop, so Elizabeth returned to the table. When the emotionalism had run its course, the talk turned to what could be done to discover what was going on and what could be done to bring Tim back into the group. The group members really did value Tim and wanted him back so Mary Ann volunteered to talk to him the next day to see if she could help manage and perhaps resolve the conflict.

She planned her approach carefully and found a time when they could talk without interruption. "Tim, I wonder if we can talk about what was going on at Stan's last night."

"Well, Mary Ann, Cheryl was being absolutely impossible. She's always on my case and I'm not going to take it anymore. If she'd change her attitude and learn how to talk to people, she'd be a decent human being. I'm through with her—and the group, too!"

"I can see that you are pretty upset with Cheryl, and perhaps the group, too, Tim. I wonder if you're willing to talk about what we did to cause you to feel frustrated and angry? The group asked me to come to talk to you. We're concerned about you and want you to still be part of us."

"Do you really mean that, Mary Ann? How can I tell if you're telling the truth. Maybe you're just saying that because you need me to get a good grade in the class."

"I can't prove that I'm telling the truth, but I am. Also, I want to understand what you are thinking and feeling when you get angry with the group. I have had some frustration myself, so I can understand how you might have that kind of experience with the group. If you're willing to share with me, I'm willing to listen."

"O.K. I'll try to talk about it, but I'm not sure that you'll understand."

It seems that just living life exposes every human being to experiences similar to this one. Cheryl's behavior seemed to trigger some unexpected emotional response in Tim. Or, as Tim said, he had all that he could take of something that Cheryl was doing and decided to tell her about his frustration. It is clear here that Tim and Cheryl had a fight that was producing negative feelings and was being very unproductive for both parties. Neither party is necessarily "right," nor is conflict bad or something that should be avoided. Often, however, this kind of destructive conflict can be avoided if the people involved understand how to share their differences while remaining supportive of each other: the parties must understand and practice interpersonal skills.

Defensive Communication Behavior

Why You Defend Yourself

Carl Rogers, a therapist who has studied how to provide a supportive climate, has suggested that humans have a natural tendency to evaluate and judge others. He believes that a "major barrier to mutual interpersonal communication is our very natural tendency to judge, to evaluate, to approve (or disapprove) the statement of the other person or the other group."[1]

But why does this natural tendency exist? Perhaps your disapproval results because the other person's behavior does not square with your expectations. So you judge that person, then tell her what she ought to believe, how she should behave, or what she should do under the circumstances.

But why is it so important to try to impose your own view? Why was Tim so anxious to counter—or at least stop—Cheryl's judgment of him? The answer might be quite simple. Her judgment, her definition, of him was different from the image he had of himself. This was threatening to Tim's self-concept. You can imagine other reactions that Tim might have shown if he had not perceived Cheryl's judgment threatening. For example, he might have ignored her, or he might even laugh. But he did neither of these, and chose, instead, a dramatic way of saying, "I disagree with your evaluation."

This defense of self-concept specifically involves two areas. First, you are defending your view of the outside world. You want your view of correct behavior, correct thinking, and correct ways of doing things to be confirmed. You need to be confirmed in these areas in order to believe in yourself and to believe that you are OK. But even more important, your defense of self-concept involves your defense of your worth as a person, too. You want to *believe* that you are of worth as a person. You want to be respected as a person, to be listened to, and understood. These are areas that Cheryl was most critical of when she said, "Tim, you're being pretty hard to get along with. What's your problem?" Remember that later Tim said to Mary Ann that Cheryl needed to change her attitude and learn how to communicate better if she wanted to be a decent human being.

Your worth as a person is at the heart of your defensiveness. You believe that you cannot always be right and are willing to tolerate being wrong some of the time. Yet, you find it intolerable to be denied worth as a person *and* to be wrong, too. You cannot listen to talk that says that you do not count, that you are inferior, that you do not have the right to have an opinion. When another person evaluates you thus, you defend yourself unless you make a conscious decision not to.

People do have a choice to behave defensively or supportively, regardless of the other person's behavior. There is clear evidence of this choice in personal experiences. Everyone tolerates outbursts from the boss. Salespeople often take terrible abuse from customers and still remain supportive. You have heard children say to a parent, "I don't love you anymore. I hate you." Yet the parent remains in control. These are signs that it is possible to remain in control if you wish to do so.

When and How You Defend Yourself

There are two basic strategies you use to defend yourself. You can *avoid* or you can *confront*. There are a number of circumstances in which you decide to ignore or avoid, but two seem especially important. One such situation occurs when you decide the opinion of the other person doesn't count. In order to care about an evaluation, you must think the other person's view matters. You can decide that for yourself, or you can decide that because other people, people you value, think the opinion doesn't count. If you do not care about the other's evaluation of you, you can ignore it.

A second reason to ignore another person's evaluation is because you don't want to hear it. Going away will allow you to avoid the evaluation altogether. Can you think of anyone you avoid because you believe that they will say things you don't want to hear?

People also engage in direct confrontation when they feel and believe that they are being attacked. These people—especially those who behave aggressively toward others—take the offensive in order to defend their self-concepts. They believe the best defense is direct countering of the other person's attack. This kind of confrontation can be carried out supportively if you are willing to utilize assertive and supportive communication behaviors. But often, people engage in aggressive communication behavior. This aggressive behavior generally creates defensiveness.

Defensive Behavior

In a classic essay, Jack Gibb described the behaviors he observed while listening to groups engaged in defensive communication.[2] He noted that six behaviors appear regularly when people are being defensive.[3] These are evaluation, superiority, certainty, control, neutrality, and strategy.

First, defensive communication involves *evaluation*. Cheryl's remark, "You're pretty hard to get along with, Tim," judges Tim. It says that there is something defective in Tim. It cuts to the core of his self-concept. Cheryl's statement is not a challenge to one of Tim's ideas about the world, it is a direct challenge to his ideas about himself.

Taking a superior attitude is another characteristic of defensive communication that Gibb observed. *Superiority* is behavior that suggests that you are better than another person; that you are somehow wiser, that you can make judgments that overrule the other person's sense of who he is and how he ought to be.

Notice how closely evaluation and superiority are linked. To make a judgment about another person, to offer suggestions as to how that person ought to proceed, implies superiority. It implies that you have set yourself above the other person. Thus, the superior attitude is often a direct attack on the other's self-concept. Cheryl implied superiority when she judged Tim.

Certainty is directly related to evaluation and superiority. There was no hesitation or sense of doubt in Cheryl's judgment. She didn't say Tim's behavior *might be interpreted* as difficult to tolerate. She didn't say that Tim *might be experiencing* a problem. She said, with confidence and certainty, that Tim was hard to get along with; he had a problem. This was a direct affront to Tim's self-concept and he could not let it go unchallenged. The use of language that indicates certainty of judgment will, in all probability, cause negative reactions. Since views frequently differ, and since there seems to be no room for negotiation in certainty, the most likely response to this attitude is confrontation and challenge.

Making judgments out of a sense of superiority using language that suggests certainty is almost always an attempt to control. You want to *control* what the other person believes. You want to control the image the other person has of herself. You often imply: "I am right and you are wrong. Adopt this way of doing it. Think this about yourself. Do what I want." Most people will attempt to defend themselves against such an onslaught.

Gibb identified a fifth behavior that generates a defensive climate—*neutrality.* There are two ways this neutrality, or indifference, can be communicated. First, the indifferent person implies that he does not care about the other. A person who cares will want to uphold the other, but the person who does not care is likely to ignore the other individual. Secondly, neutrality also implies that the person does not want to understand the other person. Not wanting to hear and understand another person's view communicates that she doesn't count; her view isn't worth considering. Neutrality will surely cause the other to defend herself.

Finally, defensive behavior often involves *strategy.* If you are not interested in a person's opinion, if you want that person to believe that your opinion is the only one that counts, then you must be pursuing a deliberate plan to gain an advantage over him, perhaps to control him. He may come to the conclusion that you are involved in some strategy to manipulate him. If he decides this, then he will resent you and your motives. He will object and will do what he can to defend himself. He'll probably attack you in the same ways that you've attacked him.

Table 8.1 Characteristics of Defensive Climates

Evaluation   To make a judgment about the other; to make an assessment of the other; to raise questions about the other's viewpoint or motives.

Control   To try to manipulate the other; to attempt to impose an attitude or viewpoint on another; to try to keep the other from doing something; "implicit in all attempts to alter another person is the assumption of the change agent that the person to be altered is inadequate."

Strategy   To plan what you want and then to trick the other into thinking he or she is making the decision; to cause the other to feel that you have an interest in her or him when you do not.

Neutrality   To show little or no concern for the other or his or her problems and viewpoint; to treat the other as an object rather than a person.

Superiority   To communicate that you are "superior in position, power, wealth, intellectual ability, physical characteristics, or other ways"; to suggest that the other person is inadequate in comparison to you; to convey the attitude that the speaker "is not willing to enter into a shared problem-solving relationship, that he probably does not desire feedback, that he will be likely to try to reduce the power, the status, or the worth of the receiver."

Certainty   To be rigid in your viewpoint; "to seem to know the answers, to require no additional data"; to adopt the attitude of teacher in the sense that you try to correct the other; to take on a win-lose position.

Source: Jack R. Gibb, "Defensive Communication," *Journal of Communication* (September, 1961): 142–45. Adapted by permission.

Table 8.1 lists the characteristics of each of the six defensive behavior categories. You can use table 8.1 to analyze your own communication behavior. Careful analysis may uncover some surprises. You may find, as have many people, that you have adopted certain styles of behaving but are not conscious of how you are acting. Understanding and using the list of defensive behavior categories can help you to discover where you might want to change your communication behavior.

Negative Responses to Another's Definition of Self

Watzlawick and his associates studied the issue of addressing another's definition of self.[4] These researchers claim that there are two possible negative responses to a person's definition of self: rejection and disconfirmation.

Rejection is the outright denial of a person's self-esteem (except in a case where the person seeks confirmation of low self-esteem). Cheryl's statement is an outright rejection of Tim.

Disconfirmation is very different from rejection and is, perhaps, more serious. It does not say that *you are wrong*. It says that *you do not exist* or that *your opinion does not exist*. Thus, totally ignoring Tim might also have led to his hostile behavior. There is a clear sense that ignoring defines the person doing the ignoring as superior. Moreover, neutrality is assumed to be a by-product of ignoring. Thus, the act of ignoring a person or his viewpoint is disconfirming. Defensive behavior is the most probable response.

Consequences of Defensive Behavior

When you become involved in defensive communication, you begin to focus on yourself. You plan messages for use in defending yourself. You stop listening, so you're not likely to hear the other person's position. The other person might be making some important points and might even be trying to accommodate your position, but all in vain. You find that being firm in your position often keeps you from losing, so you become more rigid in your position. Often you repeat the position as a response to whatever the other person says. Finally, if the other person persists—and the other person is likely to do so because he has stopped listening and has become rigid in his position, too—you try to lash out and hurt him. It is as if by hurting the other, you win despite what that person does.

Perhaps you can recall a similar experience. But did you actually win much of anything? More likely you regretted the event. Especially in close interpersonal situations, where people really do have a stake in the outcome, the final step is usually *regret*. People wish that they had had more control, and that they had not hurt the other. Regret, then, is another consequence of defensive behavior. You can imagine that Cheryl's willingness to have someone in the group talk to Tim about the incident was motivated by regret.

Finally, defensive behavior often leads to *hostility*. This occurs because both the aggressor and the defender are manipulating. Their strategies are calculated to achieve their personal ends. This is not to say that people shouldn't achieve their own ends. Rather, when manipulation is used to achieve personal ends at the expense of another, hostility often follows. The outcome of hostile behavior appears to be neutrality, the "I don't care" attitude. What often follows is "I want to hurt you."

Strategies and Results

Defensive behavior does serve the function of defending oneself, but seldom does it result in achieving any lasting or satisfying results. When people become rigid in their positions and stop listening, there is no way to resolve the differences. At least there is no way that is likely to be satisfying to those involved. Certain strategies are often employed by a given individual, but the results are generally damaging. For examaple, you might *lash out—hurt the other person* so badly that she lets you have your way. This is winning only in the sense that you got your way. You lose in the sense that you may have damaged the relationship.

Another strategy that is often employed is *pulling rank*. This strategy is imposing your own viewpoint on the other person because you are in a position of power. Resentment is generated by this strategy and the relationship is probably damaged. In the work place, this means that the damaged worker is likely to be less productive and may even sabotage the work effort. Even though the boss "won," he also lost.

Alternatives to Defensive Behaviors

Is it necessary to engage in defensive behavior? We believe that it is not. You can select an alternative and can then be more in control of your own behavior. You can decide not to use defensive behaviors once you understand what they are, and once you understand the alternative behaviors. Knowing the general outcomes of defensive behavior may be helpful in persuading you to remain supportive. If you know that in most cases "winning" also means losing, then you might be more likely to choose behaviors that have a greater "winning" potential.

At a second level, many of your interpersonal transactions are *reflexive*. What you do will have an effect on what the other person is likely to do. This principle operates when you decide to become defensive. But you can decide *not* to become defensive. In this case, the other person will find it difficult to continue the attack. Thus, the other is forced into more reasonable and perhaps supportive behavior.

Your refusal to accept the definition of the situation as defensive can have a profound effect on the other person's ability to define the situation. It's difficult to fight with a person who will not fight! But in addition to not fighting, you are also countering the wrong definition of a situation with your own definition. Remaining supportive (instead of being defensive) is saying to the other person, "I want to talk about the situation. I want to talk in a way that won't damage our relationship. I want us both to be satisfied with the outcome. Let's cooperate in deciding."

Many interpersonal transactions are reflexive, especially when the parties involved have some commitment to the relationship. This commitment may spring from liking and affection, or it may spring from interdependency. The boss needs you to get the work done; and you need the boss—or at least you need a job. When there is such a commitment, it should make some difference in how the other person is treated. If one person ignores the other's attempts to "be fair," the commitment is damaged. If both parties behave badly, then both have ignored the commitment. Then, to the degree that the people involved understand the commitment, one party remaining supportive should have an influence on the outcome.

This was essentially what happened with Cheryl and Tim when their communication broke down. Both behaved defensively and so damaged their relationship. In this case, however, the relationship extended beyond these two. The group had a stake in the relationship even though the other members did not participate in the exchange. Other group members could legitimately demand that an attempt be made to restore the relationship. This is why Mary Ann could approach both Cheryl and Tim with some expectation of success. She could hope to control Tim's behavior to the extent that she could remain supportive. She managed to do so and seemed to make some progress.

Supportive Communication Behavior

Supportive communication behavior, like defensive communication behavior, reflects an attitude toward the other person and the relationship. But as you might imagine, there is a definite contrast between supportive and defensive behaviors. *Supportive communication* affirms the other person; *defensive communication* disconfirms the other person.

Carl Rogers captured the essence of the supportive attitude in his term, "unconditional positive regard." He explained the attitude and its effects on the other person.

> [A supportive attitude] means that he prizes the client in a total, rather than a conditional way. I mean that he does not simply accept the client when he is behaving in certain ways and disapprove of him when he behaves in other ways. He experiences an outgoing, positive feeling, without reservations, without *evaluations*. The term we have come to use for this attitude is "unconditional positive regard," and we believe that, the more this attitude is experienced by the therapist and perceived by his client, the more likelihood there is that therapy will be successful and that change and development will take place.[5]

Carl Rogers is referring to the therapeutic setting and the healing that takes place when a supportive attitude is perceived by the client. This principle is also important in day-to-day communication. A supportive communication climate allows for *change and development*. It enhances the relationship by enabling the participants to understand and adjust viewpoints in a nonthreatening environment.

Characteristics of Supportive Climates

Recall the conversation that Mary Ann had with Tim at the beginning of this chapter. Mary Ann tried to be supportive. "Tim," she said. "I wonder if we can talk about what was going on at Stan's last night?"

"Well, Mary Ann, Cheryl was being absolutely impossible. She's always on my case and I'm not going to take it anymore. If she'd change her attitude and learn how to talk to people, she'd be a decent human being. I'm through with her—and the group, too!"

"I can see that you are pretty upset with Cheryl, and perhaps the group, too, Tim. I wonder if you're willing to talk about what we did to cause you to feel frustrated and angry? The group asked me to come to talk to you. We're concerned about you and want you to still be part of us."

"Do you really mean that, Mary Ann? How can I tell if you're telling the truth? Maybe you're just saying that because you need me to get a good grade in the class."

"I can't prove that I'm telling the truth, but I am. Also, I want to understand what you are thinking and feeling when you get angry with the group. I have had some frustration myself, so I can understand how you might have that kind of experience with the group. If you're willing to share with me, I'm willing to listen."

"OK, I'll try to talk about it, but I'm not sure that you'll understand."

Compare Mary Ann's communication to the six supportive categories Gibb identified: description, equality, provisionalism, problem orientation, empathy, and spontaneity. First, you can avoid evaluation by using *description*. This can be difficult since you must be able to recognize inferences in order to be able to use description and avoid evaluation. An *inference* involves a mental leap; drawing a conclusion based on your interpretation of what you observe. An interpretation of many events involves your subjective evaluation. In this case, it is close to what Gibb called evaluation: it is an opinion about what *you* observed. Thus, an inference is not a description; it's an evaluation.

There is really very little description in the conversation between Mary Ann and Tim but neither is there any evaluation. Mary Ann made only one inference: "I can see that you are pretty upset with Cheryl. . . ." Mary Ann's use of the word "are" made the inference sound like a judgment. She could have made it sound like an inference rather than a judgment by including the words "you seem to be."

Notice also that Mary Ann didn't "pull rank." She was careful not to put herself in a *superior* position, by either her verbal or nonverbal communication. She picked a time and place when she could talk to Tim "on his own ground." She went to him even though she could have called him and asked him to come over to her place to talk. She also did not offer him advice or tell him what was going on in the communication at Stan's. She tried to remain an equal. *Equality,* the second supportive category, dictates that she minimize any differences in status and position. Remaining equal helps a person feel supported.

Mary Ann also tempered her approach with *provisionalism*. She included several tentative statements in her dialogue. For example, she said, "I wonder *if* we can talk . . . ," and ". . . talk about what was going on at Stan's last night." The use of "if" in the first sentence fragment allows Tim to choose not to talk. In the second sentence fragment, Mary Ann avoids certainty by suggesting that she is open to interpretations other than her own.

Consider that Mary Ann also said, "I *can see that you are* pretty upset." No provisionalism exists in this statement. Instead, she exhibited certainty, one of the communication behaviors most likely to yield defensiveness. She could not *see* that Tim was upset. She could see Tim's facial expressions, bodily posture, and tension, perhaps. And she could observe the tone of voice, the phrasing, and the pausing Tim used. But Mary Ann could not see that Tim was upset. She had to *guess* that her observations meant something, and she called that something "upset."

This analysis may seem extreme, especially since Mary Ann's guess was correct—Tim *was* upset. But what if her guess had been incorrect? Suppose your interpersonal communication instructor meets you outside the classroom. She knows that your mark on the midterm examination was low. She also believes that you will not like the mark because she has an image of you as an achievement-motivated individual who takes pride in a consistently high grade-point average. So she hands you your paper before class begins and says, "I know you'll be upset with the grade. Would you like to talk about it?" What does her guess do to your relationship? It puts you on the defensive.

You now have to process the low grade in her presence and, perhaps, in the presence of other students. You have to do so on very short notice, and moreover, you have to deal with your emotional condition using language she has placed upon it—*upset.* She has *seen* that you are upset, so, clearly, you are upset. You aren't allowed any other options, such as, for example, surprise; or relief (you didn't get the *F* you expected); or confusion. Or suppose the paper she handed you was not your paper. Does this mean that in all the other interactions you've had, she didn't know who you were?

To defend yourself, you may do a number of things. You might, for example, play the passive role that some educational systems teach their members. Play it cool. Don't let anyone know what you are experiencing. Above all, do not involve yourself with the teacher, since that individual carries all the power in the teacher-student relationship.

You might also defend yourself by attacking her. You might use strong language or attempt to "get her goat." For instance, you might judge the quality of the test, complaining about the vagueness of the questions and the unfairness in selecting certain subjects covered in the test. If she buys into your game, then your low mark would be her fault, and you would have successfully defended yourself.

The exchange with Tim also exhibits some characteristics of a *problem orientation.* Mary Ann's offer, "If you are willing to share with me, I am willing to listen," indicates a problem orientation. A problem orientation suggests to the other person that you are willing to share in the process of arriving at a solution to the problem. With her behavior, Mary Ann seems to be saying, "Let's work together so that we can understand this and come to an agreement on how you can come back and be part of the group." She makes no attempt to control Tim by suggesting either an interpretation of what was going on or by giving him a preconceived solution to the conflict. She makes clear that she expects to engage in joint problem solving with Tim.

You can tell that this suggestion of joint problem solving met with a little skepticism. Recall that Tim said, "How can I tell if you're telling the truth? Maybe you're just saying that because you need me to get a good grade in the class." Tim's response is fairly predictable. Willingness to be supportive and to engage in joint problem solving is often met with some surprise by those who expect an attempt to control. When an individual becomes accustomed to others' attempts to control his behavior, it may require a considerable amount of reassurance from you that you do not mean to control, and that you are telling the truth.

Mary Ann replied, "I can't prove that I'm telling the truth, but I am. Also, I want to understand what you are thinking and feeling when you get angry with the group." It's clear that she was attempting to reassure Tim.

Gibb recommended a fifth supportive behavior, *empathy.* Genuine empathy is very powerful because to the other person it represents more than merely "putting yourself in another's shoes." It represents an attempt to understand the other person's position and may even represent an attempt to identify yourself with the problem. Empathy requires effort on the part of the listener. But when empathy is recognized by the person with whom you are talking, it's usually valued and viewed as supportive. Notice Mary Ann's attempt to empathize with Tim. She said, "I have had some frustration myself, so I can *understand* how you might have that kind of experience with the group." Tim recognized her effort. Thus, Mary Ann had established a caring atmosphere. She reduced Tim's sense of threat to his self-concept.

Keep in mind that an empathic attitude is largely communicated nonverbally. The face and body can signal that you are "tuned in"; that you do care about the other person. False concern can produce mixed messages; you can say you care with your words but that you don't care with your actions. Where messages are mixed, the nonverbal behavior is usually that which is believed.

Finally, Gibb identified *spontaneity* as a quality of supportive communication. Spontaneity is direct, honest, and straightforward behavior. It is impossible consciously to decide to be spontaneous. Doing so causes you to think about your behavior. And in thinking about your behavior, you become much less spontaneous. Thus to tell someone to "be spontaneous" is a contradiction since it is a demand for behaviors that cannot be performed at the same time.

This paradox can be serious, depending upon the importance of the need expressed.[6] For example, there used to be a love song in which the singer, a woman, yearned for little signs of affection from her lover. She sang, "Touch my hair as you pass my chair; little things mean a lot." There is no way that

the lover could fulfill her need for spontaneous shows of affection, although the request seems reasonable enough. By making it, the singer unintentionally places the lover into a situation sometimes called a *double bind*. The term is applied to messages that must be disobeyed to be obeyed. Thus, the meaning of the message cannot be known because it is impossible to know which command the originator of the message wishes to be obeyed. In this case, if the lover ignores the singer's request, then she may feel somewhat frustrated and dissatisfied.

Although asking is sometimes necessary to fulfill a need, the trade-off is diminished spontaneity. Self-initiated behavior sometimes is an expression of how the person is feeling at the time. Prompting the other person may initiate the same feeling, but because it is not self-initiated, it is not spontaneous and so may have a different effect. If the lover touches her hair the next time he passes her chair, then the singer feels frustrated and dissatisfied because he did it on request and not of his own spontaneous choice.

Perhaps a more serious example is the rearing of female children. Loving parents want the little girl to compete with the other children, both intellectually and physically. They want her to be active, to play sports and to climb trees. At the same time, they dress her in frilly skirts and blouses; allow her hair to grow long, and caution her not to get it mussed; and in general, enforce behavior of cleanliness and daintiness that places the child in a double bind. This double bind is implied in the parents' statement, "Go outside and play with the other kids, but be a lady!" The little girl is left with only two alternatives—both of which are unacceptable. She can do as she is told, and go outside and play with the others, roughhousing, getting dirty, and competing, or, she can do as she is told and be a lady. She can't do both.

American boys, too, are subjected to double binds. By cultural rule, they are supposed to display a certain freedom of spirit and aggressiveness that adults consider the beginnings of "manly independence" and "rugged individualism." The child tries to follow the wishes of his parents. The parents wish him to be more assertive, so they tell the boy, or in some other way signal the command, "Don't be so well behaved." In this double bind, the boy has only two choices. He can continue to be well-behaved, in which case his parents will be dissatisfied because he has not obeyed them. Or he can be more self-assertive. In that case, his parents will be dissatisfied because he has obeyed them, but for the wrong reasons. His behavior has sprung from their command and not from his "budding manly independence." For the boy, and for the parents, the situation is one in which nobody wins.

So instead of suggesting that you "be spontaneous," we advise you to be reasonably direct, honest, and straightforward with another person. The perception of genuineness may lead to trust. If it does, then progress can be made on the issue and in building the relationship.

Table 8.2 summarizes defensive and supportive behavior. The two types of behavior are presented in column form so that you can compare them.

Table 8.2 Characteristics of Supportive and Defensive Climates

Defensive	Supportive
Evaluation	*Description*
To make a judgment about the other, to make an assessment of the other, to raise questions about the other's viewpoint, motives.	To be nonjudgmental, to ask straightforward questions, to request factual information, to present "feelings, events, perceptions, or processes that do not ask or imply that the receiver change behavior or attitude."
Control	*Problem Orientation*
To try to manipulate the other; to attempt to impose an attitude or viewpoint on another; to try to keep the other from doing something; "implicit in all attempts to alter another person is the assumption of the change agent that the person to be altered is inadequate."	The antithesis of imposing one's view; to communicate "a desire to collaborate in defining a mutual problem and seeking its solution"; to suggest by your words and actions, that you have no preplanned solution, viewpoint, or behavior to impose on the other; to give the opportunity for "the receiver to set his own goals, make his own decisions, and evaluate his own progress—or to share with the sender in doing so."
Strategy	*Spontaneity*
To plan what you want and trick the other into thinking he or she is making the decision; to cause the other to feel that you have an interest in her or him when you do not.	To express straightforward, "above the table" behavior; to avoid deceiving; to have unhidden, uncomplicated viewpoints and motives; to be honest.

Source: Jack R. Gibb, "Defensive Communication," *Journal of Communication* (September, 1961): 142–45. Adapted by permission.

Benefits of Supportive Communication

Supportiveness can have a positive effect on the communication providing two requirements are met. First, the behavior must be perceived as genuine. For example, if a person is being so frank that it is out of character or beyond the bounds of normal behavior, then the spontaneity may be seen as a phony strategy to gain the other's trust. In this case, the spontaneity seems manipulative and is apt to produce defensiveness.

Second, the quality of the relationship may affect the success of an attempt to be supportive. Some caring, or at least some dependency, must exist in the relationship if the attempt is to matter to the other person. If you don't care what a friend thinks about you, you can treat him in almost any way you want. You can, for example, try to hurt him without worrying about the effect on yourself or on your relationship.

Table 8.2—*Continued*

Defensive	Supportive
Neutrality	*Empathy*
To show little or no concern for the other or his or her problems and viewpoint; to treat the other as an object rather than a person.	To identify with the other person's problems and feelings; to show respect for the other's value system; to affirm the other's worth as a person.
Superiority	*Equality*
To communicate that you are "superior in position, power, wealth, intellectual ability, physical characteristics, or other ways" to the other; to suggest that the other person is inadequate in comparison to you; to convey the attitude that the speaker "is not willing to enter into a shared problem-solving relationship, that he probably does not desire feedback, that he will be likely to try to reduce the power, the status, or the worth of the receiver."	To avoid "pulling rank"; to show the other respect; to minimize differences in ability, status, power, and intellectual ability.
Certainty	*Provisionalism*
To be rigid in your viewpoint; "to seem to know the answers, to require no additional data"; to adopt the attitude of teacher in the sense that you try to correct the other; to take on a win-lose position.	To be willing to be tentative with your behavior, attitudes, and views; to convey the attitude that more data might change your mind; to solve problems with the other rather than to impose your own view; to share data and work jointly on a task in a give-and-take fashion.

Again, providing these two requirements are met, four important benefits are possible from supportive communication. These four are encouragement, acceptance, dialogue and understanding, and growth.

Supportive Behavior Provides Encouragement

It is easy to be discouraged about yourself and your ability to handle your interpersonal relationships. (For example, when another person disagrees with or attacks your position.) Supportive behavior counters these sources of discouragement. Instead of discouraging, supportive behavior improves interpersonal encounters and affirms the other person in an encouraging way. It also provides a greater chance of achieving your goals because it encourages you to talk through your differences without feeling threatened.

Supportive Behavior Enhances the Possibility of Acceptance

The person who causes another to "give in" wins the argument but does not gain either real acceptance of the outcome *or* of himself. But supportiveness can produce acceptance in both areas. A person who conveys acceptance of the other and acceptance of the other's ideas as *legitimate* is likely to produce a feeling of trust and confidence. Even if the final decision is not to the other's liking, such a feeling of trust and confidence is beneficial to the relationship between the two.

Supportive Behavior Encourages Dialogue and Understanding

Defensive behavior often leads to ineffective listening and rigidity. Obviously, rigidity and closed-mindedness do not encourage dialogue or understanding. Supportive behavior offers a far greater chance of success because it causes people to sit down as equals and to engage in joint problem solving. Even though it requires careful listening (You can't express empathy without careful listening!), the result is honest, straightforward communication.

Supportive Behavior Encourages Growth

Supportive communication promotes self-esteem, self-disclosure, and growth of the people involved and of their relationship. Supportive behavior allows a person to feel more confident of his ideas and worth. Trust is developed in the relationship. This trust promotes sharing. The sharing helps an individual to understand himself more fully, to be more confident, to try new things, and to grow as a person. A person who engages in defensive communication, also engages in potentially negative consequences, both for himself and for the relationship. The attack on the other person's self-concept, the lashing-out behavior that often accompanies defensive communication, causes a disengagement process.[7] Obviously, there is no growth when this situation develops.

Growth and engagement are the result of sharing made possible by the trust the participants have developed in each other. They are able to decrease risk because they believe that there is a greater likelihood of support. Trust allows self-disclosure. The opportunity to get to know another person in a nonthreatening environment, even when there is disagreement between viewpoints, provides an opportunity for those involved to find commonalities. This, in turn, promotes liking and attraction. Thus, supportive behavior is a key to a growth-promoting atmosphere in an interpersonal relationship.

Choosing to Remain Supportive

Sometimes a student will say, "You folks talk about being supportive as if it is easy. It is not as easy as you make it out to be." We agree. It isn't as easy as it sounds. So we want to provide you with some additional pointers on how to use supportive behavior.

You Can Disagree and Remain Supportive

You don't have to suppress your viewpoint and accept the other person's in order to be supportive. Supportiveness is not a matter of right and wrong. You can disagree and still work out an understanding without attacking the other person. For example, you might say, "I disagree with your position, but I do understand how you can believe as you do. Can we work out a cooperative position?" A statement like this says that, while you disagree, you know the other person has a legitimate viewpoint and that you are willing to cooperate in coming to a decision. Remaining supportive does not mean that you can't disagree.

Understand the Need for Interdependency

Try to figure out if there is some sort of caring or mutual need in your relationship. Every relationship has some degree of interdependency, although some have very little while others have a considerable amount. Understand, too, the strength of this interdependency. If there is strong interdependency, then there is a chance that a particular need will cause the person to be concerned about how he treats you. Interdependency helps check the other's tendency to treat you badly in the face of your supportive behavior. There is no guarantee that the other person will recognize and respond to your supportive behavior. You are dealing with probabilities, but these probabilities are in your favor if there is an important interdependency.

Look for the Best Time to Talk

Sometimes people get caught up in the "heat of the moment." If a person is caught in an emotional rage, she is unlikely to be able to respond to supportiveness. Under such circumstances it is better to withdraw because she is probably incapable of listening. Perhaps, too, she has already drawn a rigid stance on a position. You could say, "I can see that we do not agree, so I would like to say that it is OK with me to leave matters as they are right now. I would like to talk more about this later, but now is not a good time for me. I hope we can talk again sometime in the next several days." Notice that this example is structured to disengage and to follow the principles of supportive communication. The goal is to withdraw from an unproductive moment without doing damage to the relationship, while making a commitment to talk later. If you select this option, you should be sure to carry through with your stated intentions by approaching the person at a later, more appropriate time.

Practice the Skills, Especially Empathy and Equality

Because incorporating supportive communication skills into your routine behavior may be a slow task, we recommend that you try being supportive at the very next opportunity, and that you practice the skills aloud. Doing so will better equip you for success.

How many ways can you think of to say or suggest:

1. The behavior in question may be described as . . .
2. We share this problem. Let's work at solving it cooperatively.
3. I understand and can relate to your problems and feelings.
4. You and I have equal status, power, and ability. We're both OK just the way we are.
5. Your position is legitimate. You have a point of view. I am willing to discuss the issue at hand with an open mind. I am not certain . . .

Remember that the natural tendency to be critical is difficult to overcome. As you increase your skill with language and nonverbal communication, practice in more difficult relational settings. Students report that practice can be very instructive and liberating. They discover that they can be supportive, that it does make a difference, and that discovering this gives them a new and welcome freedom.

We recommend that you focus especially on empathy and equality because they are key behaviors. If you are empathic, you will listen more carefully. If you avoid "pulling rank," you will avoid the notion that "I am better than you." These two attitudes generate a definition of the relationship that promotes the other supportive behaviors.

Summary

This chapter focuses on the behavior displayed when you are engaged in supportive and defensive communication. Carl Rogers argues that people engage in defensive behavior because there is a natural tendency to evaluate others. He concludes this is a major barrier to effective interpersonal communication. This tendency to evaluate is often met with defensiveness from the other person. Evaluation seems to suggest some defect in the other person, who may feel a need to defend his self-concept—to say that his view counts and that he has a right to his perspective.

Sometimes you defend yourself by ignoring the other person or by avoiding the person altogether. But if these choices are unavailable, you may attack. American culture teaches that "the best defense is a good offense."

Defensive behavior involves six categories of communication: evaluation, superiority, certainty, control, neutrality, and strategy. The consequences of defensive communication behavior, as seen in the following list, are numerous.

1. Defensive communication may signal rejection or disconfirmation. Rejection is an outright denial of the person's definition of self. Disconfirmation suggests that the person or person's opinion does not exist.
2. Defensive communication may lead a person to stop listening, become rigid in her position, and perhaps lash out at the other person.

3. Defensive communication may lead to hostility. When others do not seem to care, when they do not seem to take you into account, you become hostile.

The alternative to defensiveness is supportiveness. Supportive communication is characterized as descriptive, equal, provisional, problem-oriented, empathetic, and spontaneous behavior. Supportiveness produces many important benefits for both the person and the person's relationship with the other. Supportiveness gives encouragement, enhances the possibility of acceptance, encourages dialogue and understanding, and promotes interpersonal growth.

There are four ways that you can improve your supportive communication. Tell yourself that you can disagree and still remain supportive. Understand the need for interdependency. Look for the best time to talk. Practice the supportive skills that Gibb suggests. If you learn to communicate supportively, your relationships will be better, more satisfying, and more productive. These benefits seem worth the effort necessary to obtain them.

Discussion Questions

1. In what social contexts are you likely to behave defensively? What behavior in particular do you use to express defensiveness? Given what you have learned in this chapter, how will you work to alleviate defensiveness?
2. Identify three people you might call "close"—people you know well. What causes them to behave defensively? Does your behavior ever fall into this list of causes?
3. Using Gibb's six categories to analyze defensive situations in which you have been involved, do you think he is right or wrong? Are your behaviors consistent with what Gibb says will produce defensiveness/supportiveness? Give some examples of your defensive and supportive behaviors.
4. What can you do to help yourself remain supportive in a stressful communication situation? How can you help another person remain supportive under similar circumstances?

Endnotes

1. C. R. Rogers and F. J. Roethlisberger, "Barriers and Gateways to Communication," *Harvard Business Review* (July-August, 1952): 28–34.
2. J. R. Gibb, "Defensive Communication," *The Journal of Communication* 11, no. 3 (September, 1961): 141–48.
3. Gibb's theory has received considerable support from textbook authors because it makes sense and is easily applied. Some empirical support for the theory is beginning to appear. See J. V. Civikly, R. W. Pace, and

R. M. Krause, "Interviewer and Client Behaviors in Supportive and Defensive Interviews," *Communication Yearbook I,* ed. B. D. Ruben (New Brunswick, NJ: Transition Books, 1977), 347–62; W. F. Eadie, "Defensive Communication Revisited: A Critical Examination of Gibb's Theory," *The Southern Speech Communication Journal* 47 (Winter, 1982): 163–77.

4. P. Watzlawick, J. H. Beavin, and D. D. Jackson, *Pragmatics of Human Communication: A Study of Interactional Patterns, Pathologies, and Paradoxes* (New York: W. W. Norton and Company, Inc., 1967).

5. C. R. Rogers, "The Therapeutic Relationship: Recent Theory and Research," in *The Human Dialogue: Perspectives on Communication,* ed. F. W. Matson and A. Montagu (New York: The Free Press, 1967), 248–49.

6. See P. Watzlawick, *How Real Is Real? An Anecdotal Introduction to Communication Theory* (New York: Vintage Books, 1976). Chapters 2 and 3, especially, describe this interesting and frightening phenomenon.

7. I. Altman and D. A. Taylor, *Social Penetration: The Development of Interpersonal Relationships* (New York: Holt, Rinehart and Winston, 1973), 173–80.

Managing Conflict and Stress

Preview

American society defines most conflict situations as winning or losing situations. Winning and losing, however, constitute but one part of effective conflict management. Conflict situations can, in fact, present creative opportunities for interpersonal growth and development. Similarly, stress situations are generally considered to be negative situations. When stress and conflict are combined into a negative definition of yourself and your world, you are limited by the resultant tension. This has a dramatic effect on your ability to function and communicate. In this chapter, we propose an alternative set of skills for such situations so that your functioning and communication are not impaired.

Objectives

After reading this chapter you should be able to complete the following:
1. Distinguish among the various locations of conflict.
2. Identify each of the three kinds of intrapersonal conflict.
3. Suggest several intrapersonal intervention techniques.
4. Formulate a definition of interpersonal conflict.
5. Construct and explain Pondy's model of a conflict episode.
6. Explain when conflict may be dysfunctional.
7. Identify each of the interpersonal intervention techniques, and classify each as to its win-lose potential.
8. Discuss the typical use of conflict strategies in an interpersonal relationship.
9. Develop a plan for managing interpersonal conflict that makes use of the confrontation/problem-solving technique.
10. Identify the possible adverse effects of stress on the body.
11. Construct a personal stress management plan.

9

P hil believes that conflict is harmful so he tries to avoid conflict in the group as much as possible. Tim had been showing up late for group meetings and Phil could tell that something was going to happen soon. Cheryl was frequently saying in private that she "had had about all of this lateness." Phil kept trying to calm her down and once even dared to suggest that she needed to keep her feelings to herself for the good of the group. He said, "After all, Cheryl, you know that if you tell him off and make a big deal out of his being late, he might get mad and not come to the meeting at all. He might even cause trouble. Let's just plan to start fifteen minutes late."

You can imagine how Cheryl reacted to this suggestion since she never holds much back. She let Phil have it with both barrels. "What do you mean start the meeting fifteen minutes late! You must be crazy. How can you say such a thing? Are you trying to defend Tim because you and he are both men? I'm not going to let either of you mess up our group project just because Tim can't get here on time. You give him a message from me next time you get a chance. Tell him to either start getting to the meetings on time or I'll make a formal motion in the group to 'fire' him!"

Phil said no more. All he was trying to do was to make things go smoothly. Now he was going to have to talk to Tim. He knew that Tim would be just as upset as Cheryl and that he would be right in the middle. Now he was even more anxious than he was before he had tried to help. He could feel the anxiety in the pit of his stomach, and when he left the meeting, he thought that maybe he would be sick.

Phil's experience is not unusual for those who believe that conflict is bad and ought to be avoided. Phil tried to smooth over the conflict in the hope that it would go away. Cheryl, on the other hand, realized that the conflict resulting from Tim's failure to attend the meeting on time and the group's need to have him there on time was necessary in order to discover some reasonable way for the group to proceed. When Phil tried to smooth over the conflict, Cheryl would not let him do so. Thus, conflict broke out over the attempted cover-up.

If Phil believed that conflict can be beneficial and that the problem would not just go away by covering it up, he could have made the first step toward managing the situation. Of course, he would need to understand some basic conflict management techniques in order to address the problem completely. Finally, he needed to know how to manage the stress on his own body created by the conflict.

Some people in American society have grown up with the unwritten rule to "Avoid conflict if you can because it leads to hard feelings and damage to relationships." This would be a good rule to follow if it were possible. But most people find that it is not realistic to believe they can avoid conflict. It is also false that interpersonal relationships are necessarily damaged by the conflict experience. In fact, most individuals can point to many situations in which conflict strengthened a relationship. Finally, the belief that conflict should be avoided might increase the frequency of stressful situations if the conflict is, indeed, unavoidable.

Conflict Locations

It is clear that Phil was experiencing a great deal of conflict in this situation. The conflict is inside of Phil's head. This "head conflict," or intrapersonal conflict, is the most common and perhaps the most difficult kind of conflict to handle. *Intrapersonal conflict* happens as a result of how the individual perceives situations and how he talks to himself about the situations. There are three categories of intrapersonal conflict: (1) approach-avoidance conflict; (2) avoidance-avoidance conflict, and (3) approach-approach conflict. Each of these categories describes what happens inside an individual's head in particular conflict episodes.

Sometimes individuals conflict with each other, as in the case of Cheryl and Phil. This *interpersonal conflict* may be very complex, since it may stem from any one or more of five possible causes: differences in goals, competition for scarce resources, differences in status, differences in perception, or games played for particular payoffs.

Although some conflict is dysfunctional, or not useful, there is some conflict that is useful. Where the conflict is dysfunctional, you need a method for identifying the useless behaviors and for changing them. (These "intervention skills" are detailed later in the chapter.) Where the conflict is useful, you need a method for identifying and encouraging the useful behaviors.

As stated earlier, there are different contexts in which conflict is found: inside individuals who are having to make alternative choices, or between individuals who conflict for a variety of reasons. The first of these contexts is, by nature, different from the other. Intrapersonal conflict revolves around how you think and talk to yourself about a conflict situation. The other context involves interpersonal skills.

Intrapersonal Conflict

When an individual develops a thirst for a drink of water, moves toward the fountain in order to get a drink, but finds that the door out of the room has just jammed shut, the individual will experience frustration. If Mary Ann decides to go to a movie and drives to the theater, only to discover that the movie is no longer playing, she will experience frustration. If you have to choose between having and eating cake, you will experience frustration. If Phil comes to the meeting expecting all to go well, only to find Cheryl raising the question about Tim's continual lateness, he will experience frustration. Each of these situations is similar.

In each case there is a felt need, followed by some drive toward a goal. And in each case there has been a barrier. But look at the three examples carefully. You will see that there is a fundamental difference between the frustration Phil and Mary Ann experience and the one you experience. The source

Figure 9.1 Approach-Avoidance Conflict

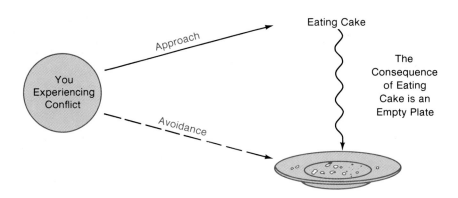

of the blockage Mary Ann experiences, when she cannot see the movie, and that Phil experiences when his expectations are not fulfilled, lie outside themselves. The source of the blockage you experience when you cannot both have and eat the same piece of cake lies inside your head. Mary Ann may experience frustration in not seeing the movie she selected. Phil may experience frustration by not getting the results he had hoped for in the meeting. But neither of them will experience *conflict.* Only you, in these three situations, experience any intrapersonal conflict.

Approach-Avoidance Conflict

Approach-avoidance conflict is produced when a single object, idea, or activity is both attractive and unattractive at the same time (fig. 9.1). You would like to eat the piece of cake, but you know that the consequence of that action is an empty plate. The cake will be gone, so you will not be able to have all that you want. Approach-avoidance conflict is very common, and is also the most difficult of all intrapersonal conflict types to manage.

Consider a more serious example of approach-avoidance conflict. If you are offered an opportunity to move up in your company (something you want very much), but you can only do so at the expense of your best friend, what will you do? If you have ever experienced anything like this, pause to consider the ethical bind. Then you know what approach-avoidance conflict can mean to you.

Still another example, a very common one, is the fear of sexual contact instilled in the young. American culture judges such contact "bad" or immoral. But a youngster cannot avoid or escape the factors that make sexual contact attractive. The resulting conflict sometimes becomes so severe that it causes personal anxiety.

Figure 9.2 Avoidance-Avoidance Conflict

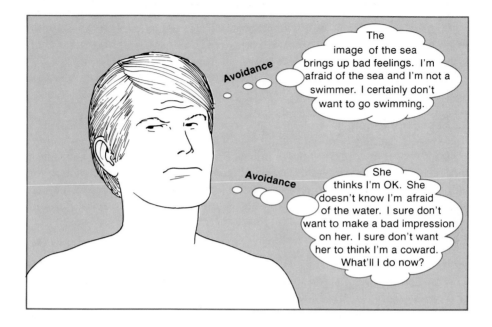

Avoidance-Avoidance Conflict

Avoidance-avoidance conflict (fig 9.2) is produced when you must choose between two objects, ideas, or activities that are both undesirable alternatives. If you find yourself in ten-foot-deep water at the sea, and if you are not a swimmer, you have no difficulty expressing your fear. You move toward shore quickly if you can. But if you are afraid to re-enter the water later, and you are asked by your best opposite sex friend to go swimming in the sea, you hesitate to express your fear because you do not want to encounter disapproval. This is a case of avoidance-avoidance conflict, where the alternatives are both repulsive.

A soldier, wishing to avoid the danger of combat, might resist his desire to run because he wishes, also, to avoid the consequences of running. His buddies would call him a coward. His officers might actually shoot him. At the very least, he would be court-martialed.

An employee who has made an error might experience this double avoidance conflict, too. She might hesitate to report an error to her superior because she fears the superior's disapproval. At the same time, she knows that she must report the error because the consequences of not sharing this information will cost the company a good deal of money and inconvenience.

Individuals working in groups often experience the same dilemma in the form of role conflict. *Role conflict* is the result of expectations by two or more persons or groups that are inconsistent. A line manager may want more resources for his work unit—and indeed his subordinates may expect this—while upper management expects that he will attempt to implement the latest cost-cutting plan.

In each of these cases, the double avoidance conflict derives from the necessity of choosing. Frequently, an individual resolves double avoidance conflict by moving in a direction that avoids both negative or undesirable choices. For example, a youngster who does not want to do his schoolwork, but who also wants to avoid the punishment that this implies, may elect merely to stay away from school—to play hooky. Soldiers have done the same thing: hundreds of young men fled to Canada during the Vietnam War to escape the alternatives of their double avoidance conflict. This kind of behavior can be viewed as *delinquent behavior,* or behavior that is not socially approved, and so is considered inappropriate. Yet, for some of the persons involved, the behavior was a carefully planned strategy of "not playing the game."

One way society controls its members is to broker guilt feelings. For example, the directive "Stand up and take your punishment like a man" creates both conflict and guilt in a youngster in trouble. He doesn't want to be punished; he doesn't want the implied disapproval of avoiding the punishment; he *can't* behave like what he *is,* a boy, or he'll be guilty of not behaving like what he is not—a man. Through an understanding of this conflict, you will be able to recognize it and, perhaps, to make intelligent decisions about it. You may be able to avoid it. Or you may only be able to understand it, and so have an idea of what to expect.

Approach-Approach Conflict

Approach-approach conflict is generated when a person is faced with choosing between two objects, ideas, or activities that are equally attractive. The individual is torn between two appealing goals. For example, a small boy at the movies may have to choose between spending his money for a candy bar or a soft drink (fig. 9.3). Approach-approach conflict is the easiest of the intrapersonal conflicts to resolve.

Individuals often do not have great difficulty making a priority decision in an approach-approach conflict situation. Sometimes, individuals experiencing this type of conflict resolve the trouble by discovering a larger goal that is achieved by either choice. The small boy, for instance, might realize that his real goal is to have something sweet during the Saturday matinee. Indeed, the only situation in which approach-approach conflict might be considered personally serious is if the chooser considers the loss of one of the alternatives as serious enough to be avoided. This would bring the chooser full circle, for the situation has developed into an approach-avoidance conflict.

Figure 9.3 Approach-Approach Conflict

The problem with approach-approach conflict is the impact of the person's choice on others. Suppose you ask your supervisor to purchase a piece of equipment for your work, perhaps a typewriter with a memory bank, then you would have a vested interest in his choice. Suppose another of his employees asks him to spend about the same amount of money for a television camera and recorder. He, too, would have a vested interest in the boss's choice. The boss is attracted to the idea of getting a memory bank typewriter *and* of purchasing a television camera and recorder, but he doesn't have enough money in his budget to buy both items. He is faced with an approach-approach conflict. You or the other employee, however, will be dissatisfied by his choice.

Intervention Techniques

Intrapersonal conflict, as you recall, occurs when an individual believes it is necessary to choose from among alternatives, and when there are unpleasant consequences involved in the choosing. This intrapersonal conflict is inside the individual's head. Remember, too, that the reality inside an individual's head is a function of the words used to talk about the objects, phenomena, or events outside of her. It is reasonable, then, to say that a viable way to manage intrapersonal conflict is to work with your own communication patterns. You can, for example, examine the ways you understand and describe situations. You can talk to yourself in tentative language—instead of in certainty—about your inferences. You can seek and find more explicit ways of expressing what is happening, or you can temper the negative consequences of the choices by manipulating those things that bear on the conflict, such as timing. You can apply all of these techniques in talking to yourself about intrapersonal conflict.

Remember, also, that the first understanding of a situation is not always the best understanding, and it is never the only understanding. It is extremely beneficial, then, to examine not only the perceptual alternatives in the conflict situation, but also the language alternatives. You might ask a trusted friend to help you identify alternative understandings of a particular conflict. This different perspective may help you see alternatives you had not previously considered. Once you identify and analyze other possibilities, you can make informed decisions about how to manage conflict more successfully.

Suppose that Phil had understood some of these intervention techniques when he was trying to decide what to do about Tim's tardiness. He might have realized that the tension he was feeling about an impending conflict was not necessarily felt by others. He might have asked himself if he was being too categorical in labeling the situation. For example, the pronouncement "conflict is disruptive" and "creates hard feelings and damages relationships" seems like an all-or-nothing statement. If Phil could have realized that he was being too categorical, he may have been able to talk and think in more tentative terms. Talking and thinking in more tentative terms may have led him to consider another option such as alerting the whole group to the situation, rather than trying to smooth over the difficulty himself. He may also have been able to use Mary Ann, as we suggested, as a sounding board for some alternatives to his immediate perspective and plan. He may have then pursued the issue in a more supportive environment. This kind of examination might have led to a redefinition of the situation.

We believe that intrapersonal conflict cannot be avoided. But we also believe that it is possible for you to intervene—if you are careful about how you talk about the conflict. It may also be helpful for you to seek a trusted friend with whom to share some of these concerns. The friend's fresh perspective can help you to consider alternatives that might not otherwise occur to you. We believe that if Phil had attempted this kind of analysis, he might have avoided much of the stress that he felt after fighting with Cheryl.

Interpersonal Conflict

Frost and Wilmot have defined *interpersonal conflict* as an expressed struggle between interdependent parties.[1] There are several implications in this definition. In particular, the word *struggle* implies that the parties perceive that they have incompatible goals; that the goals are scarce; and that the other person (or persons) involved are keeping them from achieving their goals. The aim of the people involved is to prevail or to gain the rewards. Opponents in intense conflict may even attempt to damage, neutralize, or even eliminate their opponents.

The important words in the definition are "perceived" and "incompatible goals." There must be differences between the individuals as well as striving for goals or scarce resources. If there is no striving, there is no motivating force

Figure 9.4 A Conflict Episode

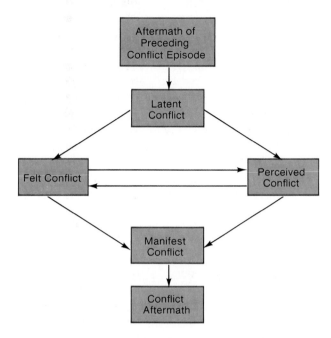

for the conflict. Note that sometimes the difference is real; other times it is merely imagined. Yet, in one sense it doesn't matter if the difference is imagined. If the persons involved in the situation *believe* that there is a difference, real or imagined, they will act on what they think is true.

The Conflict Episode

Louis R. Pondy thought that interpersonal conflict has a pattern.[2] This pattern is made up of a sequence of *conflict episodes,* with each episode following a pattern of development. The conflict follows this pattern across the sequence of episodes. Pondy's model is useful in understanding what happens when you become involved in conflict. The model of a single sequence of a conflict event is shown in figure 9.4.

Each conflict episode must be considered in the context of any preceding conflict that might have taken place. Thus, Pondy's model begins with the aftermath of preceding conflict episodes. He is taking into account that the resolution of past conflict affects the person's current conflict and its management. For example, if you have a history of unhappy conflict management with a friend, you will approach the current conflict situation with the expectation that you're about to encounter another unhappy experience.

Latent Conflict

A second element in the model is the probable source of tensions in your environment. *Latent conflict is potential conflict.* Latent conflict between peer-peer, supervisor-subordinate, or group-group might involve perceived limited resources, status differences, or incompatible goals.

An illustration of the development of latent conflict into observable conflict is helpful. Many proposals have the potential to produce conflict among Cheryl, Elizabeth, and Phil. They could have conflict over perceptions of limited resources. Anything can be perceived as one of these resources: food, money, position, power, equipment, materials, and even intangible items. In fact, Miller and Steinberg state that a reward is "any positively perceived physical, economic, or social consequence."[3] Thus, anything that satisfies one of our needs or wants is a resource. Power and self-esteem are two resources that are often perceived as limited and so are a common source of interpersonal conflict. Suppose Phil begins to believe that Cheryl is favoring Elizabeth over him with regard to a project on which the group is working. You can see that the potential for conflict in this situation stems from understanding esteem as a scarce resource. Conflict can erupt with Cheryl or Elizabeth, or both. Phil would be unhappy, and would certainly experience some intrapersonal conflict in the bargain.

Another source of common interpersonal conflict is *interpersonal interdependence.* If you depend on your friend, and she depends on you, each of you has to live up to the other's expectations. If you fail to live up to her expectations, or she fails to live up to yours, the result may very well be conflict between you. On the other hand, the same interdependence can yield unusual cooperation. You may see that, in order to achieve your goals, you must help your friend to achieve hers.

One obvious example of interpersonal interdependence is a dinner date. Suppose you and a friend have agreed to meet for dinner at a certain restaurant at 7:00 P.M. You arrive at 7:00 and find that your friend is not there. By 7:30, you'll probably begin to fret. By 8:30, you'll have left the restaurant—probably feeling betrayed.

Perceived Conflict

Latent conflict becomes a problem when it is perceived, but *perceived conflict* does not necessarily result in interpersonal conflict. If you perceive that your goals are incompatible with your friend's goals—whether they are, in fact, or not—then you have a potential for conflict. If you were to express a struggle over these incompatible goals, then you have an actual conflict. For instance, suppose your supervisor wants to buy a new typewriter with some of the money she has set aside. A co-worker thinks that the expenditure is foolish since each of you has a fairly good typewriter and other equipment is needed. Clearly, the *potential* for conflict exists *because* the co-worker perceives incompatible goals. But notice that no interpersonal conflict has actually developed. The co-worker has not responded to the supervisor's well-intended proposal.

Felt Conflict

Pondy's model shows that latent conflict can lead to *felt conflict* instead of perceived conflict. The felt conflict can then become perceived conflict. *Felt conflict is personalized conflict.* You sometimes take the problem as your own, so it influences your affection for the person involved. Sometimes you experience hostile feelings that may not even relate to the particular situation at hand. These feelings probably result from anxieties related to your daily life outside of the immediate relationship. To illustrate, imagine that you have been rejected by a friend. You may displace the hostility, transfer it from the real cause, to one of the latent sources of conflict in your life. It then appears that the hostility was generated by, say, a co-worker, when it was actually generated by your friend. This transfer is illustrated in the Pondy model by the arrow from felt conflict to perceived conflict.

The double arrow ($\rightleftarrows$) suggests the possibility of movement in either direction. You might perceive conflict and then internalize it through tension and anxiety (felt conflict). Or you might move from a general feeling of hostility to perception of some incompatibility.

Manifest Conflict

If you and a friend are angry with each other, and you both perceive it, something can be done about the anger. But suppose you are angry with your friend— perhaps because you think he has somehow betrayed you—but he doesn't know it. He goes about his business acting like nothing happened, and indeed, nothing *has* happened from his perspective, but you continue to fume and burn. Thus, you are experiencing a felt conflict that is not yet manifest, or outwardly visible. When this conflict is expressed, it is observable to the other and thus becomes manifest.

Interpersonal conflict happens when two or more people interact about a perceived or felt conflict; it cannot happen at any other time. Thus, interpersonal conflict can be considered communication behavior. Such a consideration is beneficial to the development of a communication perspective.

Conflict can be expressed either with or without language. For example, you may hotly or cooly disagree with another in the context of some meeting. The expression, in this case, is verbal. You are able, also, to state, "I don't want to talk to her about the matter. In fact, I don't want to talk with her at all. Please tell her I'm not in." Your friend would certainly get the message that you are experiencing conflict with her—especially if she knows and believes that you are, in fact, in your office.

The expression of conflict may, likewise, be blunt or subtle. The point is, conflict must be communicated if you are to deal with it interpersonally. Otherwise, it is an intrapersonal problem.

Functional and Dysfunctional Conflict

There can be both positive and negative outcomes from the exercise of conflict. Morton Deutsch pointed out that destructive conflict exists when all involved parties believe they have lost as a result of the conflict and so are dissatisfied with the outcome.[4] But if the participants are *satisfied,* the conflict has been successful. Although most conflict management does not result in either of these extremes, the goal of conflict management is to make the outcome as functional as possible.

In *destructive conflict,* the participants expand the conflict step-by-step even though there are other options. In fact, the participants often lose sight of the initiating causes altogether. This expansion in conflict often includes an increase in the size and number of issues; the number of participants; the number of principles involved; negative attitudes; and in changes in a participant's willingness to bear costs. Reliance upon control, threats, force, and deception increases dramatically. There is also a movement toward uniformity in position. Pressure is applied on members of a side who might listen to the other point of view.[5] This reliance on control, threats, force, and deception is destructive to relationships and, therefore, dysfunctional.

Productive conflict is managed so that some satisfaction is achieved and the relationship is not seriously damaged. It is usually controlled, whereas destructive conflict is usually out of control. *Control* is the careful management of both the relationship between the individuals and of the resolution of the basic inconsistency. It is productive conflict if (1) some personal and organizational goals are accomplished by some of the participants, and (2) the relationship is not injured in a way that will cause permanent damage or lashing out behavior.

Furthermore, destructive conflict is fostered by what Alan C. Filley calls "the ethic of the good loser."[6] He describes the good loser ethic as embodied in this logic:

- In a disagreement, there must be a winner and a loser;
- The loser is not going to be me;
- So you will have to lose;
- But losers can make trouble;
- So I'll tell you that you are bad (or evil) if you complain about your loss.

Filley concludes his discussion of the good loser ethic by pointing out its evil and the problem in resisting it. He states:

> The argument against the Good Loser Ethic may be made on
> economic as well as moral grounds. If the result of the Good Loser
> Ethic is a reduced self-esteem on the part of the recipient, then the
> cost may well be reduced energy, reduced creativity, and lower levels
> of measured intelligence. The lower self-esteem results in less
> motivation and less personal resources for those affected. On the other

hand, where individuals resist the Good Loser Ethic in power-oriented systems, preserving their self-esteem, the alternative consequences may be less cooperation and greater conflict in the social unit.[7]

So Filley presents a two-sided problem. He suggests that the good loser ethic is evil, but that resisting it may lead to greater conflict and less cooperation. If cooperation is important, and it is, some kind of conflict management scheme is needed to preserve energy, creativity, intelligence, *and* to enhance cooperation.

Intervention Techniques

Research into conflict management has produced a list of methods that people use in managing conflict: withdrawal, smoothing, compromise, forcing, and confrontation or problem solving.[8] Briefly, these methods involve the following:

1. *Withdrawal*—retreating from the argument
2. *Smoothing*—playing down the conflict (differences) and emphasizing the positive (common interests), or avoiding issues that might cause hard feelings
3. *Compromise*—looking for a position where each gives and gets a little, splitting the difference if possible; no winners and no losers
4. *Forcing*—using power to cause the other person to accept a position; each party tries to figure out how to get the upper hand and cause the other person to lose
5. *Confrontation* or *problem solving*—energies are directed toward defeating the problem and not the other person; open exchange of information is encouraged; best solution for all: the situation is defined, the parties try to reach a mutually-beneficial solution, and the situation is defined as win-win

Although Burke lists these methods as those supervisors use in managing conflict with their workers, these techniques clearly are those used in other interpersonal settings.

You can imagine that these strategies for managing conflict are likely to have a variety of results. Filley grouped these methods by their probable outcome in his book on conflict management.[9] Some of these are win-lose methods, others are lose-lose methods, and one is a win-win method.

Win-Lose Methods

Two methods are classified as win-lose. With either method, one person will win, and the other person will lose.

Forcing is usually a win-lose strategy as it uses power (or perhaps majority rule in the case of a group) to cause the other person to accept the goal. The loser is forced to abandon her goal. Often the mechanism for keeping the other person in line here is "the good loser ethic" described previously. It is not nice to complain when, in the case of a vote, the majority votes against you.

Withdrawal may not seem like it involves conflict at all since the method does not necessarily involve direct communication. But in most cases of withdrawal, there is likely to be some nonverbal communication, maybe some interpersonal communication, and certainly intrapersonal conflict on the part of the person who retreats. The winner here wins because the loser, by her actions, is giving permission for the other person to proceed.

Lose-Lose Methods

Both people give up something in a lose-lose situation. There are two lose-lose methods that are often applied in interpersonal situations.

Compromise is a lose-lose method because both parties give up something and so avoid confronting the issue. Compromise should not necessarily be avoided, but there are better ways to approach an issue. It is, however, certainly better than forcing, withdrawal, or smoothing.

Smoothing also falls into the lose-lose category because the people involved settle nothing. Sometimes people can "bury the hatchet," but this is not the usual case. More frequently, one or both of the individuals continue to suffer intrapersonal conflict because they are unable to put the issue aside. Sometimes this intrapersonal conflict becomes so intense that it reappears; the parties involved were only able to put it aside because they did not confront the issue openly.

Win-Win Method

There is an alternative to these "losing" strategies. This win-win method is confrontation/problem solving.

Confrontation/problem solving is practiced when the participants get the problem out in the open and try to use a joint problem-solving approach. This problem solving may take various forms. If the parties are not too far apart in their positions, they may merely need to focus on the goals and sort through the information that each has about the problem. In such cases, it may be relatively easy for the parties to reach agreement. If, however, the individuals are far apart on an issue, they may need to go through a more careful step-by-step, decision-making process. The important consideration here is to get the people involved to focus on goals each hopes to achieve, to reach agreement, then to focus on solutions to goals.

Mary Anne Fitzpatrick and Jeff Winke[10] examined how people act, specifically, when they want to address conflict in an interpersonal setting. They used the Kipnis' Interpersonal Conflict Scale to determine factor categories, then provided representative tactics for each conflict strategy. The result of their work is shown in table 9.1.

Table 9.1 Factor Categories and Representative Tactics for Interpersonal Conflict Strategies

Factor Category	Representative Tactics
Strategy of Manipulation	Be especially sweet, charming, helpful and pleasant before bringing up the subject of disagreement Act so nice that he/she later cannot refuse when I ask him/her for my own way Make this person believe that he/she is doing me a favor by giving in
Strategy of Non-negotiation	Refuse to discuss or even listen to the subject unless he/she gives in Keep repeating my point of view until he/she gives in Appeal until this person changes his/her mind
Strategy of Emotional Appeal	Appeal to this person's love and affection for me Promise to be more loving in the future Get angry and demand that he/she give in
Strategy of Personal Rejection	Withhold affection and act cold until he/she gives in Ignore him/her Make the other person jealous by pretending to lose interest in him/her
Strategy of Empathic Understanding	Discuss what would happen if we each accepted the other's point of view Talk about why we do not agree Hold mutual talks without argument

Source: Mary Anne Fitzpatrick and Jeff Winke, "You Always Hurt the One You Love: Strategies and Tactics in Interpersonal Conflict," *Communication Quarterly* 27:1 (1979), p. 7.

Forcing Strategies

Notice from table 9.1 that the first four of these strategies are related to forcing. The tactics involved in the category *manipulation* are attempts to use a particular behavior in order to get the other person in "a good frame of mind." Such behavior is an attempt to build a climate that will permit less open conflict. But, in fact, the behavior is manipulative because it puts on a false image to achieve a particular end.

The second strategy, *non-negotiation,* either avoids open confrontation by refusing to discuss the issue, unless certain conditions are met, or it avoids confrontation of the other's view by repeating a viewpoint until the other gives up. This strategy assumes that the other person will become so frustrated by the stalemate that he will give up in order to relieve the tension. This strategy denies the other person's view with the tactic of avoiding or ignoring the individual altogether. The attitude that the other person has no right to be in disagreement is often part of the tactic, too.

The strategy of *emotional appeal* relies on the use and abuse of the affection the other person has for the actor. The person may promise love and affection in return for achieving an end. One kind of emotional appeal is *displaying*. Tactics for this strategy include crying, pouting, or even the outpouring of anger in order to cause the other person to agree. An appeal might be, "If you really love me, you will give up studying for the test and go out to dinner with me." This is an attempt to force a viewpoint by demanding that you do what the person wants as a sign of affection.

Personal rejection is the final forcing strategy. Fitzpatrick and Winke suggest this strategy is an "attempt to make their partner feel stupid, absurd, and worthless." The message is, "You are not good enough for me to love, to give my attention to, or to be interested in, unless you give in to me. Thus, this strategy involves such tactics as attacking the other person's self-worth in order to achieve an end.

Confrontation and Problem-Solving Strategy

Empathic understanding is the fifth and final strategy presented by Fitzpatrick and Winke. This is a cooperative strategy that is in line with Burke's confrontation and problem-solving approach. It is a win-win strategy in the sense that the individuals attempt to understand each other and to accept the other's point of view if possible. You'll recognize this as falling into Carl Rogers's and Jack Gibb's supportive communication climate. The goal of this approach is to manage the conflict without damaging the relationship and thus to promote interpersonal growth. In using this strategy, you might discuss what would happen if you accepted the other person's viewpoint. You might even discuss why you seem to be disagreeing. You would attempt to remain supportive and avoid argument based on personal opinion.

Typical Use of Interpersonal Conflict Strategies

Fitzpatrick and Winke entitled their essay, "You Always Hurt the One You Love: Strategies and Tactics in Interpersonal Conflict." This title expresses their major discovery about use of conflict strategies: people hurt the ones they love. They use strategies that inflict pain more frequently than they use empathic understanding.[11] The subjects in Fitzpatrick and Winke's study who were involved in the most committed relationship, or those who were married, were more likely to use emotional appeal or personal rejection to win their way. People in less committed relationships were likely to use conflict avoidance techniques. They would divert the person's attention by using a strategy of manipulation or non-negotiation.

The apparent inconsistency in "always hurting the one you love" is simple to understand. Those involved in a more committed relationship can use more harsh, even pain-inflicting tactics because of the strength of the relationship. The bonds of the relationship are strong enough to withstand the risk of destroying the relationship altogether. Less committed people are more concerned about their relationship. Think of a committed relationship you are experiencing. For example, do you or your parents use these tactics in relating to each other? How do you work out differences? Compare your style in these relationships to that in your dealings with friends. Is there a difference? We think, if you're honest, you'll find that Fitzpatrick and Winke were right.

Recall the difference that Tim and Cheryl had at the beginning of chapter 8. Remember that they were at Stan's Pizza House and Cheryl approached Tim with the remark, "Tim, you're being pretty hard to get along with. What's your problem?" Tim met that conflict with a personal rejection of Cheryl.

Recall, also, the conflict episode at the beginning of this chapter. This time Cheryl and Phil were experiencing conflict. Cheryl threatened personal rejection of both Phil and Tim this time. Cheryl could do these things without much risk because there was a forced commitment in the relationships. Their group is bound by a need to cooperate in order to get a good grade. Cheryl could risk hurtful behavior because of the nature of the commitment. Had this been a voluntary group, Cheryl could not have acted so without destroying or damaging her relationship with the group.

In examining tactics used with same-sex best friends, Fitzpatrick and Winke found typical patterns for males different from typical patterns for females. Males were more likely to use non-negotiation strategies. Females use personal rejection, empathic understanding, or emotional appeals. These behaviors are explained by sex differences discovered by various researchers. Fitzpatrick and Bochner found that males rate themselves as more detached and controlling in their same-sex friendships.[12] Women on the other hand, have greater social skill. Although generalizations, these may explain the differences. Non-negotiation techniques do offer a greater degree of control. In contrast, the techniques women seem to favor require the social skill of empathy.

One annoying problem remains. Why is the empathic understanding strategy not the most-used tactic for managing interpersonal conflict? Although not substantiated by research, it may be that forcing tactics are viewed as more likely to be successful, easier, and less time-consuming than empathic understanding or confrontation and problem solving. Forcing tactics that avoid direct conflict, or those used most often when the relationship is less committed, allow the participants to think what they want. They also allow each person to stand fast in a viewpoint.

This kind of behavior occurs in dating relationships. Suppose that you are dating a person who holds fast to his or her beliefs and refuses to even discuss an issue unless you are willing to "see his or her viewpoint," or until you give in. You may be very careful about timing, too. Do you pick the time, and are you sure to be especially helpful and pleasant before bringing up the issue? It is as though you hope your behavior will keep the other person from rejecting you and being emotional.

Amazingly, people seem to think such efforts will be more successful than if they actually tried to understand the other person's viewpoint. There is irony in the statement: "If you understand the other's view, you might be forced to give up your own view in favor of one that seems more reasonable!"

A strong need or desire to maintain a committed relationship appears to be the factor that makes forcing seem like a more successful alternative. It is difficult to withdraw from such a relationship since most people do not want to experience the pain of a broken relationship. Therefore, they give in to the other person's view because it seems easier than suffering the pain of withdrawing. In this context, forcing becomes a powerful way of achieving a goal. The only casualty appears to be a slightly damaged relationship and pain for one or the other. In most instances, the damage is short-lived. But what accounts for the high rate of divorce? Is there a connection? If a connection does exist, then learning and practicing an alternative strategy—empathic understanding or confrontation and problem solving—can be very useful.

Managing Interpersonal Conflict

Confrontation and problem solving is a conflict *management* technique. It is not a conflict resolution technique. Management implies working with a conflict situation in a way that allows for a variety of solutions. Not all efforts will resolve a problem. Sometimes, in fact, differences cannot be settled satisfactorily. So while the following plan might lead to the resolution of the difficulty, it might also lead to understanding the other's position in a way that allows for empathy. Either of these is a desirable alternative to hostility.

Begin by understanding your typical conflict management strategy and the consequences of using it. The place to begin learning a win-win conflict management strategy is a careful examination of the conflict behavior you use now. If you assume that the behavior you presently display in conflict situations is not useful to you, and if you want to change that behavior, then you need to know what you are trying to change. Although this prerequisite seems obvious, people do tend to engage in conflicts over and over again, sometimes using the same language and the same behavior in each episode.

For instance, father and sons often experience conflict over the use of the family car. Dad wants son to be able to use the car, but he also wants the son to put some gas in the tank when he's through using the car. And, of course, dad wants him to bring the car safely home by a reasonable hour. Son wants to use the car, but knows that he is often short on cash. And, sometimes, he forgets the time, and returns home after the gas stations are closed. Thus, the conflict episode between the father and the son over the use of the car often repeats itself.

"Dad, can I use the car tonight?" Son sees the muscles in father's face tighten.

"Uh . . . well . . . uh . . . Son, I want you to be able to use the car, but I want you to bring it in at a reasonable time. And I want to find gas in the thing in the morning." Dad sees his son's posture change from relaxed to tense.

"Okay, Dad." Son heads for the doorway.

"Remember," says father. "Come in at a reasonable hour. And put some gas in it." This sounded like a "zinger" to his son.

Son turns, asking a question that guarantees the same old conflict. "What time is reasonable?"

"We've been all through that over and over." Dad is getting hot. "I think you know what reasonable is. Can't you take some responsibility for yourself?" That does it. Father and son have the same fight again.

The key to managing such conflict behavior begins with knowing what you actually do. Otherwise it is impossible to *change* your behavior or to develop some ground rules between yourself and the other that might help you to avoid the conflicting behaviors.

Or else, suppose that you and your best friend find that you often engage in the strategy of personal rejection. You treat each other to the "cold shoulder." You ignore each other when you engage in conflict. You might say, "It seems as if we tend to ignore each other when we are having a disagreement. When I do this, I feel frustrated afterward. I don't like the frustration. And besides, it doesn't do anything for the problem. What do you think?" If the other person agrees, you might make a suggestion. "I suggest that we try to sit down and understand each other, instead of ignoring each other. Would you be willing to do that?"

If you can agree to a basic ground rule like this, then you are well on your way to changing your conflict style. You may need to go further and establish other agreements. If, for example, either or both of you engage in emotional appeals, you may have to agree to hold those back, also. Of course, rules are broken and sometimes hard to follow, and you may not be totally successful in sticking to your agreements. Nevertheless, agreements are an important first step to successful conflict management.

Agree upon general, overriding goals. Each party in a conflict has a goal for any particular disagreement. This goal probably centers around gaining the other person's agreement. If this goal is the motivating factor in your current conflict style, then you are more likely to engage in one of the forcing behaviors we described. If you wish to avoid forcing, you can begin by stating your goals for the relationship dimension: "We want to understand each other's positions and talk in ways that show that we value each other." You can also set goals to counter your previous, unwanted conflict strategy: "We will sit and hear each other out. We will avoid the ignoring behavior we engaged in before."

Don't despair if you and your friend are unable to keep your new goals always in sight. Sometimes the habits you've depended upon in conflict situations are very well-learned. Even a very much desired goal can get lost in the shuffle of words in a conflict episode. Breaking such a learned habit is impossible. You have to replace it with a new and more desirable behavior. If you find that you are having difficulty in keeping your general overriding goals in mind during conflict episodes, write them down, carry them about, and refer to them frequently.

This mechanical device was once recommended to a friend who often engaged in conflict with his wife over the same things. At first he thought the suggestion was silly. But repeating a conflict episode over and over again, especially one which left both him and his wife unhappy, and one that they didn't want to repeat, was even more silly. He agreed to introduce the idea to his wife that weekend. Three years later, this friend said that he and his wife always write down the goals they have when they're in conflict, then share these goals with each other, make copies for each one to keep, and then bring them out each time they find themselves falling into the trap of habit. They still have conflict, but, reports the friend, they don't play the same old tapes over and over. Both he and his wife agree that their relationship has matured and grown.

Allow each person an opportunity to state his own position on the question at issue. Each person in a conflict episode should *describe* his or her position as clearly and fully as time permits. Each person needs a chance to talk, and needs to be as specific as possible. Stating positions is important because it can lead to some areas of progress by clearing up misunderstandings.

Suppose your friend had committed himself to helping you study for a geography exam, but didn't show up for the session. If you were a bit concerned about the outcome of the exam, and if you needed two pages of his notes, then conflict might develop. You begin by saying, "I am afraid to talk to you about this problem because I can't trust you anymore."

"I am surprised that you say that. I think we need to talk. Can we agree to hear each other's side of this?"

"OK. You promised to bring your notes over last night and to help me study for geography. I am sure that I didn't pass the exam today. You broke your promise."

"I am really sorry about the test," your friend responds. "I am willing to help you study, but I thought that I said that I would help you *if you wanted me to do so.* You didn't say anything, so I assumed that you didn't want help. I'm sorry." Each person might go on to state the circumstances surrounding the conversation and the expected commitment, a detail that could be useful for future commitments of this type.

The dialogue illustrates our point. If you believe your friend, it is clear that each of you had a different understanding of the commitment. Now you work out a way of being clearer about commitments. Perhaps your friend says, "Will you agree to call me next time something like this happens? I intend to do what I say I will. So if I fail to do it, it is because something beyond my control has happened or I do not understand what I am supposed to do."

Engage in active listening. Active listening encourages understanding because the other person must listen carefully enough to be able to repeat your position to you. You can also correct any apparent misunderstanding because you will hear the other person's interpretation of what you have said.

Often errors in hearing and understanding surface when you take the time to use this kind of feedback. Remember that active listening has some real advantages, so try to incorporate it as a step in conflict management. (You may want to review some of our suggestions for active listening in chapter 4.)

Suggest a range of ways of approaching or avoiding the difficulty you are experiencing. You force yourself to think of various perspectives when you name a variety of approaches to managing a conflict situation. Many people get stuck in a particular definition of a situation. When they are stuck, they are unable to achieve the flexibility necessary for productive discussion. Give yourself the freedom to adopt different positions by forcing yourself to consider alternatives to your favored plan.

Consider also that your initial positions might be far apart. Other alternatives might be closer to what the other person can accept. When both persons are thinking of alternatives, you may be able to come up with some position that both persons are willing to accept. Win-win outcomes are related to discovering alternatives that allow both persons to accept the position without feeling as if it were necessary to give in to the other's position.

Implement the final plan by specifically stating who does what, when, and where. Commitment involves action. It is an important step to decide what action will be taken by whom. Beyond "what," and equally important, are "when" and "where." Some plans never are begun because there is no commitment as to when to begin. Set a time. Set a place. Set a time to talk again with each other about how the plan is going. These steps may be quite important to your success.

This is not a world of fantasy where all differences can be managed through communication. Sometimes you will find disagreements that cannot be resolved. For example, one of the ongoing problems for some college students is a parent who is providing financial support, and so feels justified in imposing controlling behavior that treats the student as a child. Sometimes this relational problem is impossible to solve. Further discussion of the issue might only lead to a more impossible situation.

In cases like this example, the decision to withdraw from the conflict may be the best answer. Avoid withdrawal, however, that is intended to hurt the other person. Some people part saying, "I am not going to listen to reason. I will move out and never see you again." This attitude says, "The conflict cannot be managed. The issue is impossible. The problem will never be solved. I will make sure of that by completely breaking off contact." This is both an unnecessary and an unfortunate announcement. Try to keep the communication channels open for the future.

Finally, we want to remind you that in all of the conflict situations in which you are involved, you should keep the relationship in mind. One way to do this is to remember to include statements about the relationship. For example, you might say, "I am feeling a little frustrated right now, but I know that we will be able to work out our differences. We have been good friends for a long time and have been able to settle problems." Or you might say, "I'm glad that we are able to talk about this without getting angry with each other." Comments like this make a positive statement about both you and the other person. They also help to keep the relationship at a conscious level. You can imagine how this might help both of you keep the differences under control so that you can avoid hurtful remarks.

Stress

Recall the group's conflict at the beginning of this chapter. Phil was caught in the middle. "Phil said no more. This was more than he could take. All he was trying to do was to make things go smoothly. Now he was going to have to talk to Tim about being late for the meetings. He knew that Tim would be just as upset as Cheryl and that he would be right in the middle. Now he was even more anxious than before he had tried to help. He could feel the anxiety in the pit of his stomach. He left the meeting thinking that he was going to be sick."

Phil was experiencing stress. The anticipation of conflict became a *stressor.* Conflict itself can be a stressor. But conflict and the anticipation of it are not the only stressors. Stress is generated by deadlines, by performance requirements, and by many other events in life.

Stress is a necessary physical and psychological adjustment to the interpretation of an external event that makes special requirements of a person. Phil suffered stress. The external event, anticipation of conflict, placed a requirement on Phil. He was to give a message to Tim that might result in conflict. His body reacted by psychological tension and physical illness.

Consequences of Stress

Stress results in a number of reactions, some positive and others negative. Positive consequences include increased effort, increased state of alertness, and generally high motivation. Some negative consequences are even dangerous to a person's health. A representative list of negative outcomes of stress, compiled by Cox, includes the following:

1. *Subjective effects:* Anxiety, aggression, apathy, boredom, depression, fatigue, frustration, guilt and shame, irritability and bad temper, moodiness, low self-esteem, threat and tension, nervousness, and loneliness
2. *Behaviorial effects:* More accidents, drug use, emotional outbursts, excessive eating or loss of appetite, excessive drinking and smoking, excitability, impulsive behavior, impaired speech, nervous laughter, restlessness, and trembling
3. *Cognitive effects:* Inability to make decisions or to concentrate, frequent forgetfulness, being overly sensitive to criticism, and mental blocks

4. *Physiological effects:* Increased blood sugar level, increased heart rate and blood pressure, dryness of the mouth, sweating, narrowing of the pupils, difficulty in breathing, hot and cold spells, lump in the throat, numbness and tingling in parts of the limbs
5. *Organization effects:* Absenteeism, poor industrial relations and poor productivity, high accident and labor turnover rates, poor organizational climate, hostility at work, and job dissatisfaction[13]

Different individuals react differently to stress, but for the most part, we believe that all people experience stress and would like to avoid it. Thus, we present a plan for managing stress.

Managing Stress: A Plan

Many approaches to *stress management* are highly individualized. This is the case because most individuals are problem solvers: they are naturally going to look for some way to manage stress. The fact that individuals experience and cope with stress differently makes it difficult to propose any plan that will work for all people. But a general plan, such as the following, can be adapted to the individual. This plan begins with self-analysis.

Self-Analysis
List on a piece of paper four or five of the most obvious stressors in your life. Some of these are communication related, some are deadline-related, and some are performance-related. Concentrate, now, however, on communication-related stress.

Three communication stressors that I experience frequently are

1. _____
2. _____
3. _____

Now ask yourself some questions about goals related to these situations. Begin with the first stressor and follow through with it. Think of a specific situation involving this stressor. The situation under which you experienced this stressor was _____
_____. My goal in this situation was
_____ .

Analyze your goals by answering these questions:

1. Is the goal difficult but not impossible?
2. Is the goal clear?
3. Is the goal important to you?
4. Did you have a plan to achieve the goal?
5. Did your plan include an appropriate time frame or deadline?

If you answered "yes" to the first three, you are ready to proceed. If you answered "no," you need to go back and restructure the goal so that it is difficult, but not impossible. It must also be clear and important to you.

Structure Your Plan
How successful was your plan? We assume that it was not as successful as it might be. If this is true, then you need to restructure your plan. Try to talk over your plan with a friend who might be able to spot problems. When you restructure the plan, be sure that you set an appropriate time frame and deadlines. Briefly, sketch a plan on your paper.

First, I will _____

_____

_____ .

Then, I will _____

_____ .

Continue this process until you have completed the plan.

Check Your Plan
Since you are dealing with a communication problem, look for key words that describe the communication difficulty. Now turn to the Self-Help Guide at the end of the book. Find the references and pages that talk about the type of communication and the skills necessary to carry out that communication. Does your plan follow the suggestions? If not, it doesn't mean your plan is faulty. Use some judgment about what is right for you. Now check your final plan with a trusted friend. If you have determined that it is your best plan, then proceed with it.

Evaluate Your Progress
If you expected to confront your stressful situation and achieve first-time success, you may be disappointed. Most often you make progress, but need to repair your plan and try again. Skillful communication and stress management require practice and, often, repeated effort. Don't be discouraged. Note your progress. Now evaluate how you fell short of your goal. In which areas did you fall short? What might have caused the difficulty? What are some possibilities for changing your plan? Which one(s) seem the most promising? You may want to restructure your plan.

Restructure Your Plan
Now that you have additional experience with the stress-producing situation, go back and repeat steps two and three. Anticipate a greater understanding of the situation. You now have additional experience. We expect that you will be able to make more progress when you encounter the situation again.

Stress and Body Relaxation

There is considerable evidence that learning how to relax your body is an effective stress management technique. Studies have focused on particular relaxation techniques and their effect on bodily stress. It is assumed that reduced heart rate, lowered blood pressure, and other lowered physiological responses are signs of reduced stress.

Monitoring and Controlling Muscle Tension

Formal and informal programs have been developed that attempt to control muscle tension. Formal plans have been structured and their effects monitored. One such plan was discussed by James McCroskey to help students cope with speech anxiety.[14] His plan, and other formal plans, focus on muscle relaxation in situations that are not stress-producing. Then the person is asked to imagine a series of stressful communication situations, beginning with the least stressful situation. At each step, the person practices until he or she is able to control the resultant muscle tension. Research indicates that this technique significantly reduces anxiety.[15]

Experience: **Relaxing Muscle Tension**

You can achieve an effect similar to the systematic relaxation program on your own. Begin by discovering which muscles you tighten when you encounter a stressful situation. Say, for example, that you tighten your jaw muscle. Next time you find yourself in a stressful situation, discover if you are tightening your jaw muscle. Then concentrate on relaxing it. The key is to become aware of what you do and then to develop the habit of relaxing those muscles.

You can even create a more formal program modeled after that used in teaching people to relax in stressful situations. First, produce a list of situations that cause you anxiety. Arrange the list from the least stressful to the most stressful. Find a comfortable chair or recliner, get comfortable, and practice relaxing the muscle group that you seem to tense during anxiety-producing situations. After you have learned to relax without thinking of a stressful situation, begin work on the list. Master the least stressful situation first, then proceed through the list. As you progress through the list, you are gaining more and more control of your muscle tension.

Meditation

Again, there are both formal and informal meditation techniques. Daydreaming, listening to music, prayer, and watching the sunset are all informal forms of meditation. *Meditation* is simply redirecting the mind's activities away from the source of stress toward some other activity. You probably engage in some of these forms of meditation already.

One of the most popular formal meditation techniques is Transcendental Meditation. The Maharishi Mahesh Yogi introduced Transcendental Meditation (TM) to the United States in the early 1960s. With TM, the individual selects a particular word, a *mantra,* and concentrates upon the word while shutting out all other distractions. The person selects a place where she will not be disturbed, assumes a comfortable position, and concentrates on her mantra. Usually, those who practice TM will do so twice daily for fifteen to thirty minutes.

TM does work. A number of researchers have shown that TM reduces heart rate, lowers oxygen consumption, and decreases blood pressure.[16] Kuna has even found evidence in reports from TM students that this meditation also produces positive results in an individual's work adjustment, job satisfaction, work performance, academic performance, recall ability, and other areas.[17]

Physical education trainers and professors have believed for years that exercise is not only good for the body, but is also a good relaxer. Physicians have also recommended a systematic exercise program as an important step in maintaining body health. But does exercise really reduce stress? If you have engaged in such a program, you will likely agree. You are right. There is test evidence that supports your experience. Lynch and others[18] conducted an experiment in which they tested a group of men who did not exercise and a group of men who did. They found that those who did exercise scored better than those who did not in reducing three stress emotions—anxiety, depression, and hostility.

Be careful if you decide to exercise this as a method of stress management. No person should begin a vigorous program of physical exercise without assessing the body's endurance. If you are reasonably young and healthy, you could begin with a moderate program. But if you have any doubt about your physical condition or if you are an older person, you should first see your physician who can recommend a program that is designed for you.

Summary

Conflict can be damaging to a relationship, but is often a source of strength, too. This is especially true if it is managed carefully. There are three settings for conflict: intrapersonal, interpersonal, and group contexts. The intrapersonal setting involves any one of three kinds of conflict: approach-avoidance, avoidance-avoidance, or approach-approach. These kinds of conflict can be managed by being tentative about your conclusions and with consideration of alternatives. The language you use to talk to yourself is one important factor in managing these types of conflict.

Interpersonal conflict takes place in both one-to-one settings and in group settings, and follows the episode pattern. Sometimes this conflict is not useful and sometimes it is functional. Functional conflict manages the situation without damaging the relationship. Nonproductive conflict often damages the relationship. People employ various strategies for intervention in such conflict.

Lose-lose and win-lose strategies are often not productive. Forcing strategies are win-lose methods that are frequently employed to manage conflict. The major forcing strategies are manipulation, non-negotiation, emotional appeal, and personal rejection. In close relationships, you most often use strategies in this group that will hurt the other person and thereby allow you to gain your way. An alternative strategy is confrontation and problem-solving, a win-win strategy.

Stress is related to conflict because conflict, or the anticipation of conflict, is an important interpersonal stressor. Unmanaged stress can be a factor in physical and mental illness, although different people react to stress differently. You can develop a system for managing stress by following a five-step plan: self-analysis, structuring a plan, checking the plan, evaluating progress, restructuring the plan. Successful stress management also often involves body relaxation. Three relaxation techniques are monitoring and controlling muscle tension, meditation, and exercise.

Discussion Questions

1. In the preview of chapter 8, it was suggested that we frequently hurt the ones we love. Is this true in your experience? Why is this done? How might it be avoided?
2. Describe what you believe to be your most successful conflict management method. Would you describe this strategy as win-win, win-lose, or lose-lose? Why? Having studied this chapter, how satisfied are you with your method? What do you like about the method? What do you dislike?
3. Which of the intervention techniques that we've suggested in this chapter do you think you would be most comfortable using?
4. How does your method for managing conflict compare to the method recommended in this chapter?
5. Why is so much time spent giving yourself and others pain when trying to manage conflict?
6. How are conflict and stress related? Are they under cognitive control?
7. How do you manage stress? How does this compare with our suggestions?

Endnotes

1. J. H. Frost and W. W. Wilmot, *Interpersonal Conflict* (Dubuque, IA: Wm. C. Brown Publishers, 1978), 9.
2. L. R. Pondy, "Organizational Conflict: Concepts and Models," *Administrative Science Quarterly* 12 (1967): 296–320.

3. G. R. Miller and M. Steinberg, *Between People: A New Analysis of Interpersonal Communication* (Chicago: Science Research Associates, Inc., 1974), 65.
4. M. Deutsch, "Conflicts: Productive and Destructive," in F. E. Jandt, *Conflict Resolution Through Communication* (New York: Harper and Row Publishers, Inc., 1973), 158.
5. Ibid, 160.
6. A. C. Filley, "Conflict Resolution: The Ethic of the Good Loser," in R. C. Huseman, C. M. Logue, and D. L. Freshley, *Readings in Interpersonal and Organizational Communication,* 3d. ed. (Boston: Holbrook Press, Inc., 1977), 234–35.
7. Ibid., 235.
8. R. Burke, "Methods of Resolving Superior-Subordinate Conflict: The Constructive Use of Subordinate Differences and Disagreements," in R. C. Huseman, C. M. Logue, and D. L. Freshley, *Readings in Interpersonal and Organizational Communication,* 3d. ed. (Boston: Holbrook Press, Inc., 1977), 234–255.
9. A. C. Filley, *Interpersonal Conflict Resolution* (Glenview, IL: Scott, Foresman and Company, 1975).
10. M. A. Fitzpatrick and J. Winke, "You Always Hurt the One You Love: Strategies and Tactics in Interpersonal Conflict," *Communication Quarterly* 27:1 (1979): 3–11.
11. Ibid., 7.
12. M. A. Fitzpatrick and A. Bochner, "Insider and Outsider Perspectives on Self and Other: Male-Female Differences in the Perception of Interpersonal Behaviors," *Sex Roles* 7:5 (1981): 523–35.
13. T. Cox, *Stress* (Baltimore: University Park Press, 1978).
14. J. C. McCroskey, D. C. Ralph, and J. E. Barrick, "The Effect of Systematic Desensitization on Speech Anxiety," *The Speech Teacher* 19 (1970): 32–36.
15. R. M. Meyers, "Validation of Systematic Desensitization of Speech Anxiety through Galvanic Skin Response," *Speech Monographs* 41 (1974): 233–35.
16. See, for example, H. Benson, *The Relaxation Response* (New York: William Morrow and Co., Inc., 1975), J. F. Gavin, "Occupational Mental Health—Forces and Trends," *Personnel Journal* (1977): 198–201.
17. D. J. Kuna, "Meditation and Work," *Vocational Guidance Quarterly* 23 (1975): 342–46.
18. S. Lynch, C. H. Folkins, and J. H. Wilmore, "Relationships Between Three Mood Variables and Physical Exercise" (Unpublished data, February, 1973). Cited in J. M. Ivanevich and M. T. Matteson *Stress and Work* (Glenview, IL: Scott, Foresman and Company, 1980), 221.

Caring for the Relationship

Preview

Growing, healthy relationships are a great source of pleasure. Relationships that are deteriorating, however, have quite the opposite effect. This chapter helps you to promote growing, meaningful, and happy relationships. It introduces a method by which you can analyze the current status of a relationship and offers practical suggestions on intervention.

Objectives

After reading this chapter you should be able to complete the following:
1. Describe the developmental stages of "coming together" in an interpersonal relationship.
2. Explain why renegotiation is often necessary before two people enter the bonding stage of relationship.
3. Describe the stages of a relationship that is "coming apart."
4. Identify the function of definition and rules in relationship development.
5. Specify why people initiate the engagement process.
6. Suggest how the basic interpersonal needs of inclusion, control, and affection affect the decision to engage in a relationship.
7. Discuss the five specific ways you can promote relational growth.
8. Formulate a plan for combating relational decay.

10

P erhaps the most frustrating experiences are relationships that "just didn't work." In fact, people insulate themselves by expecting only a few relationships to grow, mature, and prosper. But in spite of this emotional preparation, they are surprised and even saddened at times when they value a person and a relationship with that individual, but discover that the relationship is failing.

We believe the ability to care for a relationship is a skill that is central to happiness. But the alarming rate of divorce in America attests to the difficulty of maintaining healthy, growing relationships. In fact, in 1983, one of every two marriages ended in divorce.[1] If it is assumed that people do not enter marriage expecting failure, then what happens? Why do half of the American marriages break up? There is surely no simple answer to such a complicated question, but we believe that skill in caring for the relationship contributes significantly to its success or failure.

Relational Development

The concept of developmental stages in interpersonal relationships has been investigated by a number of people.[2] One of the most sensible models of interpersonal development—and the easiest to understand—was presented by Mark Knapp.[3] Knapp says that there is a "coming together" process and a "coming apart" process. The coming together process occurs in five stages: (1) initiating, (2) experimenting, (3) intensifying, (4) integrating, and (5) bonding. Coming apart involves (1) differentiating, (2) circumscribing, (3) stagnating, (4) avoiding, and (5) terminating. Table 10.1 presents these stages and a representative conversation for each category.

Initiating

You initiate a relationship by making decisions about a person's attractiveness to you. You observe the person from afar, and make a decision as to whether you will invite the person to interact. This decision is based on at least two factors. First, the *situation* may encourage or inhibit communication. Social situations such as parties, for example, give you permission to mingle and involve others in casual conversation. The odds that you will talk to people you have never met before increase. Likewise, you are more likely to initiate a conversation when the situation gives you something in common with the other person.

If you are interested in sailing and attend a boat show, you'd be likely to talk sailing with some of the other people in attendance. On the other hand, recall being a brand new college student. As a freshman college student attending orientation, it may have been difficult for you just to walk right up to people and engage them in conversation. The newness of the situation and

Table 10.1 Interaction Stages

Process	Stage	Representative Dialogue
Coming Together	Initiating	Hi, how you doin'? Fine. You?
	Experimenting	Oh, so you like to ski. So do I. You do? Great! Where do you go?
	Intensifying	I . . . think I love you. I love you too.
	Integrating	I feel so much a part of you. Yeah, we are like one person. What happens to you happens to me.
	Bonding	I want to be with you always. Let's get married.
Coming Apart	Differentiating	I just don't like big social gatherings. Sometimes I don't understand you. This is one area where I'm certainly not like you at all.
	Circumscribing	Did you have a good time on your trip? What time will dinner be ready?
	Stagnating	What's there to talk about? Right. I know what you're going to say and you know what I'm going to say.
	Avoiding	I'm so busy, I just don't know when I'll be able to see you. If I'm not around when you try, you'll understand.
	Terminating	I'm leaving you and don't bother trying to contact me. Don't worry.

Source: Mark L. Knapp, *Social Intercourse: From Greeting to Goodbye* (Boston: Allyn and Bacon, 1978), 13.

your doubts about appropriate behavior may have acted to constrain the acquaintance process. But suppose that during this orientation period, you shared a college dormitory room with another student. The fact that you are living in such close proximity is going to enhance the likelihood that you will initiate a relationship with your roommate.

Attraction is the second factor that may invite or inhibit you from initiating communication. Consider what you know about people without talking to them and you will understand why attraction is a key ingredient. For example, you can observe physical appearance or the type of clothes and hairstyle worn. You observe the appearance and then compare it to your own personal likes and dislikes. Perhaps you like people who are close to your age, who smile frequently, or who have medium-length hair. Our guess is that many of the characteristics you like are very similar to your image of yourself. If you think of yourself as having average "looks," you will probably pick people who have average looks, rather than those you define as "too good looking."

Usually your decision is influenced by what you want from the situation, too. If you are looking for someone you would like to date, you apply one set of standards; if you are looking for advice about sailboats, you are likely to apply quite different standards. It is interesting to note that although there is very little concrete data available at this early stage on which to base a decision, you still make decisions about continuing or breaking off the relationship.

Once your decision is made, you search for an appropriate opening line. The message you send may be, "I'm a nice person, and I'm fun, too. Let's talk." This message may be sent by making a friendly inquiry that is often related to the situation. You might say, "I see you are taking interpersonal communication, too." Or you might say, "What kind of boat do you like to sail?" With such statements, you suggest that the communication channel is open and that you want to discover a topic for conversation.

This inviting process takes only about fifteen seconds, but the outcome is crucial to further relational development. At this point, you again decide whether or not to continue. Your decision is one of three: (1) disengagement, (2) keeping the relationship at a superficial level, or (3) moving the relationship to the next developmental stage.

Experimenting

Exploration of the unknown characterizes the experimenting stage in relationship development. You want to know who this other person is and what you have in common. Strangers often begin *experimenting* by collecting some standard information—they exchange names, names of hometowns, and places of employment. Students often exchange their major, year in school, and perhaps social organizations to which they belong. Since most people realize the superficial nature of this kind of talk, you search for some common interest or experience to which you can shift the talk. This moves the participants to a new depth of disclosure and to more meaningful, but risky topics. This more personal, more revealing level of talk becomes the basis for important comparisons; comparisons that allow you to make decisions about the future of the relationship.

Relationships are not sustained and do not grow if they are fed only by "small talk." You must discover significant areas of common interest as well as cognitive similarity if the relationship is to prosper. Research has shown that common interests, and especially similarity of attitudes, values, and beliefs, are most important for maintaining interpersonal attraction.[4] For example, if you believe that doing well in classes is important, you may want to discover if the other person believes this, too. If you think that he or she should be anxious about nuclear weapons, and if this is a major agenda item in your life, then it is important for the other to believe this, too. If you think it is important to have a particular religious belief, you will want the other person to value that belief, too. You experiment with and explore more and more topics as you work through this experimenting stage. You are disclosing yourself, demonstrating trust, and making decisions about the other person's compatibility.

While all this checking and double-checking is going on, the commitment level remains limited. People stay at the *acquaintance level* throughout the experimenting stage. And as is true of the initiating stage, there are several possible outcomes. You may decide that the two of you don't have enough in common to sustain interest, so you may break off the relationship. Or you might decide to maintain the relationship on the acquaintance level. In fact, most relationships operate at this level. You share something in common and enjoy talking about it—occasionally. The third possibility, of course, is to intensify the relationship.

Intensifying

Intensifying signifies a change in relationship from acquaintance to friend. Intimacy and trust increase as the partners commit themselves more fully to the relationship. Self-disclosure increases dramatically in amount and kind. You and your partner begin to share information that is generally withheld from acquaintances. You may talk about problems you are experiencing in relationships with others. You may reveal your fears and even your personal failures. This willingness to make yourself vulnerable is a sign of trust, and a very significant contributor in the intensification of a relationship.

Knapp suggests that there are numerous verbal cues that the relationship is intensifying.[5] Some of these cues are listed here.

- Forms of address become more informal: first name, nickname, or some term of endearment.
- Use of the first person plural becomes more common: "*We* should do this" or "*Let's* do this."
- Private symbols begin to develop, sometimes in the form of a special slang or jargon, sometimes using conventional language forms that have understood, private meanings.
- Verbal shortcuts built on a backlog of accumulated and shared assumptions, expectations, interests, knowledge, interactions, and experiences appear more often: one partner may request that a newspaper be passed by simply saying, "Paper."
- More direct expressions of commitment appear: "We really have a good thing going" or "I don't know who I'd talk to if you weren't around." Sometimes such expressions have an echo: "I really like you a lot," or "I really like you, too, Elmer."
- Increasingly, your partner will act as a helper in the daily process of understanding what you're all about: "In other words, you mean you're . . ." or "But yesterday, you said you were. . . ."

Changes also take place in nonverbal behavior. There is usually more touching and closer interpersonal distances at the intensifying level. Sometimes greater attempts are made to coordinate clothing styles, and more time is consumed in your interactions.

Integrating

When intensification of your relationship is satisfying, you may move beyond viewing yourself as separate and begin *integrating*. It is at this stage that you will move closer together. Partners spend more time talking to each other and may even share a house or apartment. This allows them to increase their contact.

These partners, however, are enjoying their relationship so much that they often distort their perceptions of one another. Often the distortions can even be heard in their talk about each other. One might say, for example, "This is the most wonderful person I've ever met," "He is so nice; I'm so lucky," or "We never fight because we see everything the same way." Obviously such statements are gross generalizations and distortions of reality.

An integrating relationship develops unique roles, rules, and definitions. For instance, one partner may generally have the last word in arguments. Thus, a definition of the relationship as superior/subordinate is evolving. On the other hand, partners may share in the decision making and hear each other out. Equality defines this relationship.

Characteristic conflict management techniques may also emerge. If partners start to "manage" conflict by yelling at each other, making cutting remarks, and lashing out to hurt the other, this style of conflict management may be accepted as "appropriate." But if problem solving is adopted as a style of conflict management, the partners will adopt certain rules related to this style.

Activities and hobbies are integrated into the relationship during the integrating period. If, for example, you like to go fishing and your partner doesn't, then he or she probably will not think of that activity as part of your relationship. But usually partners don't mind giving up things and adopting particular interaction patterns that they would not generally display. People sometimes do this just because they find each other attractive. They feel excited about each other. Sometimes they perceive the relationship and their activities within it selectively, changing, for them, the nature of that activity. A young woman in our department reported that her boyfriend loves to sail, but that she is afraid of the water. Nevertheless, she goes sailing with him almost every weekend. We asked her to account for this apparent inconsistency in her behavior. "I just feel so safe when I am with Charlie," she answered.

Julia T. Wood suggests that such distortion presents a special irony. Individuals are less attentive to the communication patterns and rules at a time when many important understandings and rules are developing.[6] For example, you begin to form unsatisfying methods for handling conflict that could lead to deterioration later in the relationship when the incompatibilities in managing conflict are discovered. Wood suggests that "the critical process of generating rules and roles for the relationship, thus, proceeds almost without partner's awareness."[7]

The verbal and nonverbal behaviors that characterize the integrating stage can be described as intensifying, sharing, and minimizing differences. You share where possible, and minimize differences between you and your partner. Knapp found that this sharing and minimizing process has several forms.[8]

- Attitudes, opinions, interests, and tastes that clearly distinguish the pair from others are vigorously cultivated. "We have something special; we are unique."
- Social circles merge, and others begin to treat the two individuals as a common package. They send one present, one letter, and one invitation.
- Intimacy "trophies" are exchanged so that each can "wear" the other's identity. They exchange pictures, pins, rings.
- Similarities in manner, dress, and verbal behavior also accentuate the oneness.
- Actual physical penetration of various body parts contributes to the perceived unification.
- Sometimes common property is designated: "our song," a joint bank account, or authoring a book together.
- Empathic processes seem to peak so that explanation and prediction of behavior are much easier.
- Body rhythms and routines achieve heightened synchrony.
- Sometimes the love of a third person or object will serve as glue for the relationship. "Love me, love my dog."

Knapp stated that these behaviors do not characterize only male/female relationships. Any relationship in the "integrating" stage will exhibit some of these behaviors.

Interaction in this stage is characterized by increased self-disclosure both in scope and in intimacy. Self-disclosure allows people to know each other in new ways. They are able to share their worlds, and even create a new, shared world in the process. This leads to deeper trust, which then enables the partners to risk sharing themselves even more.[9] Frank Dance has illustrated this process as a spiral (fig. 10.1).[10] The act of sharing reflects the commitment that has developed during the integrating stage of the relationship.

Language patterns change during the integrating stage, too. You will hear more use of "we," "us," and "our,'" instead of "I," "me," and "mine."[11] Integrating partners develop their own language to describe reoccurring situations. For example, in a work situation, one partner might say, "Let's go fishing." What he really means is, "Let's quit work early and go play." Partners may also develop nicknames for one another.

Figure 10.1 Characterization of the Trust—Self-Disclosure Spiral

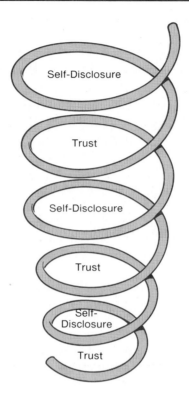

Talk about the relationship also develops. You hear signs of both integration and optimism if you listen carefully. Two sisters might say, "It's so wonderful the way we are able to talk to each other. I can't imagine it being any
better for us." Or two lovers might say, "I can't believe the way I feel when I'm
away from you. We just seem to fit together. I can't imagine not being together
forever." These are statements that describe being together, as well as optimism about the relationship. The decision to examine the relationship more
closely moves the pair to the next stage.

Renegotiating

Questioning the relationship signals a new stage. Julia T. Wood has termed
this stage *revising communication*.[12] Although Mark Knapp does not include
this stage, it is important if his *bonding stage* is to make sense. Bonding represents public, and perhaps, legal commitment. Before you make a public commitment, you will examine the relationship more carefully than you did during

Figure 10.2 Options for Renegotiating the Relationship

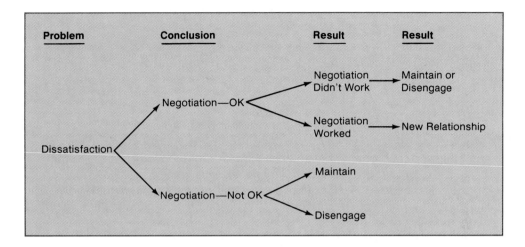

the earlier integration stage. Furthermore, you are likely to negotiate changes in the things you do not like. If this is not possible, you may begin the disengagement process.

The first step in *renegotiating*, then, involves a private examination of the relationship. Many questions and thoughts are raised: "Can I tolerate this person who wants to take a dominant role?" "I wish she didn't argue so negatively." "Can this relationship really last?" "Do we really have enough in common?" Such examination is vital to the decision to make a public commitment.

The answers and conclusions from this examination often generate dissatisfaction with various elements of the relationship. We have listed some options for renegotiating a relationship (fig. 10.2).

The model begins at the point of discovering the pain created by dissatisfaction with the relationship. Suppose you begin to weigh alternatives. "Should I ask her to try to change her ways? Should I offer to change my ways? Should we both give up a little in order to smooth things out?" You conclude that negotiation is OK if you believe that there is a good chance of success *and* that the success is worth the potential pain involved. "She's certainly the best woman I have ever known. So what if she doesn't do this the way I'd prefer. Her compromise makes sense, and my own part of the bargain may be better than what I was doing before." When you think that there is not much chance of success, or that the pain is too great, you may put the relationship on hold or begin the disengagement process. "She'll probably never change. Anyway, she says she won't change, and I believe her. Humm. That leaves me with no alternative, because I just can't stand to be around that behavior."

Taylor and Altman said that this process is like a movie shown in reverse.[13] You may see the relationship move backward through the successive stages. This means less disclosure and less contact. If you and your partner decide that negotiation is reasonable, you may begin discussion of differences, but fail to come to agreement. This might then result in either a "holding pattern" or disengagement. But if you and your partner successfully negotiate your differences, you are ready for the final developmental stage—bonding.

Bonding

The *bonding stage* is different from the stages already discussed because all the others are part of a process rather than an event in themselves. This process is relationship evolution. Bonding, however, is something different. It is a special kind of commitment, but not necessarily intimacy in the sexual sense—although this would be the situation in the case of lovers. Bonding is a voluntary, ongoing commitment to the renegotiated relationship.

There is some disagreement about the public nature of the commitment represented by bonding. Knapp suggests that it is "a public ritual which announces that commitments have been formally contracted."[14] In contrast, Wood suggests, "Bonding may occur privately between partners or it may be public, as in a ceremony."[15]

Public bonding can create a different kind of relationship than private bonding. Private bonding must rely more on the strength of the relationship to keep it intact. The fact that outsiders have witnessed a public bonding can help to keep the relationship intact.

The important features of bonding are its voluntary nature, its indefinite length of commitment, and the special rules attached to it. The voluntary nature of this commitment, and the fact that it is undertaken for an indefinite period, are symbolically important. They signify a powerful force that changes the nature of the relationship.[16] Bonding permits you and your partner to deal with each other with new freedom because you no longer need to be concerned that minor infractions of the rules will destroy your relationship. You can be yourself in ways that were previously impossible because of your commitment to the future. Thus, new rules of behavior are generated based on the new definition of the relationship.

Relational Deterioration

As has been discussed, various stages characterize the evolution of a "pair-bonded" relationship. Each of these stages seems to us—and we hope, by now, to you—to be a useful measure against which you can judge the current status of your own relationships.

But what about the situation in which the relationship doesn't work out? What if, somewhere along the way, the partners determine that their relationship is not a happy one for them. How can individuals "measure" when a relationship is coming apart?

Many relationships slip somewhat during the process of evolving. Sometimes this happens intentionally. Of course, there are also times when deterioration occurs while you are totally unaware of what is going on. And there are still other times when you know your relationship is coming apart, but you either do not know how to stop it or are powerless to do so.

This section can be very helpful to you for two reasons. First of all, when you know the stages in the *relationship deterioration* process, you will often find that you can reduce the chances of their happening unaware. Second, understanding this process can help you discover what to do when you want to counteract the deterioration process. You may be able to give new life to a relationship if you understand the process and some of the options for reversing the process.

To understand more completely the stages of a relationship breakup, examine the following relationships. Neither is a "typical" case, but the two serve to illustrate much of what is known about the process of breaking up.

Case I

Kathy and Joe had gone together during the year she was a sophomore and he was a junior. Both of them agreed that Kathy was the one who wanted to break up. She felt they were too tied to one another, and that Joe was too dependent and demanded her exclusive attention. Even in groups of friends he would draw her aside. As early as the spring, Joe felt that Kathy was no longer as much in love as he, but it took him a long time to reconcile himself to the notion that their relationship was ending. They saw less and less of each other over the summer months, until finally she began to date someone else. The first time the two were together after the start of the next school year, Kathy was in a bad mood, but wouldn't talk to Joe about it.

The following morning Joe told Kathy, "I guess things are over with us." Later, when they were able to talk further, he found out that she was already dating someone else. Kathy's reaction to the breakup was mainly a feeling of release—both from Joe and from the guilt she experienced because she was secretly dating someone else. But Joe had deep regrets about the relationship.

For some months afterward, he regretted that they didn't give the relationship one more chance. He really thought they might have been able to make it work. He said that he had learned something from the relationship, but hoped he hadn't become jaded by it. "If I fall in love again," he said, "it might be with the reservation that I'm going to keep awake this time. I don't know if you can keep an innocent attitude toward relationships and keep watch at the same time, but I hope so." Meanwhile, however, he had not begun to make any new social contacts, and instead focused on working through the old relationship, and in learning to be comfortable in her presence since Kathy and he sometimes see each other at school.

Case II

David and Ruth had gone together off-and-on for several years. David was less involved in the relationship than Ruth, but it is clear that Ruth precipitated the final breakup. According to Ruth, David was spending more and more time with his own group of friends, and this bothered her. She recalled one night in particular when they were showing *The Last Picture Show* in one of the dorms, and they went to see it.

"I was sitting next to him, but it was as if he wasn't really there. He was running around talking to all these people and I was following him around. I felt like his kid sister. So I knew I wasn't going to put up with that much longer." When she talked to him about this and other problems, he apologized, but did not change. Shortly thereafter, Ruth wanted to see a movie in Cambridge and asked David if he would go with her. He replied, "No, there's something going on in the dorm." This was the last straw for Ruth, and she told him she would not go out with him anymore. David started to cry, as if the relationship had really meant something to him, but at that point it was too late. At the time we talked to her, Ruth had not found another boyfriend, but she said she had no regrets about the relationship or about its ending.

"It's probably the most worthwhile thing that's ever happened to me in my twenty-one years, so I don't regret having the experience at all. But after being in the supportive role, I want a little support now. That's the main thing I look for." She added, "I don't think I ever felt romantic [about David]—I felt practical. I had the feeling that I'd better make the most of it because it won't last that long."[17]

Differentiating

In the first stage of deterioration, differentiating, the partners make clear the differences they see in each other. Recall that in the later stages of the engagement process, the partners ignored these differences and focused on commonalities. The partners were preoccupied with making new language patterns that showed unity. Differentiating, however, represents a change in the relationship's focus.

The focus during the differentiating stage is on the individual, instead of on the partners. If you perceive yourself as separate from the other person and the relationship, you gain the necessary distance to differentiate effectively. If you have "glossed over" important differences between you and someone else, these differences may resurface and become the subjects of conflict during the differentiating stage.

Signs of differentiation turn out to be the opposite of what you would witness in the integration stage. The "we," "us," and "our" language returns to "I," "me," and "mine." The shared possessions and friendships return to their "owners" or become less important. Conversation turns from the values, activities, and interests you shared, to questions about why the partner doesn't share values, activities, and interests. Too often, *why* isn't even asked. Rather than talk about their relationship, the partners privately dwell upon the awareness of differences.

Circumscribing

People involved in deteriorating relationships engage in circumscribing. They tend to avoid both topics and intimacy because either might lead to self-disclosure. Partners avoid the expected response by substituting some less appropriate topic for talk about their relationship. You can actually count a decrease in the partners' total number of interactions, in the number of subjects they discuss; in the depth (intimacy) of the subjects; and in the length of the communications.[18] This, you recall, is just the opposite of the engagement process.

Mark Knapp found that partners try to avoid risky topics when circumscribing.[19] But as the relational deterioration progresses, this becomes increasingly difficult to do. Knapp points out that "any new topic becomes dangerous because it is not clear whether the new topic may, in some way, be wired to a previous area of static."

Another characteristic of circumscribing is the lack of reciprocal behavior. While this is true of self-disclosure of all kinds, it is especially true of relational disclosure. The statement, "I know we are not agreeing, but I want you to know that I still like you," may be met by a neutral statement or perhaps even by silence. A statement about a concern may be similarly met. For example, you might say, "I feel bad about our disagreement last night. Let's talk about it." Your partner might either reply, "I don't want to talk about it," or meet your suggestion with silence. Either way, the effect is to isolate, cut off, and disconfirm the other—something you would not do if the relationship were healthy.

Stagnating

The term stagnating is used to describe the third stage in relational deterioration because it is characterized by motionlessness and inactivity. Verbal silence in the other's presence is indicative of this stage. Even though partners may be physically together, they close off verbal communication. But nonverbal messages are not so easily extinguished. Discomfort and negation can often be detected by the partner.

Silence means that something is happening in the relationship. Partners often carry on conversations in their heads, imagining how the other would respond. They also continue to make judgments about the other person. Many of these are negative judgments, which lead to further resentment and separation. They rarely check these thoughts out with the other person because they want to avoid the potentially negative outcome. These persons are saying to themselves, "I really can't bring any of this up because I know just what will happen, and I'll feel worse if I try."

Avoiding

While some people remain in the stagnating stage with hopes of reviving the relationship, people in the avoiding stage are in the process of breaking off the relationship. In this stage, you might hear, "Quit calling me. I don't want to talk to you any more," or "Can't you see that it is all over? I don't want to even see you anymore." Statements can be as blunt as these, but they can also be quite subtle. For example, "I don't really have time to see you today" is an avoidance communication. You might also hear, "I'm sorry, but I really can't stay long." Sometimes avoidance is evidenced in a put off, as with, "I'm busy tonight." The other person then replies, "How about tomorrow?" The invitation for tomorrow is avoided with, "I told my boss I'd work late." The person may persist, "When can I see you?" To which is replied, "I'll call you when I'm free."

Rain
Pierre Henri Delattre

I can't see you this afternoon.
It's beginning to rain,
And I have to look at the rain
All afternoon with my window open,
Hold out my hand to it,
Touch sorrow, come in again.

How can I explain that my time
Is taken up with rain? It's like
Indifferent sadness
Watching from a train.

The sky is getting late
But the night is slow.
I shall sleep for a while
And wake for a while
And look out again
At the rain.

There were ten things we had to do
Between noon and nine.
Postpone them. The rain
Is taking up my time.

Terminating

It is not clear that the terminating "stage" is really a stage at all. It seems to be more an ending point or announcement, which can be made in several ways. People who are living together may physically separate. They may even sever all contacts by moving to a different part of town, or perhaps a different city. At this point, the relationship is usually dead and both parties know it. They want to publicly acknowledge this fact. Generally, some parting statement about expectations regarding contact is made. This might be, "I want to make it clear that you are not welcome in my house," "We'll stay in touch by phone about the children. But don't come over to the house unless you call and I agree."

The relationship is over, but in situations where there has been a lengthy commitment, there is a *grieving period.* As with physical death, people experience loss when a relationship dies. Partners will frequently go through a period of intense negative feelings and blaming. Although painful, this seems to be a necessary part of the healing process for many people.

Two Important Relational Elements

Underlying this developmental view of communication in interpersonal relationships are two fundamental elements—*definition* and *rules.* These two elements are found at every stage of the process. The extent of the agreement on these elements by the partners becomes an important measure of the relationship's stability.

Relational Definition

The partners have a definition of the relationship at every point in its development. A typical definition is "We enjoy each other, but we are mere acquaintances." Another couple might define their relationship by saying, "We are best friends." An eighteen-year-old said, "You'd have to say we're friends—special friends—but just friends."

The main reason for considering these definitions is that they indicate the stability of the relationship. A *stable relationship* is one in which there is agreement about the kind and nature of the relationship. Thus, when both say that they are "best friends," they are in agreement about the kind and nature of the relationship. That agreement undoubtedly assumes that they have talked about, and agreed upon, what it means to be best friends.

William W. Wilmot presented three aspects of relational stability:

1. Relationships stabilize because the participants reach some minimal agreement (usually implicitly) of what they want from the relationship.
2. Relationships stabilize at different levels of intimacy.
3. A "stabilized" relationship still has areas of change.[20]

Outsiders may not understand why the relationship is stable, as, for example, when parents evaluate the relationships their offspring have with others. This does not matter if the partners agree on the nature of the relationship. Outsiders may believe some aspect of the relationship is crucial, while the participants see that aspect as unimportant. For example, consider the marriage that is stable because the participants value the financial resources they can give each other. For them this security is important. The fact that they hold few interests in common may not matter.

People will not be satisfied unless they can achieve a minimal positive agreement about what they want from their relationship. For example, mere acquaintances may want to receive a happy greeting when they meet each other. They may not need any particularly meaningful conversation.

Wilmot's second aspect of stability is that individuals fix the relationship at a particular level of intimacy that they find satisfying. When partners agree to a particular level of intimacy in a relationship, they stabilize it at that level. This kind of agreement is important if the relationship is to be satisfying. Suppose you meet a professor who shares your particular academic interests. You think that it would be nice to get to know him as a friend. He, however, thinks that the acquaintance level is enough for a student-teacher relationship. You have a definitional problem that could generate some awkward moments: you try to be a friend and he brushes you off as an acquaintance.

Finally, Wilmot's third aspect of stability suggests that stability does not mean stagnation. There is always some change in a relationship that requires negotiation. As time passes, people want different things from a relationship. If these wants are met, a new definition is struck and the relationship takes on new stability. If they are not met, the resulting instability might lead to relational deterioration.

Relational Rules

Most people behave according to a set of societal rules governing what they can and cannot do to others when they talk. Society dictates a certain level of politeness, for example. Moreover, people are also expected to keep the conversation at a certain level of intimacy, usually a safe, nonintimate level for strangers.

But how do you know *what* these societal rules are? The answer lies in the concept of *prediction*.[21] (Review chapter 7, which bears directly on this discussion.) You predict how the other person might act based on social and cultural cues you get from the person's verbal and nonverbal behavior. "How it's supposed to be" governs what happens. Gerald R. Miller and Mark Steinberg classify this kind of relationship as impersonal.[22]

As members of a relationship become acquainted through self-disclosure, they become aware of each other's personality. This gives them an additional basis for predicting behavior, and may be more reliable since it takes into account the uniqueness of the person. Now the relationship has moved from the impersonal level to the *interpersonal* level.

A change in level, from impersonal to interpersonal, allows the partners in a relationship to set rules based upon their respective preferences. For example, it might be OK for Tim to tease Cheryl about her being overweight. And the group might permit Tim to express his "hotheadedness" when he is angry. They may also establish the informal relational rule that allows Mary Ann to dominate all the others during a crisis. Each of these relational rules is based upon a knowledge of the members' peculiarities and agreeing to rules that will allow the group to succeed. The more often the group members adopt rules based on their relationships, the more predictable, interpersonal, and intimate they become.

Initiating Relationships

All relationships have a beginning. But *why* do people engage other people in relationships? Knowing *why* will help you to understand *how* the process actually works. This should help you to manage your relationships more effectively when you want to do so.

Why You Engage

Interpersonal attraction is the most obvious response to the question, "Why do people decide to engage others in conversations that lead to interpersonal relationships?" This attraction might be physical, social, or task-related.

Physical attraction is clearly an important factor in initiating communication. You are more likely to start a conversation with a person you find physically attractive. But defining just what physical attractiveness means is a difficult assignment. Everyone has some ideal image of an attractive person. But often, when it comes to deciding about interaction, you choose to apply a definition of attractiveness that favors someone much like yourself. You know that you don't fit the ideal image, but you do think of yourself *within the range* of what you would call attractive.

Other than mere attractiveness, people might want to engage in conversation because of an attribute they believe is related to attractiveness. Researchers find that certain inferences are drawn regarding attractive people. Attractive people are thought to be more sexual, personable, persuasive, popular, happy, kind, interesting, confident, sociable, serious, and outgoing.[23] You might engage an attractive person in conversation because you suppose the person possesses some of these attributes.

Socially attractive people seem to draw others into engagement. Social attraction, like physical attraction, is highly dependent upon the individual's frame of reference. You might feel attracted to a person with a sense of humor, a storyteller who can carry the conversation. On the other hand, another might feel attracted to a person who is direct but less forward, and who can carry on a conversation about woodworking. Generally, if you look around your social circle, you will discover something about your definition of socially attractive. You are drawn to a socially attractive person because his behavior meets your need for social stimulation. Your needs are particular to the persons involved.

A person is *task attractive* if you enjoy working with him or her. When you appreciate the way people work on a project, whether in a club, social organization, or on the job, you seek more contact with them. Working with them brings enjoyment as well as productivity. Both of these elements, enjoyment and productivity, are important parts in task attraction. So, even if you believe that the person is efficient and productive, but also boring, you are not likely to engage in conversation with that individual.

Basic Interpersonal Needs

People experience three basic interpersonal needs that affect their decision to engage: inclusion, control, and affection. Each of these needs may be present in a degree range of high to low. Moreover, you both give and receive these needs. For example, you have some need to include others and a need for yourself to be included. You have a need to control others and a need to be controlled. You have a need to love and a need to be loved. Table 10.2 will help you to imagine how basic interpersonal needs can affect the likelihood of engagement.

Expectations of Relational Benefits

In *intimate relations,* M. S. Davis suggests that there are four motivations for interpersonal engagement:

1. The impulse to receive stimulation
2. The impulse to express experiences
3. The impulse to assert oneself
4. The impulse to enhance enjoyment of certain activities[24]

Because of their importance, these require individual discussion.

College students often experience the impulse to receive stimulation when Saturday evening comes along and they don't have plans to share the evening. The impulse to receive stimulation is also strongly felt when a dating relationship ends and a person feels alone.

Sometimes this impulse for stimulation is generated by a relationship that has become too routine; the people do the same things over and over. They become bored and this boredom gives them the initiative to begin new relationships. Each of these situations presents a context in which people experience an impulse to receive stimulation from others.

The second motivation for engagement is the impulse to express experiences. To illustrate the impulse to express experiences, suppose you've been

Table 10.2 Interpersonal Needs and Initiating Relationships

Needs	Intensity	Impact on Initiating
Need to include	High	May give parties and include new acquaintances
	Low	May stick to own circle of friends; may avoid initiating
Need to be included	High	May seek opportunities to initiate; may "push" self on strangers
	Low	May avoid initiating contact; may enjoy being alone
Need to control	High	May initiate contact with those who appear to be easily controlled
	Low	May initiate contact with those who appear to be equal or able to "hold their own" in a relationship
Need to be controlled	High	May initiate contact with those who appear to dominate others
	Low	May initiate contact with those who do not control others; may avoid contact with those who appear to control
Need to love	High	May initiate contact with those who need "warmth;" may avoid contact with those who appear to be "cold" and uncaring
	Low	May initiate contact with those who appear to need little affection; may avoid initiating contact
Need to be loved	High	May initiate contact with those who appear to give "warmth;" may avoid contact with those who appear to be "cold" and uncaring
	Low	May initiate contact with those who appear not to give too much affection; may avoid initiating contact

out looking for a car to buy and have just found the right car at the right price. Your immediate impulse is probably to share the news with someone else. Everyone has had a similar experience of having good news to share. You feel frustrated and perhaps even a little cheated if nobody is available to share your news. The joy of sharing such an experience is important.

The same is true about bad news. If the boss has been grumpy and you received the brunt of it, you will want to share this experience. This sharing is an opportunity for you to receive empathy and encouragement from another person. It may even prompt the other person to share a similar experience. This reciprocal sharing provides a basis for comparing your experiences to those of others.

Or else, can you recall a time when you felt that you did not do well on a test? We'll guess that you do remember such a time, and that it didn't take you long to seek out others in the class with whom you could commiserate! "That was some kind of a test," you say. "Yeah. I think it was the hardest one yet. What did you think of that essay question?" You both shudder at the thought of the essay question before you add, "I'll study harder next time."

The third motivation, the impulse to assert oneself, is not related, as you might suspect, to assertiveness. Rather, it refers to the expression of an idea that needs testing. People have impulses to express ideas of which they are unsure, ideas for which they need feedback. This expression and its related feedback undoubtedly serve the purpose of developing an individual's identity and self-concept. You may not be particularly interested in confirming your ideas, but you want to discover how others react to them. You are acting on an impulse for both social contact and comparison when you seek people out for this purpose.

Finally, people are motivated to engage others because being together enhances their enjoyment of an activity. You join together to play games and to engage in certain kinds of recreational activities. You join together to celebrate our important events. Imagine celebrating your birthday by yourself. Or perhaps you can picture yourself trying to celebrate Independence Day, July 4th, by yourself. Being together allows you to share your joy, your excitement, and your thoughts so that you gain more enjoyment from the activity.

Engaging Another Person

Mere talk is not necessarily interpersonal communication. Interpersonal communication moves beyond the impersonal application of societal rules. Impersonal talk is important, of course, but it relates only minimally to engagement. William and Judith Pfeiffer suggested that the important last step in the engagement process is *contact*.[25] They illustrated the engagement process in four steps, as shown in figure 10.3.

Very simply, this process progresses from becoming aware of the person, to being excited by the prospect of the conversation, to acting on that excitement, and finally to making contact. Real contact is never made if there is an intent to remain impersonal. Only an intent to get to know the person psychologically moves you to make interpersonal contact.

Promoting Relational Growth

Relational growth is something that can happen naturally, without any particular effort from the partners. However, relational growth is more often the result of active effort on the part of one or both of the people involved. Further, informed effort, that which is based on understanding of what promotes growth, is likely to yield a healthier and more satisfying relationship.

Figure 10.3 The Engagement Process

Awareness — — — — — — →Excitement — — — — — — → Action — — — — — — → Contact

Based upon what we've said previously, it won't surprise you to discover that we think there are five specific ways you can promote relational growth:

1. Appropriate self-disclosing
2. Achieving role and rule agreement
3. Giving support
4. Demonstrating affection and liking
5. Managing conflict constructively

Appropriate Self-Disclosure

Sidney Jourard said that you cannot possibly love another person unless that person is fully disclosed to you.[26] He meant that you must know a person in order to develop affection for that person. This knowledge is important for at least three reasons.

First, knowing provides a basis to discover similarities, or common areas of interest. Discovering similarities is very important to the development and growth of a relationship. Obviously, people feel more comfortable with those who are similar to themselves. Self-disclosure allows the discovery of similar areas of interest and beliefs. Not only do you feel comfortable in knowing that an individual is like you, but you also trust the person because that person's behavior seems predictable. You might say, "I understand Jean. I know how she is likely to react. These things help us get along."

Second, the act of disclosing promotes disclosure. When a person shares with you, and you see the disclosure as appropriate, you generally respond by disclosing yourself. Over time, this kind of talk leads to greater intimacy. Each knows more of the other's experience (breadth) and more of the personal and private parts of the other's experience (depth).

Finally, self-disclosure is stimulating to the relationship. A stagnant relationship may be characterized, in part, as one in which there is no "news." When disclosure drops off to the point that the partners stop learning about each other, the relationship does not—cannot—grow.

Achieving Role and Rule Agreement

Satisfaction in a relationship is contingent upon the achievement of role and rule agreement. But once these are negotiated, continued satisfaction depends upon successful change. As relationships mature, the partners' ideas of what is appropriate for the relationship must mature as well. When there is no room for renegotiation, the relationship will probably cease to grow. Negotiation is a function of many of the skills discussed in previous chapters, but conflict management is especially important. When a partner introduces dissatisfaction with some aspect of role or rules, conflict is introduced into the relationship.

Giving Support

Supporting another person involves two particular kinds of activities. First, the partner needs to be supported as a person, affirmed as a person, and valued as a person. Carl Rogers called this kind of support "unconditional positive regard."[27] Such valuing on a day-to-day basis results in a positive climate for relational growth.

Second, a partner needs support and confirmation when the pressures of daily living create a need for bolstering. Earlier you learned that people are motivated to engage others because of a need to share. One particular kind of sharing is bad news. When the activities of the day have been disappointing, you feel a need to share so that you can be supported. You may recall how much psychologically easier it is to handle a problem when you can share that problem with a friend. Active listening and empathy are the two main vehicles for such support. Support is essential to growth in a relationship and contributes directly to the psychological health of the partners.

Demonstrating Affection and Liking

In William Schutz's model of interpersonal needs, one of the three primary interpersonal needs is *affection*.[28] Each person in a relationship has some particular need for being liked. If a relationship is to grow and prosper, the partners should pay attention to meeting this need in each other. The first step in being able to give affection is to discover the nature of this need for your partner. Some people want affection to be demonstrated more frequently and more directly than others. You need to know the expectations of your partner.

In Eric Berne's theory of transactional analysis, a display of affection is called *stroking*.[29] When you give strokes to an infant, you physically touch the child. Adult stroking behavior does not always involve such overt acts as touching. Of course, touch stroking may happen in intimate relationships, but it does not usually occur in others. Instead, people in the American culture tend to engage in verbal stroking. You might make it a point to remember to tell the other person from time to time how much you appreciate him or her. Be sure, also, to recognize the positive achievements of the other person. Noticing how good the other person feels is a powerful way of stroking.

Therapist Muriel James suggests that good friends give each other this kind of stroking. She recommends that you agree to help each other when needed by directly signaling the need. You might say to a good friend, "I really feel beat down today. Things have just not gone right for me." The partner then might reassure you about his or her affection. This kind of reassurance is also very important to the relationship, since knowing that you can share your disappointments and still be liked will almost certainly enhance the growth of the relationship. But keep in mind that the individual who repeatedly asks for support can become "needy." That is, this partner may be seen as forever dependent and the other may come to resent this overdependence. Each pair must decide how much of this kind of sharing is healthy for their particular relationships.

Managing Conflict Constructively

Partners who are not successful in managing conflict cannot expect their relationship to grow. In fact conflict that is not managed carefully can promote resentment and bitterness. A history of resentment and bitterness is a serious relational problem, for it promotes differentiating, circumscribing, stagnation, avoiding, and finally, terminating of the relationship. Successful conflict management, on the other hand, provides a sense of accomplishment, growth, and optimism. It is important, therefore, to sharpen your conflict management skills. (The material in chapter 9 will help you.)

Confronting Relational Problems

Preventing Stagnation

Relational stagnation occurs when a relationship ceases to be stimulating. The solution to this difficulty, therefore, is to find ways to increase stimulation. We could never complete a list of suggestions for increasing stimulation in your relationships, but we can list three of the most important ones.

Set a time for sharing
You often get so busy doing things that you do not spend enough time on sharing and self-disclosure. Sometimes, when you think you are sharing, you really are not. Joint activity may include little sharing at all. For example, going to the movie together, watching your favorite television program together, or taking classes together may not give you the opportunity to engage your partner interpersonally.

Sharing through disclosure is an important source of stimulation for the relationship. Without it, a relationship will soon be in trouble: conversations become predictable, and if there is no news, listening becomes almost impossible. Such situations are deadly to relational growth.

You can avoid this situation by creating and taking advantage of opportunities for sharing. Find activities that allow for time alone with the other person: have lunch together; walk together; go to the beach together. When you are involved in such activities, be willing to share yourself. However difficult this may seem, self-disclosure is worth the price, for it creates reciprocal self-disclosure.

Agree to do something new together

Another way to stimulate your relationship is to move off in a new direction together. Take stock of potential interests and set aside a time to plan something new. Learning to do something together can provide stimulation and a refreshing experience for you and your partner.

Express your caring for the other person frequently

Often you forget to say what you are thinking. This is especially true in long, established relationships. You assume that the other person knows you care about him or her. There is no substitute for saying you care! You must make it known to the other that you are thinking about him or her and about the relationship.

These three ideas can go a long way in preventing relational stagnation. The first two create stimulation. The third tells the other person you care.

Combating Relational Decay

Relational decay is something everyone has experienced. This is not particularly a problem when neither partner wants to remain in a relationship, but it is painful when one, or both, of the partners wants to keep the relationship alive. People who find themselves in this position are sometimes frustrated because they don't know exactly what is happening, and they don't know what to do to discover the difficulty. This section can be used as a diagnostic tool to help you understand what might be going wrong in a relationship. We also offer some advice on developing a constructive course of action.

Assessing and Understanding the Problem

Sometimes an effort to improve a relationship can be cooperative because both parties recognize a need and want to participate. Clearly, this is the best possible situation for successful problem solving. But it is possible to work on a relationship even under less-than-optimum conditions. If possible, both partners should first fill out a diagnostic form (fig. 10.4).

Completing the following exercise in identifying relational problems will bring you closer to an understanding of each other's view of the relationship. Only when you both understand are you ready to develop a course of action.

Figure 10.4 Diagnose Your Relationship

Step 1

Working separately, put your initial on the continuum line in response to each statement. Take as much time as you need to think about each item. Do not discuss your responses while you are working. When you finish, proceed to step 2 on the bottom of this page.

1. Cooperation

A. We identify, define, and solve our problems together. We respect each other's competence.
Rarely < ---> Often

B. We work together as a team without competing or putting each other down.
Rarely < ---> Often

C. We make decisions together. We make the most of what each of us has to contribute.
Rarely < ---> Often

D. We share our opinions, thoughts, and ideas without becoming argumentative or defensive.
Rarely < ---> Often

E. Overall, I am satisfied with our mutual respect and cooperation in thinking, deciding, and working together.
Rarely < ---> Often

2. Compatibility

A. We accept and work through our differences to find a common lifestyle with regard to social and public images.
Rarely < ---> Often

B. We accept and work through differences to find common values with regard to religion, morality, social concern, and politics.
Rarely < ---> Often

C. We accept and work through differences with regard to our social life and choice of friends.
Rarely < ---> Often

D. We accept and work through differences so that we are able to share a basic approach to roles and rules.
Rarely < ---> Often

E. Overall, I am satisfied with the way we deal with our differences, maintain a lifestyle, and share values.
Rarely < ---> Often

3. Intimacy

A. We often play together. We put fun into what we do together.
Rarely < ---> Often

B. We express our feelings openly and freely. We say that we are scared, sad, hurting, angry, or happy.
Rarely < ---> Often

C. We tell each other what we like and dislike. We ask openly for what we want from each other.
Rarely < ---> Often

D. We "let go" with each other. We play, relax and enjoy each other.
Rarely < ---> Often

E. Overall, I am satisfied with the level of openness and intimacy in our relationship.
Rarely < ---> Often

Figure 10.4—*Continued*

4. Emotional Support

A. We listen, understand, and empathize with each other's disappointments, hurts, or problems.

Rarely < --> Often

B. We encourage and support each other when one of us is making basic life changes or trying new behavior.

Rarely < --> Often

C. We take responsibility for nurturing when either of us is sick or hurting.

Rarely < --> Often

D. We are emotionally supportive of each other when either of us feels anxious, dependent, or wants to be cared for.

Rarely < --> Often

E. Overall, I am satisfied with the nurture and support we give and receive from each other.

Rarely < --> Often

Step 2

A. Still working separately, review each item and let yourself get in touch with how *satisfied* you feel. You may have marked an item low on the continuum—and *like* it that way. Or you may have marked an item high but feel uncomfortable about it. One person's intimacy is another's anxiety. In the margin next to each item, put one of the following: S = satisfied, OK = acceptable but not exceptional, or D = feel some disappointment.

B. One at a time, take turns telling each other how you marked each item on the continuum and why you marked it the way you did. Also tell about your "S," "Okay," and "D." Give examples to illustrate your explanations.

Developing a Course of Action

Relational problem solving can be a difficult task because it usually involves conflict management. Each of the differences you uncover in a diagnosis of your relationship is a source of conflict. (We're assuming that the process of understanding each other didn't alter the differences you originally uncovered.) Here is a way to proceed that may prove helpful.

1. *Review what you've learned about conflict management.* The tools of conflict management are very important in an examination of relational problems.
2. *See if you and your partner can agree that change is important in the particular area.* This is important because unless you and your partner agree that change is desirable, further discussion will only be frustrating. If you can't agree at this time, you might agree instead to think more about it and to talk again later.

3. *List as many concrete proposals as you can for achieving the desired end.* Suppose you discover that you and your partner want to share opinions, thoughts, and ideas more often, without becoming argumentative. Some things you might do are (1) set aside a specific time for sharing, (2) write down what you think and make a date to discuss what you have written, (3) agree to discuss whatever is on your mind before the end of the day, or (4) wait until the other person says "I've finished presenting my side" before you talk. List your ideas and even write them on a piece of paper if that will help. The more ideas you can generate for achieving your desired goals, the better.

4. *See if there are any particular ideas that the other person doesn't understand.* Exchange lists. Before you get into talking about your ideas, you need to be sure that you understand each other. If one partner doesn't understand, he or she should mark the item and hand it back. Confer until all marks are eliminated.

5. *One partner should now look over the list and make a proposal.* This proposal might even include a statement of expectations about the other's behavior. For example, you might say, "I'd be willing to set aside a time to talk, if you'd be willing to allow at least thirty minutes for us to talk."

6. *Now the other partner may consider the proposal and respond.* It is helpful for the partner to limit the response to one of three types:

   a. an acceptance of the proposal
   b. a specific modification of the proposal
   c. a specific counterproposal

   These responses can be translated as the proposal is OK, the proposal is basically OK, but here are some additional suggestions, or the proposal is unacceptable and I'd like to suggest a different one.

7. *Continue modifying or making counterproposals until you can both agree.* As your partner makes a modification or counterproposal, make sure that you fully understand what he or she is saying. A good way to do this is to engage in active listening. Usually, if partners are willing to stick with this kind of negotiation, they will be able to come to agreement.

The negotiation process will go much better for you if you and your partner are able to be flexible and open to change. There is no magic formula we can give you that will *cause* you to be flexible and open to change. You and your partner must resolve to be so. One way to try to promote these behaviors is to begin your conversation by talking about the need for give and take. You might also talk about and try to agree that there is a need for change. If you can gain some agreement, then you have laid the groundwork for successful negotiation.

·   You can also encourage agreement by avoiding extreme positions. As soon as one of you takes a position that involves absolutes, such as, "I want you to *guarantee* that you will *always* do . . . ," the other person is likely to become defensive. When this happens, a counterproposal that is just as absolute and rigid will likely come from the partner.

Finally, recognize that you can agree to talk at another time if tempers flare. This is not *always* a good idea, of course, because avoidance can develop into a habit. Avoidance does not solve the problem, nor does it cause the difficulty to go away. Use it only to allow tempers to cool and to give you and your partner time to think about the issue privately.

Summary

Sometimes relationships do not seem to work very well but you can improve your success in relationships by knowing how to care for them. This involves both understanding how relationships develop, as they grow and as they come apart, and being able to promote relational growth.

Relationships move through stages of growth. The pattern usually appears as follows:

Initiating – – ►Experimenting – – ►Intensifying – – ►Integrating – – ►Renegotiating – – ►Bonding

Initiating involves making a decision to engage the other person in conversation based on the situation and on your attraction. If the situation seems right and there is sufficient attraction, then initiation is likely. Since there is still much that is unknown at this stage, the pair moves to the next stage, *experimenting.* Here they exchange information in order to discover common interests. Generally, this talk moves from superficial to more meaningful disclosure. The disclosure allows comparisons that are useful in deciding about the future of the relationship.

Intensifying signals a change in the relationship from acquaintance to friend. Self-disclosure increases dramatically as partners are willing to make themselves vulnerable by discussing personal problems and failures. Nonverbal behavior becomes intensified in this stage as more touching and closer interpersonal distances are desired.

Integrating suggests coming together in ways that create increased contact. This could be living together or just more frequent contact. Activities that the partner does not enjoy may be dropped, as the emphasis is on doing things together. There is an infatuation with the other person.

Renegotiation takes place as the persons involved in the relationship try to decide if they want to make this friendship more permanent and committed. At this stage, partners are conducting a private examination of their relationship. When attempts to negotiate the dissatisfactions fail, disengagement may begin. Successful negotiation leads to a new relationship and bonding.

Bonding signals a special kind of commitment to intimacy, a voluntary commitment to the partner for an indefinite period, with new rules. These rules are the result of successful renegotiation of the relationship.

Signs of relational deterioration are characterized by differentiating, circumscribing, stagnating, avoiding, and terminating.

Differentiating emphasizes the individuals and their differences. Differences that were previously unnoticed or unimportant become a source of irritation, and perhaps, conflict.

Circumscribing is avoiding behavior. Partners avoid topics that might lead to intimacy and self-disclosure. If a partner self-discloses, the other person will likely not disclose. Attempts to solve problems may be met by statements like "I don't want to talk about it. Let's talk about something else."

Stagnating is descriptive of the relationship in which the partners are silent, rather than talking to each other. One may be irritated with the other, but says nothing. Each is thinking, though, and especially about the other's motives. Often they rehearse in their heads how they would respond if they were to talk about the situation.

Avoiding is the first clear sign that the relationship is breaking off. The previous stage, stagnating, closed off communication, but not physical presence. In the avoiding stage, partners try to stay away from each other. Each may even tell the partner that "I do not want to see you."

Terminating, like bonding, is more of a signal than a stage. The relationship is dead and both partners know it. Therefore, they sever all contact. This might be characterized by a statement like "I want to make it clear. You are not welcome in my house!"

Underlying this developmental view of communication in interpersonal relationships are two fundamental elements: definition and rules. Partners have a definition of the relationship at each stage of the process. The extent of agreement on this definition is a measure of the relationship's stability. Rules of conduct regulate the behavior and provide predictability. Relationships in the early stage are guided by *impersonal,* societal rules. More developed relationships are guided by *interpersonal* rules, based on each other's knowledge of the partner.

Relationships are initiated for a number reasons. Some of the most important reasons are interpersonal attraction, physical attraction, social attraction, task attraction, and basic interpersonal needs. Motivation also comes from the impulse to receive stimulation, express experiences, assert oneself, and enhance enjoyment of activities.

There are some specific activities you can use to promote this growth. These include appropriately disclosing, achieving role and rule agreement, giving support, demonstrating affection and liking, and managing conflict constructively.

A plan for combating relational decay first requires that you understand your relational problems using assessment. Next, you develop a course of action by using good conflict management skills and by working together.

Discussion Questions

1. Choose one of your long-term relationships. Trace it through the stages of development that were outlined in this chapter. Discuss in class how closely your relationship mirrored these stages. Did it skip any stages? Did it backtrack? Were there stages in your relationship that we didn't mention at all? If there were differences, how do you account for them?

2. What happens in a relationship if the stage we call "renegotiation" is skipped before the "bonding" stage takes place?

3. Can you make a relationship work? If possible, how would you accomplish this? Can you renegotiate a relationship more than once? How?

4. More than half the marriages in America end in divorce. Where do these relationships go wrong? What information in this chapter will help you to identify the pitfalls in such ongoing relationships?

5. Are working relationships in business any different from working relationships at home? If so, how? If not, why aren't the home relationships as successful as the working relationships? Does the definition of the relationship and the rules applied make the difference?

6. Can a person make you love him or her? Can you make someone love you? Does this have anything to do with attraction? Does attraction have anything to do with loving?

7. Can you disclose yourself too much in a relationship? How much is too much?

Endnotes

1. Source: National Center for Health Statistics, Public Health Service.

2. For information on the investigation of stages in interpersonal development, consult the following: C. R. Berger and R. J. Calabrese, "Some Explorations in Initial Interaction and Beyond: Toward a Developmental Theory of Interpersonal Communication," *Human Communication Research* 1 (1975):99–112; S. W. Duck, *Personal Relationships and Personal Constructs: A Study of Friendship Formation* (New York: The Free Press, 1973); T. M. Newcomb, *The Acquaintance Process* (New York: Holt, Rinehart and Winston, 1961).

3. M. L. Knapp, *Social Intercourse: From Greeting to Goodbye* (Boston: Allyn and Bacon, Inc., 1978), 17–28.

4. T. M. Newcomb, *The Acquaintance Process* (New York: Holt, 1961); W. Griffitt and R. Veitch, "Preacquaintance Attitude Similarity and Attraction Revisited," *Sociometry* 37 (1974): 163–73.

5. Knapp, *Social Intercourse*, 20.

6. J. T. Wood, *Human Communication: A Symbolic Interactionist Perspective* (New York: Holt, Rinehart and Winston, 1982), 177.

7. Ibid., 177.

8. Knapp, *Social Intercourse,* 21.
9. G. L. Wilson, "Trusting and Self-Disclosure in Dyads." (Ph.D. diss., University of Wisconsin, 1979).
10. F. E. X. Dance, "Toward a Theory of Human Communication" in *Human Communication Theory: Original Essays,* ed. F. E. X. Dance (New York: Holt, Rinehart and Winston, 1967), 288–309.
11. Murray S. Davis, *Intimate Relations* (New York: Free Press, 1973), chapter 3.
12. Wood, *Human Communication,* 178–80.
13. I. Altman and D. A. Taylor, *Social Penetration: The Development of Interpersonal Relationships* (New York: Holt, Rinehart and Winston, 1973), 174.
14. Knapp, *Social Intercourse,* 21.
15. Wood, *Human Communication,* 180.
16. Knapp, *Social Intercourse,* 21–22.
17. G. Levinger and O. C. Moles, eds., *Divorce and Separation: Context, Causes and Consequences* (New York: Basic Books, 1979), 71–72.
18. Knapp, *Social Intercourse,* 24.
19. Ibid.
20. W. W. Wilmot, *Dyadic Communication,* 2d ed. (Reading, MA: Addison-Wesley, 1979), 152.
21. Review chapter 7, which discusses predictions.
22. G. R. Miller and M. Steinberg, *Between People* (Chicago: Science Research Associates, 1975), 22–25.
23. See Keith Gibbins, "Communication Aspects of Women's Clothes and Their Relation to Fashionability," *British Journal of Social and Clinical Psychology* 8 (1964): 301–12; E. Berscheid and E. Walster, "Physical Attractiveness," in *Advances in Experimental Social Psychology* 7, ed. L. Berkowitz (New York: Academic Press, 1974); C. L. Kleinke, *First Impressions: The Psychology of Encountering Others* (Englewood Cliffs, NJ: Prentice-Hall, Inc., 1975).
24. M. S. Davis, *Intimate Relations* (New York: Free Press, 1973).
25. W. Pfeiffer and J. Pfeiffer, "A Gestalt Primer," in *The 1975 Annual Handbook for Group Facilitators,* eds. J. W. Pfeiffer and J. E. Jones (La Jolla, CA: University Associates, 1975), 183.
26. S. M. Jourard, *The Transparent Self* (New York: Van Nostrand Reinhold Company, 1971), 5, 49–57.
27. C. R. Rogers, *On Becoming a Person* (Boston: Houghton Mifflin Company, 1961), 62, 283–84.
28. W. C. Schutz, *Firo: A Three-Dimensional Theory of Interpersonal Behavior* (New York: Holt, Rinehart and Winston, 1958).
29. One of the best treatments of Berne's idea of stroking is found in M. James and D. Jongeward, *Born to Win: Transactional Analysis with Gestalt Experiments* (Reading, MA: Addison-Wesley Publishing Co., Inc., 1971), 44–67.

Epilogue

Interpersonal growth should be a constant, ongoing process. This text has detailed the basic skills for you to continue developing your relationships. Like most skills, you must practice daily to perfect them. Work at your relationships. Success will encourage you to continue your efforts.

By far the largest number of relationship problems among adults result from the inability to be open, honest, and constructive. Better communication is definitely needed. Our experience with students who complete a good interpersonal communication course is that they feel better about their ability to relate to other people. But they do not all relate to others more effectively. The difference lies in active practice. You have to work at making your relationships better, but it can be done.

We congratulate you on your growth and encourage you to continue growing. Your future will be brighter and more promising because of your improved interpersonal skills.

Self-Help Guide

Interpersonal growth requires active practice, particularly since you will continuously encounter situations that require effective interpersonal communication. We know, however, that after you have completed your course, you may rarely have the opportunity to have a professional help you to improve your interpersonal skills. So that you are able to consult a resource when you feel you need help with a skill, we have constructed a self-help guide. The guide includes over seventy-five questions or statements about interpersonal communication and relational development. We have indexed these so that you can turn to the appropriate spot in *Interpersonal Growth through Communication* for the information that will help you.

Using the Question-Answer Index

1. Form a statement or question about the situation that is puzzling you. Try to word the statement using the terms you have learned from this text.
2. Look for key words in your statement. Then locate your key words in the directory. We have listed in this directory the key words we used in the guide.
3. Turn to the key word in the *guide* and look at the questions and statements under it. Select the one that most closely resembles your concern.
4. Turn to the page in the text that addresses your concern.
5. If the concern is not addressed by a key word in the directory, you may find an index entry that will help you.

Directory

active listening
assertiveness
attending
agreement
conflict
decision making
defensive communication
emotions
fact/inference confusion
feedback
feelings
hearing
interpersonal communication
interpersonal needs
language
meaning
nonverbal communication

perception
relational
   definition
   deterioration
   rules
relationship
reification
remembering
roles
self-concept
self-fulfilling prophesy
stereotyping
stress
supportive communication
symmetry/complement
understanding

Problem Category and Questions

active listening

What can I do to listen more carefully when a friend
    just wants me to be a good listener?   113–15

assertiveness

I seem to be a person people like to push around. I
    want to do something about this. What can I do?   179–80

attending

Why is it that sometimes I don't even hear what the
    other person said?   101–3

agreement

I get frustrated when someone tells me they don't
    understand when they really just don't agree.
    What's going on here?   103–4

conflict

I fear conflict because it sometimes seems very
    destructive. Is there any way to tell if conflict is
    going to be destructive?   262

Is there any relationship between how I fight and the
    likely outcome?   263–64

Sometimes, especially in an important relationship, I
    seem to be particularly nasty to the other person.
    Why?   266–68

How do I know what kind of conflict management
    strategy I usually follow?   268–72

Can you give me a plan for productive conflict
    management?   268–72

decision making

Sometimes I have trouble making decisions. It is like I
    don't know what's going on. Is there any help?   258–59, 263

defensive communication

There are times when I really feel the need to defend
    myself. What's going on here?   231–32

Why does what another person says make me feel
    defensive?   232–33

Sometimes I feel put down by the other person;
    personally rejected. Why?   234–35

What alternatives do I have to returning the other
    person's defensive behavior?   236–37

emotions

Isn't it best to ''play it cool'' by not showing emotions?   207–8

fact/inference confusion

Sometimes I confuse what I observe with what I think
    I've seen. Can anything be done about that?   17–27

feedback

Sometimes there are problems in communication
    because the person doesn't tell me enough. How
    can I encourage the person to say more?   112–13

feelings

I often have the feeling that I must depend on
    someone, but I don't want to. And I don't want to
    feel that way.   125–26

Sometimes when I'm with (*Name*) I am confused by
    strong feelings that I can't identify. Where will I find   125–26, 138–39,
    help in this book?   144–49, 152–53

I want to expand my own emotional range—to
    experience more feelings and emotions. Will this
    book help?   130–32, 147–52

I'd like to find better ways to deal with the frustrations
    I'm having.   133–34

hearing

Why is it that sometimes I don't even hear what the
    other person said?   97

interpersonal needs

One of my best friends has been getting on my nerves
    lately. When we are together with other people, he/
    she demands attention and dominates the group.   173–74

Lately, my spouse has been taking charge of
    everything. This leaves me feeling useless.   52–54

One of my co-workers seems moody and apathetic
    these days. How can I help him/her in a way that
    will also improve our relationship?   52–54

language

Sometimes I have to work hard to understand what a
    person is talking about because words are used
    differently than I define them.   166–72

My boss surprises me sometimes with the language I
    hear him using.   169–70

When we argue, my co-worker takes a "for me or
    against me" attitude. What can I do about that?   183–84

listening

I know I have trouble listening sometimes, but I don't
    know why.   95–97

What does the listening process involve? What do I
    do?   98–100

What can I do to improve my listening?   108–18

What can I do to listen more carefully when a friend
    just wants me to be a good listener?   113–15

meaning

I sometimes have trouble expressing exactly what I
   mean.   160–62

Although we talk about our relationship, my friend and
   I don't seem to connect. It's as if we're talking
   about different things.   163–64

I sometimes have trouble reporting events to others.
   They frequently misunderstand me.   170–71

My neighbor thinks that because I have a job as a
   secretary, that's all I can do. How can I deal with
   this problem?   174–77

My best friend isn't acting like much of a friend these
   days. What might be the problem?   177–78

nonverbal communication

I am sometimes confused about the meaning of
   nonverbal messages that are sent. How can I learn
   to "read" these?   193, 204–7

Does my clothing send the "right" message?   195–98

How can I "read" a room for important nonverbal
   signals?   196–97, 210–12

How can I use nonverbal messages to protect myself?   199–200

Is there a best way to stand?   202–4

Isn't it best to "play it cool" by not showing emotions?   207–8

Can I learn to touch people for a particular
   communicative effect?   208–10

Where should I sit for the best effect? Is there a best
   place to sit for different purposes?   215–17

Suppose someone is always late. Is he/she telling me
   something?   218–21

perception

I don't understand why my friend and I see things so differently.	39–40
I would like to learn more about the way I see myself and the way others see me.	49–51
Sometimes I lose my train of thought. What might be causing this?	70
I have to make a demonstration as part of a program. What can I do to make it stand out and be noticed by the people there?	71–73
I sometimes remember events differently than they are remembered by others. How can this happen?	77–78
How can I improve my perception of other people?	85–88

relational definition

I think of us as friends; my friend thinks of us as "being together." What's going on here?	295–96

relational deterioration

Everything was really great with (Name), but now that we're getting ready to marry, it has all fallen apart. Why?	288–90
What are the signs that my relationship is deteriorating?	290–95
Suppose I know my relationship is in trouble. What can I do to try to save it?	303–4

relational engagement

Why are people attracted to some attempts at relationship initiation but not to others?	297–98

relational rules

Sometimes it seems like everyone is playing some sort of game. "Society" is calling the shots. At other times (Name) seems to act more naturally. I can't figure this out.	296–97

relationships

Sometimes, especially in an important relationship, I seem to be particularly nasty to the other person. Why?	266–68
Is there a "checklist" I can use for an agenda when I want to talk about my relationship with someone?	19–26
I need a single piece of good advice to help me manage my relationship with (Name).	26–27
I often have the feeling that I must depend on someone, but I don't want to do so. And I don't want to feel that way.	125–26
I feel confused about my priorities and goals in several of my relationships.	177–78
I get upset when one of my co-workers talks down to me. What could be the cause of such behavior?	171–72
I'd like to know more about where I am in a relationship. Is there any way to tell?	282–95
What signals might tell me whether my relationship is beyond the initial stages?	285–86
Everything was really great with (Name), but now that we're getting ready to marry, it has all fallen apart. Why?	288–90
I think of us as friends; my friend thinks of us as being "together." What's going on here?	295–96
Sometimes it seems like everyone is playing some sort of game. "Society" is calling the shots. At other times (Name) seems to act more naturally. I can't figure this out.	296–97
Why do people decide to begin a relationship?	297–98
How can I help my relationship with (Name)?	300–303
Suppose I know that my relationship is in trouble. What can I do to try to save it?	303–4

reification

I have a friend who thinks that buying me things is a demonstration of affection. I don't feel that way, and want to know what to do.	182–83

remembering

I sometimes remember events differently than they are
remembered by others. How can this happen?   77–78

Why do I have problems remembering what I've
heard?   107–8

How can I improve my ability to remember what I've
heard?   116–18

roles

Sometimes my co-workers say and do things that I did
not expect them to say or do. Why?   84

self-concept

People I associate with seem to see me differently
than I think I'm presenting myself.   37–39

Lately, I find that the image I present is incorrect for
the occasion or for the person with whom I'm
talking.   39

I would like to learn more about the way I see myself
and the way others see me.   49–51

I would like to learn more about how I got to be the
person I am. What can I do?   56–58

self-fulfilling prophesy

Sometimes I get this feeling before an encounter that
things aren't going to go well. I'm usually right. Why
does this happen?   181–82

stereotyping

I get hassled a lot because of the clubs to which I
belong. What can I do about this?   84

stress

I know I'm under stress. What are some possible
    consequences?   272–73

I'd like to deal with stress more successfully. What
    would be a good plan?   273–74

What can I do to help myself relax in order to cope
    with stress?   275–76

supportive communication

What alternative do I have to returning the other
    person's defensive behavior?   236–37

I'd rather be supportive than defensive when making
    an argument. How can I do this?   237–42, 244–46

Why be supportive? Isn't defensiveness more likely to
    get me what I want?   242–44

symmetry and complement

I get upset when one of my co-workers talks down to
    me. What could be the cause of this behavior?   171–72

understanding

What can I do to better understand what others really
    mean when they talk to me?   87–88

Credits

Illustrations

Figure 2.1 From *Group Processes: An Introduction to Group Dynamics* by Joseph Luft, by permission of Mayfield Publishing Company. Copyright © 1963, 1970 by Joseph Luft. **Figure 3.3** Georges Seurat, *Sunday Afternoon on the Island of La Grand Jatte.* Collection of The Art Institute of Chicago. **Figure 3.4** Georges Seurat, *Sunday Afternoon on the Island of La Grand Jatte.* Collection of The Art Institute of Chicago. **Figure 4.2** From *Use Both Sides of Your Brain* by Tony Buzan. Copyright © 1974 by Tony Buzan. Reprinted by permission of the publisher, E. P. Dutton. **Figure 4.3** From *Use Both Sides of Your Brain* by Tony Buzan. Copyright © 1974 by Tony Buzan. Reprinted by permission of the publisher, E. P. Dutton. *Source:* Herman Ebbinghaus, *Uber das Gedachtnis: Untersuchungen zer Experimentelen Psychologie* (Leipzig: Dancker and Humbolt, 1885). **Figure 4.5** From *Use Both Sides of Your Brain* by Tony Buzan. Copyright © 1974 by Tony Buzan. Reprinted by permission of the publisher, E. P. Dutton. **Figure 5.1** Ronald Forgus, Bernard S. Shulman, *Personality: A Cognitive View,* © 1979, p. 258. Reprinted by permission of Prentice-Hall, Inc., Englewood Cliffs, NJ. **Figure 5.6** Richard Bandler and John Grinder. *The Structure of Magic I.* (Palo Alto, CA: Science and Behavior Books, Inc., 1975) p. 10. **Figure 6.1** *Source:* C. K. Ogden and I. A. Richards, *The Meaning of Meaning.* © 1923 Harcourt Brace Jovanovich, New York. **Figure 6.5** From L. Carmichael, H. P. Hogan, and A. A. Walter, "An Experimental Study on the Effects of Language on the Reproduction of Visually Perceived Form." In *Journal of Experimental Psychology* 15, 1932, pp. 73–86. Copyright © 1932 by American Psychological Association. **Figure 7.2** Loretta Malandro and Larry Barker, *Nonverbal Communication,* © 1983, Addison-Wesley, Reading, MA, p. 83, fig. 3.1. Reprinted with permission. **Figure 7.11** From *Personal Space: The Behavioral Basis of Design* by Robert Sommer. © 1969 by Prentice-Hall, Inc. Englewood Cliffs, NJ. **Figure 7.12** Reprinted from M. Cook. "Experimentation on Orientation and Proxemics," *Human Relations,* 1970, Vol. 23, p. 63. Used by permission of Plenum Publishing Company. **Figure 7.13** Reprinted from M. Cook, "Experimentation on Orientation and Proxemics," *Human Relations,* 1970, Vol. 23, p. 64. Used by permission of Plenum Publishing Company. **Figure 7.14** *Source:* E. T. Hall, "Proximecs," *Current Anthropology* 9 (1968): 93. © 1968 by the University of Chicago Press. Reprinted by permission. **Figure 9.4** *Source:* Adapted from Louis R. Pondy, "Organizational Conflict Concepts and Models,"

Administrative Science Quarterly 12
(1967): p. 306. **Figure 10.1** *Source:*
Frank E. X. Dance, "Toward a Theory
of Human Communication" in *Human
Communication Theory: Original
Essays,* ed. Frank E. X. Dance (New
York: Holt, Rinehart and Winston,
1957), p. 296. © F. E. X. Dance.
Figure 10.4 Adapted from David L.
Luecke, *The Relationship Manual*
(Columbia, MD: The Relationship
Institute, 1981), pp. 13–14. Used with
permission.

Photographs

James Ballard: *67* (top right), *194,
197, 201* (bottom). Courtesy of
Bernhardt Furniture: *211* (bottom).
Bob Coyle: *164.* Robert Eckert/EKM-
Nepenthe: *67* (lower left). John
Maher/EKM-Nepenthe: *83* (lower left),
201 (upper middle). Chris Grajczyk:
67 (lower right). Jean-Claude Lejeune:
67 (top left), *83* (top left and right;
middle left and right), *201* (top,
middle, and lower middle), *204, 206.*
Jim Shaffer: *83* (lower left). Courtesy
of Villeroy and Boch, Inc.: *211* (top).

Name Index

Aiken, L., 195, 225
Alberti, R., 179, 180, 187
Allport, G., 44, 61
Alper, T., 226
Altman, I., 248, 290, 311
Argyle, M., 225
Aristotle, 36, 132
Athos, A. G., 31, 36, 60, 172, 187
Austin, G., 167, 187

Bandler, R., 141–43, 155
Barker, L. L., 193, 225
Barrick, J. E., 278
Beavin, J. H., 248
Berger, C. R., 310
Berlyne, D. E., 73, 91
Berne, E., 302, 311
Berscheid, E., 311
Birdwhistle, R., 200
Bochner, A., 267, 278
Book, C. L., 91
Boulding, K., 25, 31
Bower, G., 180, 187
Bower, S., 180, 187
Bruner, J., 167, 187
Buck, R., 131, 155
Burgoon, M., 91
Burke, R., 263, 278
Buzan, T., 107, 108, 116–18, 120

Calabrese, R. J., 310
Carmichael, L., 175, 187
Chaffee, S., 61
Civikly, J. V., 247
Comstock, G., 48, 49, 61
Condon, J. C., 175, 177, 184, 187, 188
Cook, M., 216, 226
Cooley, C. H., 46, 47, 61
Coop, R. H., 48, 61
Cox, T., 278

Dance, F., 287, 288, 311
Davis, M. S., 298, 311
Deese, J., 120
Deutsch, G., 155
Deutsch, M., 262, 278
Dittman, A. T., 225
Dodson, G. D., 132, 133, 155
Duck, S. W., 310

Ebbinghaus, H., 108, 120
Ekman, P., 200, 225, 226
Emmons, M., 179, 180, 187

Fast, J., 200
Feistein, S., 225
Festinger, L., 46, 61
Filley, A. C., 262, 263, 278
Fitzpatrick, M. A., 264–67, 278
Folkins, C. H., 278
Freshley, D. L., 278
Friesen, W. V., 200, 225, 226
Frost, J. H., 258, 277

Gabarro, J. J., 31, 36, 60, 172, 178
Gavin, J. F., 279
Gibb, J. R., 232–34, 238, 240, 242, 247, 266
Gibbins, K., 311
Goleman, D., 91
Goodnow, J., 167, 187
Griffitt, W., 310
Grinder, J., 141–43, 155

Hall, E. T., 218–20, 226
Hamid, P. N., 225
Hanna, M. S., 13
Hayakawa, S. I., 162, 177, 180, 181, 187, 188
Heslin, N. R., 208, 209, 226
Hess, H. J., 91, 147, 148, 155
Hogan, H. P., 175, 187
Huseman, R. C., 278

Ingham, H., 37
Ivanevich, J. M., 278

Jackson, D. D., 248
James, M., 302, 311
James, W., 36, 60
Johnson, W., 181, 188
Jongeward, D., 311
Jourard, S. M., 311

Katzman, N., 61
Kelley, C., 112, 120
Kinbourne, M., 139, 155
Knapp, M., 282, 285, 287, 288, 290, 293,
    310, 311
Korzybski, A. H., 180, 181, 187, 188
Krause, R. M., 248
Kuna, D. J., 276, 278

Lehman, W. P., 187
Logue, C. M., 278
Luft, J., 37, 60
Lynch, C. H., 276, 278
Lyons, J., 174, 187

McCandless, B. R., 48, 61
McCombs, M., 61
McCroskey, J., 275, 278
McKeachie, W., 225
Malandro, L. A., 193, 225
Manis, J. G., 30
Maslow, A. H., 226
Matteson, M. T., 278
Mead, G. H., 46, 47, 61
Mehrabian, A., 225
Meltzer, B. N., 30
Meyers, R. M., 278
Miller, G. A., 159, 187
Miller, G. R., 266, 278
Mintz, N. L., 226
Morrow, L., 168, 187
Murdock, G. P., 167, 187

Newcomb, T. M., 310
Nichols, R., 101, 109, 120

Ogden, C. K., 160, 187
Oskamp, S., 43, 61

Pace, R. W., 247
Pfeiffer, J., 300, 311
Pfeiffer, W., 300, 311

Piaget, J., 91
Plax, T. G., 225
Pollio, H. R., 159, 187
Pondy, L. R., 259, 277

Ralph, D. C., 278
Richards, I. A., 160, 187
Roberts, D., 61
Rogers, C. A., 231, 237, 247, 248, 266, 302,
    311
Rokeach, M., 61
Rosencranz, M. L., 195, 225
Rosenfield, L. B., 196, 225
Rothwell, J. D., 166, 187
Ruben, B. D., 248
Rubenstein, C., 200, 225
Ruffner, M., 91

Schutz, W. C., 52–54, 61, 302, 311
Seurat, G., 75
Shannon, C., 30
Sibatani, A., 155
Siegman, A. W., 225
Smith, D. R., 171, 187
Sommer, R., 215, 216, 226
Springer, S. P., 155
Steinberg, M., 260, 278
Stevens, L., 120

Taylor, D. A., 248, 290, 311
Thayer, L., 120
Thornton, G., 225
Tucker, C. O., 91, 147, 148, 155

Veitch, R., 310

Walster, W., 311
Walter, A. A., 175, 187
Watzlawick, P., 248
Weaver, W., 30
Webb, W., 91
Weinstein, J., 131, 155
Williamson, K., 171, 187
Wilmore, J. H., 278
Wilmot, W. W., 258, 277, 295, 311
Winke, J., 167, 264, 278
Wood, J. T., 288, 290, 310, 311

Yerkes, R. M., 132, 133, 155

Subject Index

absolute present, 17–19
abstraction, 162–66, 178
    levels of, 162–66
accommodation, 77–78
active listening, 113–15
    overcoming difficulties, 114–15
affection, 53–54, 302–3
    overpersonal, 53
    personal, 53
    underpersonal, 53
affiliation motive, 125
agenda for talking about relationships,
    19–26, 111
    check out, 26
    feelings, 22
    images, 25–26
    inferences, 20–22
    intentions, 24
    latitude of acceptance, 24–25
    observations, 19–20
    wants and expectations, 22–23
agreement, 103–4
allness rules, 151
angle of interaction, 215–16
anxiety, 136–37
    behavioral consequences, 136–37
    controlling, 137
    responses, 136–37
    selective perception, 136
    withdrawal, 136–37
approach-approach conflict, 256–57
approach-avoidance conflict, 254–55
artifacts, 196–99
assertiveness, 179–80
assimilation, 77–78
attachment motive, 125
attending, 101–3
    habits, 101–2
    problems, 101–3

attitudes, 44–45, 102
attraction, 82
avoidance-avoidance conflict, 255–56
avoiding, 294

behavioral consequences of emotions,
    132–36
beliefs, 40–42
    derived, 41
    shared, 41
    unshared, 41
body cues, 204–10
body movements, 199–204
bonding, 283, 290

certainty, 233, 234
channels, 7–9
check out, 26, 115–16
circumscribing, 283, 293
closed-mindedness, 106
clothing and communication, 195
cognitive control of emotions, 130–32
communication, 7–12, 137–43
    of feelings, 137–43
    model, 7–12
complementary transaction, 171–72
conflict, 253–61
    dysfunctional, 262–63
    episode, 259–61
    felt, 261
    functional, 262–63
    interpersonal, 253
    intrapersonal, 253–58
    latent, 260
    locations of, 253
    manifest, 261
    perceived, 261–62
    potential, 260

control, 53, 233, 234
    abdicrat, 53
    autocrat, 53
    democrat, 53
coordination problems, 105–6
culture, 166–67

decoder, 7–8
deep structure, 144–47
defensive communication, 231–37
    alternatives to, 236–37
    certainty, 233–34
    consequences of, 235–36
    control, 233–34
    evaluation, 232, 234
    neutrality, 233–34
    strategies, 233–35
    superiority, 233–34
    when and how you defend, 232–34
    why you defend, 231–32
deliberative listening, 112
denial strategies, 126, 152
denotative meanings, 170–71
dependency motive, 125
description, 238, 242
differentiating, 283, 292–93
distance, interpersonal, 218
distributed practice, 117

emotions, 126–37, 139–40, 144–53
    behavioral consequences of, 132–36
    cognitive control, 130–32
    expressing, 126–37, 139–40, 144–53
    and language, 126–30
empathic listening, 111–13
empathy, 240, 243
    lack of, 104–5
    and listening, 111–13
encoder, 7–8
engagement, 297–98
environmental cues, 210–21
equality, 238, 243
evaluation, 232, 234

face and eye behavior, 204–8
feedback, 8, 11, 113–15
feelings, 126, 138–40, 147–49
    denial strategies, 126
    expression of physical, 139–40
    learning feeling words, 147–49
    recognizing, 138–39
filtering process, 10–11

filtering screen model, 10–11
forcing strategies, 265–66
frame of reference, 10, 65–66, 82, 166

gestures, 199–204
goal block responses, 133–36
    displacement, 133–36
    frustration, 133–36
    rationalization, 135–36
    substitution, 134–36

identity aspirations, 46
images, 25–26
inclusion, 52
    adaptable-social, 52
    oversocial, 52
    undersocial, 52
inferences, 20–22, 238
initiating, 282–84, 297, 300
intensifying, 283, 285–86
intentions, 24
internalizers, 131–32
interpersonal communication, 4–7, 16–17
    content dimension, 16
    reasons for study, 4–7
    relationship dimension, 16–17
interpersonal concepts, 14–16
interpersonal conflict, 258–72
    forcing strategies, 265–66
    intervention techniques, 263–66, 272
    lose-lose methods, 264
    management, 268–72
    typical use, 266–68
    win-lose methods, 263–64
    win-win method, 265–66
interpersonal needs, 302–3
interpreting response, 116
intrapersonal conflict, 254–58
    approach-approach, 256–57
    approach-avoidance, 254–55
    avoidance-avoidance, 255–56
    intervention, 257–58

Johari Window, 37–39

labeling the dominant behavior, 46
language, 17–19, 126–30, 140–44, 159–84
    assertive, 179–80
    basis of, 166–72
    complementary transaction, 171–72
    components of, 159
    constraints, 141–43
    and culture, 166–67

definition, 159
emotions and, 126–30
and experience, 160
figurative, 173–74
incomplete nature of, 140–41
limited ability of, 140–44
map and territory, 182–83
nature of, 159–66
personalizing, 17–19
problems, 180–84
referent, 160–62
and relationships, 169–72
and self, 172–80
and society, 167–69
symbol, 160–62
and symmetrical transactions, 171–72
thought, 160–62
Triangle of Meaning, 160–62
latitude of acceptance, 24–25
levels of abstraction, 178
listening, 95, 98–100, 108–18
active, 113–15
components, 98–100
deliberative, 112
empathic, 111–13
improvement, 108–18
involvement, 109–10
as a problem, 95
process, 98–100

material me, 37
meanings, 170–71
connotative, 170–71
denotative, 170–71
meditation, 275–76
message, 7, 102–3, 149–52
incomplete, 149–52
length, 103
low-intensity, 102–3
model, listening, 100–108
motives, 125
mutual experience, 82–85

naming, 177–78
overdiscrimination, 177–78
needs, 102, 289–300
neutrality, 233, 234
noise, 8–9
nonverbal communication, 193–223
allophones, 200
angle of interaction, 215–16
artifacts, 196–99
body movements, 199–204

clothing, 193–96
controlling face and eye behavior,
207–8
environmental cues, 210–21
face and eye behavior, 204–8
general body cues, 193–204
gestures, 199–204
paraverbal cues, 221–23
particular body cues, 204–10
personal distance, 218–19
posture, 202–4
space, 212–17
territoriality, 213–15
time, 218–21
touching behavior, 208
observations, 19–20
open-mindedness, 111
overdiscrimination, 177–78

paraverbal cues, 221–23
perceiving, 71–73, 81–85
act of, 71–73
others, 81–85
perception, 12–13, 73–81, 162
accommodation, 77–78
building accuracy, 85–88
building interpretive skills, 87–88
building receptive skills, 85–87
functions of, 65–66
how you perceive, 68–73
as interpretation, 73–81
physical influences, 69–71
qualities of, 66–68
sensory aspects, 68–69
polarization, 183–84
posture, 202–4
prediction, 13
problem orientation, 239–40, 242
provisionalism, 238–39, 243

qualities of perception, 66–68

receiver, 7–9
referent, 160–62
reflected appraisal, 46
reification, 182–83
rejection response, 234
relational decay, 304–8
relational deterioration, 266–68, 282–90,
292–95
avoiding, 294

circumscribing, *283, 293*
differentiating, *283, 292–93*
stagnating, *283, 293–94*
terminating, *283, 295*
relational development, 266–68, 282–90
   bonding, *283, 290*
   experimenting, *283, 284–85*
   initiating, *282–84*
   intensifying, *283, 285–86*
   renegotiating, *283, 288–90*
relational elements, 295–97
   definition, *295–96*
   rules, *296–97*
relational problems, 306–9
   assessing, *308–9*
   combating, *306–8*
relational rule agreement, 301–2
relationships, 169–72, 297–308
   basic needs, *298–300*
   engagement process, *297–98, 300–301*
   growth, *300–303*
   initiating, *297–300*
   and language, *169–72*
   problems, *303–8*
remembering, 107–8, 116–18
   increasing ability, *116–18*
   problems, *107–8*
renegotiating, 283, 288–90
risk, 12–13, 15
role, 82–84, 301
   agreement, *301*
   assignment, *82–84*
   expectations, *84*
   psychological, *84*
   sociological, *82–84*

scanning the environment, 46–47
selective attention, 79–81, 99, 101
selective exposure, 78–79
selectivity, 78–81
self, 37–38, 172–80, 234–35
   blind, *37–38*
   definition, *234–35*
   disconfirmation responses, *234–35*
   expression, *172–73*
   hidden, *37–38*
   and language, *172–80*
   open, *37–38*
   rejection response, *234*
   responding to self-definition, *234–35*
   revelation, *173–74*
   unknown, *37–38*

self-concept, 5, 39–59
   components, *39–45*
   definition, *36–39*
   development, *58–59*
   evolution process, *45–51*
   influence of significant others, *47–49*
   interpersonal needs and, *52–54*
   maintenance, *54–59*
self-confidence, 5
self-definition and naming, 174–79
self-disclosure, 14, 15, 278, 301
   appropriate, *301*
self-fulfilling prophecy, 181–82
sensing problems, 100–101
sensitivity, 12–13, 15
social comparison, 46
social me, 37
source, 7–8
space, 212–17
speech/thought differential, 109
spiritual me, 37
spontaneity, 240–42
stagnation, 283, 293–94, 303–4
   preventing, *303–4*
stereotype, 84, 137, 181–82
stimuli, 9–13
strategy, defensive, 233–34
stress, 184, 272–76
   and body relaxation, *275–76*
   consequences of, *272–73*
   definition, *272*
   management, *273–76*
structural linguistics, 144–47
surface structure, 144–47
superiority, 233–34
supportive climates, 237–42
supportive communication, 237–47
   benefits, *242–44*
   description, *238–42*
   empathy, *240–43*
   equality, *238–43*
   giving, *302*
   problem orientation, *239–40, 242*
   provisionalism, *238–39, 243*
   remaining supportive, *244–46*
   spontaneity, *240–42*
surface structure, 144–47
survival orientation, 54–55
symbol, 160–62
symmetrical transaction, 171–72

terminating, 283, 295
territoriality, 213–15
thought and meaning, 160–62

time, 218–21
touching, 208
Triangle of Meaning, 160–62
trust, 13–15
two-valued orientation, 183–84

understanding problems, 103–6
understanding versus agreement, 103–4

values, 43–44
vocalizations, 223
vocal quality, 223

wants and expectations, 22–23

Yerkes-Dodson Law, 132–33